Parachute?

FOR RETIREMENT

SECOND EDITION

What Color Is Your Parachute? FOR RETIREMENT

Planning a Prosperous, Healthy, and Happy Future

JOHN E. NELSON and RICHARD N. BOLLES

TEN SPEED PRESS
Berkeley

Publisher's Note: This book is intended to provide general information about retirement life planning. Neither the author nor the publisher is engaged in rendering legal, accounting, financial, medical, or psychological services. As each situation is unique, questions specific to your particular situation should be addressed to an appropriate professional for proper evaluation and advice. The author and publisher disclaim any liability, loss, or risk that is incurred as a consequence of the use and application of any of the contents of this work.

Published in the United States by Ten Speed Press, an imprint of the Crown Publishing Group, a division of Random House, Inc., New York.
www.crownpublishing.com
www.tenspeed.com

A previous edition of this work was published in the United States by Ten Speed Press, Berkeley, CA, in 2007.

Library of Congress Cataloging-in-Publication Data

Nelson, John E.
What color is your parachute? for retirement : planning a prosperous, healthy, and happy future / John E. Nelson and Richard N. Bolles. — 2nd ed.
p. cm.
Bolles's name appears first in the previous ed.
Includes index.
Summary: "A revised edition of the definitive retirement guide for people of all career stages"—Provided by publisher.
1. Retirement income—Planning. 2. Retirement—Planning. I. Bolles, Richard Nelson. II. Bolles, Richard Nelson. What color is your parachute? for retirement. III. Title.
HG179.B575 2010
332.024'014—dc22

2010005578

ISBN 978-1-58008-205-1

Printed in the United States of America

Design by Betsy Stromberg

10 9 8 7 6 5 4 3 2 1

Second Edition

To my mother.

You were a better role model than I knew.

—John E. Nelson

Contents

Preface

This book is part of what we call *The Parachute Library*. Like all books in that Library, it is not intended as a substitute or replacement for its best-selling centerpiece, *What Color Is Your Parachute? A Practical Guide for Job-Hunters and Career-Changers* (ten million copies in print), but as a supplement to it.

Why do we need a supplement? Well, each *time* of Life has special issues and special challenges, where we all could use a little extra guidance. The *time* of Life from age fifty, on, is one of those times. I have a friend named John Nelson, who is an expert on that *time* of Life, and therefore I have asked him to write this book.

My contribution to this book is twofold: (1) To frame some of the questions and challenges during this period, as I have done in my earlier work *The Three Boxes of Life, and How to Get Out of Them: An Introduction to Life/Work Planning* (1978). (2) To write this introduction and overview, to get us going.

The *time* of Life that we are talking about here is traditionally called "Retirement." Some people love that word. I'm not one of them. For me, it implies "being put out to pasture"—to borrow an image from a cow. It implies a kind of parole from a thing called *work*, which is assumed to be onerous, and tedious. It implies "disengagement" from both *work* and *Life*, as one patiently—or impatiently—waits to die. It thinks of Life in terms of work.

I prefer instead to think of Life in terms of music. My favorite metaphor is that of a symphony. A symphony, traditionally, has four parts to it—four movements, as they're called. So does Life. There is infancy, then the time of learning, then the time of working, and finally, this time that we are talking about, often called "retirement." But if we discourage the use of the word "retirement," then this might better be called the Fourth Movement.

The Fourth Movement, in the symphonic world, is a kind of blank slate. It was and is up to the composer to decide what to write upon it. Traditionally, the composer writes of triumph, victory, and joy—as in Beethoven's Symphony #3, the *Eroica*. But it may, alternatively, be a kind of anticlimactic, meandering piece of music—as in Tchaikovsky's Symphony #6, the *Pathetique*. There the Third Movement ends with a bombastic, stirring march. The Fourth Movement, immediately following, is subdued, meditative, meandering, and sounds almost like an afterthought.

Well, there are our choices about our own lives: Shall the Fourth Movement, the final movement, of our lives be *pathetique or eroica*—pathetic or heroic? Your call!

I like this defining of our lives in terms of music, rather than in terms of work.

To carry the metaphor onward, in this Fourth Movement of our lives, we have instruments, which we must treat with care. They are: our **body**, our **mind**, our **spirit**, and what we poetically speak of as our **heart**, which Chinese medicine calls "the Emperor."[1] Body, mind, spirit, heart. Some of these instruments are in shiny, splendid condition. Others are slightly dented. Or greatly dented. But these are the instruments that play the musical notes and themes of this time of our lives.

The traditional notes are: **sleep, water, eating, faith, love, loneliness, survival** (financial and spiritual), **health care, dreams** (fulfilled or unfulfilled), and **triumph**—over all adversities—and even **death**.

Traditionally, the themes for this period of our lives also include *planning*. But I believe the outstanding characteristic of the Fourth Movement in our lives is the increased number of things we call *unexpected*. And that can knock all our plans into a cocked hat. So I prefer to say that

1. www.itmonline.org/5organs/heart.htm

one of the notes we strike, is how to handle interruptions. Martin Luther King, Jr., perhaps put it best, just before his death:

> "The major problem of life is learning how to handle the costly interruptions—the door that slams shut, the plan that got side-tracked, the marriage that failed, or that lovely poem that didn't get written because someone knocked on the door."

Interruptions, in music, are the pauses between the notes; they are, in fact, what keep the notes from just becoming a jumble. Just listen to the first few bars of Beethoven's Fifth. Thank God for the interruptions, the spaces between the notes.

So, where have we come thus far? Well, I suggested that it is useful to think of Life after fifty as the Fourth Movement in the symphony of our lives—the movement that comes after the first three: Infancy, then The Time of Learning, and then The Time of Working. And it is useful to think that we have instruments, which play certain themes in this movement, as we have seen. That brings us to the $64,000 question: "Toward what end? What is the point of all these notes, all these themes, in the Fourth Movement? What are they intended to produce?"

Ahhh, when I think of the overall impression left with me after I hear the Fourth Movement of any great symphony, such as Schubert's Ninth, one impression sticks out, above all others. And that impression is one of *energy*. I am left with an impression of great energy. And the more the better, say I. Energy is lovely to behold, and even lovelier to possess. That energy belongs in the Fourth Movement because it brings the whole symphony to triumphant resolution.

This, it seems to me, is how people evaluate the Fourth Movement of our lives, as well. Not: Did we live triumphantly and die victoriously; but: Do we manifest *energy*? Do we manifest enthusiasm? Do we manifest excitement, still?

Ask any employer what they are looking for, when they interview a job candidate who is fifty years or older, and they will tell you: energy. They ask themselves, "Does the candidate (*that's us*) slouch in the chair? Does the candidate look like they're just marking time in Life? Or does the candidate lean slightly forward in the chair as we talk? Does the candidate seem excited about the prospect of working here?"

Energy in people past fifty is exciting to an employer. And to those around us. It suggests the candidate will come in early, and stay late. It suggests that whatever task is given, the task will be done thoroughly and completely, and not just barely or perfunctorily.

All right, then, *energy*. Where shall we find energy, after fifty? When we were young, energy resided in the physical side of our nature. We were "feeling our oats." We could go all day, and go all night. "My, where do you get all your energy," our grandmother would ask us. We were a dynamo of physical energy.

Can't say the same when we reach fifty, and beyond. Oh, some of us still have it. But as we get older the rest of us start to slow down. Physical energy is often harder to come by, despite workouts and exercise and marathons. Increasingly, our energy must more and more come from *within*. It must spring not from our muscles but from our excitement about Life and about what we are doing in this Fourth and final Movement of our Life.

That is why, past fifty, we need to spend more time on the homework of inventorying what in Life we are (still) passionate about. The questions of our youth—***what** are your favorite skills? **where** do you most enjoy using them? and **how** do you find such a place and such a job or endeavor?*—become critical when we are past fifty.[2] The nicest compliment any of us can hear as we grow older, is: "What a passion for life she still has! Or, he has! It's thrilling to be around them."

And so, it is time to turn to the body of this book. All of the *frame* that John Nelson proposes, for our looking at this time of our Life, all the *questions* he suggests we must ask ourselves, and all of the *inventory* that he suggests we should do, are essential to finding our *energy* in this Fourth and final Movement of the symphony of our Life. Come with me, as we enter the main body of the book. And we shall make beautiful music, together.

—Richard N. Bolles

2. Detailed instructions for getting at these questions can be found in my book *What Color Is Your Parachute?*, updated annually, and available in any bookstore.

What to Expect from This New Edition

You may be wondering what's new in this edition of *What Color Is Your Parachute? for Retirement.*

First, you'll notice that this edition captures the continuing evolution of retirement as a life stage. Chapter by chapter, it shows how society is irrevocably remaking the *old* retirement into a *new* retirement. But because we're still in the process of creating it, no one knows yet, for sure, what that will mean. This book helps you prepare for that shift.

Second, you'll notice that this edition provides you with additional planning tools and techniques. Even with all the uncertainty, you'll still have more freedom in retirement than in any other stage of life. This book helps you design, and take concrete steps toward, the life of your dreams.

The universal dream is prosperity, health, and happiness—otherwise known as well-being. But many feel that economic uncertainty threatens their dreams. How do all these evolving forces affect you and your plans for retirement?

Financially, we've seen our retirement accounts and home values take the roller-coaster ride of a lifetime. Traditional pensions, which offer a guaranteed monthly benefit, have increasingly shown signs of inadequate employer funding. Social Security is facing a similar problem on a larger scale. The ballooning federal debt complicates long-term fixes for Social Security and Medicare funding problems. At all levels, governments will be forced to rethink the assistance they provide to a rapidly growing number of older citizens. Uncertainty has prompted many to keep working as long as possible. Have we now come to view continued employment as an expected part of retirement?

Geographically, we've begun to think more deeply about where we really want to live. Rather than speculating on future home values, we're viewing our home and community as environments that support the life we want to lead.

Medically, we know retirement is a life stage that brings increased interaction with the medical delivery system. But the system itself will be undergoing significant changes in the coming years—just when we'll personally need more care. One effect of economic stress is to drain our biological vitality, so it's even more important for each of us to build that vitality up.

Psychologically, the concept of retirement happiness as carefree decades of leisure is now out of date and out of step. It's being replaced by our desire for a deeper sense of fulfillment and engagement in life. From now on, we're more likely to recognize that our happiness is more connected to our sense of community than to our level of consumption.

You can use this book to gain insight and make plans for *all* these areas of your life, because it's unique. It's not a finance book (although it is about prosperity). It's not a medical book (although it is about health). And it's not a psychology book (although it is about happiness). It's a well-being book.

You might think of this as an *introductory course* on all the aspects of designing your retirement life. Or if you've already studied retirement, you might think of this as your *capstone* course, pulling all of your studies together. Either way, you'll find this book to be both a philosophical and a practical resource.

Finally, here's a bit of heartfelt advice for you. The best way to use this book is to actually do the exercises, fill in the blanks, and write all over the pages. I provide you with a *process* for designing your Ideal Retirement. But you, dear reader, must provide the *content*. That's how you make this *your* book, instead of *my* book.

After all, it's your retirement, isn't it?

—John E. Nelson

"I know that someday I will die, but I will never retire."

—Margaret Mead, renowned anthropologist

Chapter ONE

Retirement Is Dead— Long Live Retirement!

In centuries past, when a king lay dying, there would be great concern among the people. They were sad about losing a ruler they knew. And anxious, too, about getting a new ruler that they didn't know. The kingdom was changing. What would happen to them? As the old king took his final breath, and his successor became king, a cry would ring out among the people:

"The king is dead—long live the king!"

That is what's happening to the life stage we call "retirement." At all levels—individual, organizational, and societal—it's dying. And it's dying sooner than we thought. The successor is a new, unknown, and quite different life stage—which will also be called "retirement." The kingdom is changing. What will happen to you?

While all these changes are going on around you, you'll be making key decisions about your next stage of life. Because there are no rules for this new version of retirement, you'll need to design it for yourself. This book will help you make those decisions, and help you design the life you want to live.

Where do you stand now? If you've been working steadily toward the *old-fashioned version of retirement*, you can probably still get there, if you really want to. If you're anxious about the uncertainties of the *new retirement*, you can take concrete steps to protect yourself. If you're curious about the new possibilities that are opening up, you can explore those. And if you don't think you'll ever have a retirement (new or old), you can identify what might keep you going. Whatever your situation, you'll discover something useful here.

You'll also discover that this book isn't about just one aspect of retirement. It's about you, and all the parts of your life. For example, most retirement books focus on finances, and come from the narrow perspective of money and managing the affairs of the world. Other books focus on health, and come from the narrow perspective of medicine and managing your physical body. Still others focus on happiness, and come from the narrow perspective of your relationship with yourself and others. *This book is unusual because it integrates all those aspects of your life.* So instead of coming from one of those narrow perspectives, this book takes your perspective. It's you-centered, rather than topic-centered!

Why You Won't Find Everything You Need within This Book

To design the life you want to live, you'll need to do some real research and make some important decisions. However, you won't find *all* the information you need within these humble pages. The world—and the world of retirement—is now simply too big and too complicated. It wasn't so long ago that there was a shortage of information out in the world, and the purpose of a book like this was to collect and preserve that scarce resource. To obtain in-depth information on a specific topic like retirement, you traveled to a repository in the physical world—a library or bookstore. There were only a few designated places where in-depth information was indexed, catalogued, and stored, so that you could obtain it when you needed it. The world was almost like a knowledge desert, and a book was like an oasis of knowledge. In that bygone era (just a few years ago), most people valued books mostly for the *content* that they offered.

But now it's the opposite! There's a *surplus* of information in the world. There's more floating around than we know what to do with. From television to magazines to advertising to bloggers to Google searches, it's simply endless. It keeps pouring in, more and more of it, every day. We are awash in information. And it's not just of a general nature. Anyone with an internet connection can drill down to find and retrieve the most specific, technical, and obscure tidbits that you can imagine. Although some of what we access is simply data, much of it is actual knowledge. That is, it's well-considered advice from people who truly know what they're talking about, within their own area of expertise. The world isn't an information desert anymore.

If the World Is Full of Information, Then What's This Book For?

Due to the ever-present, immediate, and endless electronic delivery of in-depth information, there is now more of it available *outside* of books than *inside* them. If you can obtain knowledge through your broadband connection, then what's a book for? In this case, the book you're holding has a more important job than merely providing more information. Its job is to help you understand the sea of information in a new way. As it turns out, there are *three fundamental problems* with the way the sea of information operates.

The first problem with the sea of information is that it's actually incoherent. It just splashes around, with no sense of order. So this book provides a *coherent structure for organizing information*. That way, you'll be able to bring order to the chaos of the modern information world.

The second problem with the sea of information is that it's relentless. It's like a fire hose that's forever trying to fill you up, as though you were an empty barrel. So this book provides a way to *reflect upon, draw out, and crystallize* the wisdom you already have. It's at the confluence of the information stream and your own stream of consciousness, that you'll make your best decisions.

The third problem with the sea of information is that it's fickle—the current flows one way and then another. Because there's no direction, who knows where you might end up? So this book helps you *choose your own destination* and set a course to get there, no matter which way the winds are blowing.

Unlike the stream of information, this book is something secure that you can get a hold of. Unlike that anonymous information that flows by and is gone forever, when you use this book, you'll be organizing and clarifying your own information, thoughts, and dreams. (Try doing that with Google!)

Truth be told, there really is a lot of content in this book. Most of it can't be found anywhere else. But just as important, you'll find a unique *process* for designing the life of your dreams. A process that offers a coherent structure, recognizes what you already know, and provides a constancy of vision. When you read this book and do the exercises, you'll become better and better at navigating that ever-changing sea of information out there. You'll be the captain of your own ship, sailing toward your own destination.

Retirement As a Gradual Process

So—what *is* the destination, anyway? Where are we supposed to be heading? Why are we supposed to retire? After all, for 98 percent of human history, retirement didn't really exist!

For eons, most people worked for themselves, and with their families. They were hunters or farmers or fishers or craftspeople or traders. They pretty much kept working into their later years, because they weren't wealthy enough to stop working. (There have always been a few wealthy people who could stop working, of course. But most people couldn't.) As they aged, they worked at a slower pace, relying less and less on their physical strength and stamina and more and more on their acquired knowledge and skills. If they were clever and fortunate, they found ways to do more of the work that they liked (and less of the work that they didn't). But most people couldn't afford to stop working, and so they kept on, as best they could, as long as they needed to. Except in the case of sickness or accident, withdrawing from work was a gradual process. The human life course had a long and gradual arc, with gentle transitions from one life stage to the next. It was a natural way to live, and it was like that for thousands of years.

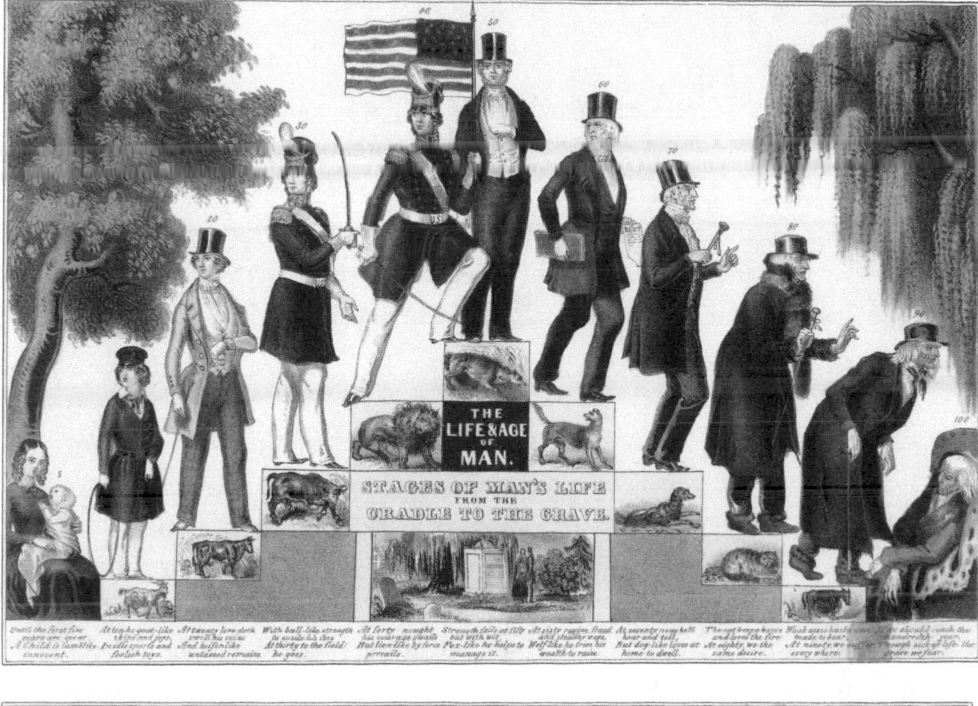

Before the industrial age, life transitions were more gradual.

The Life and Age of Man and *The Life and Age of Woman*, James Baillie, 1848.

So what happened? The Industrial Revolution! Many of the people who had worked the land or pursued their own cottage crafts went to work in factories for someone else, or for something else—a corporation. Most of them did it willingly, because they could earn more money and improve their material standard of living. The industrial laborer's life was very different, though. In factories, everything was standardized. All the machines were in rows. All the nuts and bolts were in standard sizes. And people's *activities* became standardized, too. Instead of using their unique skills, workers with the same jobs were supposed to do the same things in the same way. Also, people's working *time* became standardized. Everyone worked in shifts, with each shift's workers starting at the same time, taking a break at the same time, and quitting at the same time. At the end of the day, as one shift of workers left, another was waiting to take its place.

The work in factories was fast, demanding, and repetitive. People had always worked hard, but not in such a structured, mechanistic way. As workers aged, they couldn't gradually slow down. They couldn't focus more on using their knowledge and skills, as they had in preindustrial times. After all, factories were organized around efficient production, not around the natural life course of humans. Workers were seen almost as a part of the machines they operated. (Charlie Chaplin's movie *Modern Times* was a serious comedy on that topic.)

Factory owners decided to get the slower, older workers out of the factory by implementing a new practice: retirement. It was similar to replacing the worn-out part of a machine. After all, with an increasing population, there were plenty of younger, stronger, faster workers ready to fill those jobs. It was also pretty easy to sell the idea of retirement to workers—especially when it included a retirement pension! The jobs were physically demanding, dirty, and dangerous. Much of it was sheer drudgery, so the simple absence of this nasty work, in itself, was a reward. As general prosperity increased, more and more people were able to stop working as they got older. Given the nature of the work, who wouldn't want to retire?

THE ONE BEST WAY TO RETIRE?

In the early days of the twentieth century, the Industrial Revolution was getting up to full speed in the United States. The industrial workplace was so different from the old agrarian way of life that experts needed to develop completely new ways of thinking about work, workers, and the workplace.

A revolutionary thinker of the day was Frederick Winslow Taylor (1856–1915). He was essentially the very first management consultant. Taylor's seminal ideas were outlined in his book *The Principles of Scientific Management*. One seminal idea was to expand standardization from things (like nuts and bolts) to human behaviors. His goal was to discover the "One Best Way" to do each job and then make sure every worker did the job in that exact way. This thinking sparked a new profession—the efficiency expert—which ultimately transformed the industrial workplace. But it went way beyond industry. This way of thinking spread to construction, the military, offices, professions, and even schools. Peter Drucker, the famous management guru, suggested that "Taylorism" might have been the United States' most important contribution to new thought since the framing of the Constitution. The impact was international as well: *The Principles of Scientific Management* sold one and a half million copies in Japan.

We don't know what Taylor would have personally thought about a standardized approach to retirement. He only lived to the age of fifty-nine. However, the Taylorism movement wanted to standardize everything in its path, and that could have included retirement. Anyway, the idea of a standard approach to retirement is truly a relic of twentieth-century thinking. Isn't it time to move retirement into the twenty-first century?

A Standardized Approach to Retirement

Like everything else in the factory, though, retirement needed to be standardized. So employers selected standard ages for retirement. In fact, it was often called the "normal retirement age." It could vary, but let's take age sixty-five as an example. At that time, workers who made it to sixty-five were, in general, pretty worn-out. But not all of them. There was a huge variation in how worn-out people were at that age.

It didn't matter that at any given retirement age, one worker might be as fit as a fiddle and the next one had a foot in the grave. Or that one person loved the work he was doing and was productive, while the next one hated it and barely kept up. None of that was taken into consideration, and for the sake of standardization, retirement was based on age. After all, for employers and employees, age is easy to measure and to specify. How healthy a person is, or how much that person loves the job, is certainly more relevant to the timing of retirement—but that couldn't be easily measured.

So the die was cast. This standardized approach to retirement, based on age, meant that instead of the withdrawal from work happening gradually, as it had for most of human history, it became an all-or-nothing deal. When the idea of retirement was created, it was created as an event—a specific point in time. Before workers reached the retirement date, they went to work full time, every day. When they reached that date, they stopped working completely, all at once. Retirement was radically different than the more gradual transitions that humans had always known. But it made sense for the factory.

This standardize-everything mentality spread far beyond the factory and into offices and professions. The federal government took the same approach as the organizations that had implemented pensions. When Social Security was instituted in 1936 with a standardized age, that was the end of the story. Retirement became an all-or-nothing event. Retirement became the finish line of life.

In the old retirement, then, the idea of standardization stuck. It stuck with employees, with employers, and with the government. It has stuck around for well over half a century. But you're not stuck with it.

When you go about designing the new retirement, a good place to start is with the transition itself. Could you choose your own timing, and transition gradually, like humans did before retirement was created? Think how different that would be than an all-or-nothing event.

Is Retirement a Finish Line or Just a Marker along the Way?

Unfortunately, a retirement finish line can give us a countdown mentality: "Only five years, eight months, two weeks, and four days to go—hallelujah!" A countdown mentality can make us unintentionally put our life on hold. On a more subtle level, it can leave us feeling powerless, as if we were not in control of our lives. It can make us feel that we need to wait until the normal retirement age to become emancipated—when finally, at last, we'll be set free to do what we really want with our lives.

Or just as dangerously, a retirement finish line may induce us to retire on the standard schedule, even though we're not ready. What if we're not financially prepared to retire? What if we're as healthy as a horse with no signs of slowing down? What if we still find our work or coworkers engaging and energizing? The pressure of the standardized retirement age can make us disregard our own unique situation.

Rather than being driven by your "normal retirement age," perhaps there is another way that you can look at it. Is your work holding you up or holding you back? Sustaining you or squelching you? Is your job a leash or a lifeline? Those questions may be more relevant in deciding when and how to retire than the age on your driver's license.

Although your employer, your benefits provider, and the government all use standardized ages for retirement, that doesn't mean you have to. Instead of automatically accepting some arbitrary ages and dates, you can come up with your own. Then be sure to brainstorm with a knowledgeable expert (or two or three) on how to compromise between your own schedule and those all-important regulations. If you're short on money, you might need to customize for a later retirement age. If you're short on health, you might need to customize for more work flexibility. If you're short on happiness, you might need to customize for your sanity!

Depending on your job and your employer, you may have almost no flexibility in customizing your transition, or you may have a great deal. (If you're one of the ever-growing numbers of entrepreneurs or solopreneurs, you have carte blanche—so you can get really creative.) In some cases, employers are willing to bend over backward to accommodate workers, and in other cases they won't bend an inch. If your knowledge or skills are in high demand and low supply, your employer may be eager to entertain your creative ideas about a "flex retirement." But if your employer sees you as just one more cog in the machine and imagines that there are plenty more cogs where you came from, you don't have much bargaining power.

Your flexibility in your job, with your employer, in your industry is ruled by the particularities of your situation, rather than the generalities of the marketplace. You won't know how much you can customize your retirement transition unless you try. Also, you know best what the culture of your workplace is—and how close to the vest you need to keep your retirement cards. At some organizations, if an employee so much as admits that some day, in the far distant future, he or she might possibly want to retire, the employer will immediately suspect that the worker is starting to slack off and not taking the job seriously. If you know that to be the case at your organization, you don't need me to tell you to be discreet! If, however, your organization is one where you can be upfront about your long-term and short-term plans, that's much better for you and for your employer, too. Remember, you and your employer are both making up new ways of transitioning to retirement. You may need to be a trailblazer to customize your transition. Just be careful not to get burned!

TEN WAYS TO CUSTOMIZE YOUR RETIREMENT TRANSITION

Here's a list of ideas, just to spark your creativity. You might:

1. Change to a career you love, that you could do forever, more or less. (Probably less.)
2. Start a business on the side, and keep it going after you retire from your regular job.
3. Slash your living expenses, save like a crazy person, and take an early retirement offer. (But be ready to work again, if need be.)
4. Take early retirement like #3, but plan to try a new career. So what if it doesn't work out?
5. Refocus your job on what you do really, really well, then retire late because you're so valuable.
6. Get rid of the worst parts of your job, then work part-time to do only the best parts.
7. Negotiate a phased retirement, where your employer lets you taper off over months or years.
8. Open the door to a revolving retirement, where you come back periodically or for specific projects.
9. Take a standard retirement, then work for a customer, a supplier, or even a competitor.
10. Take a standard retirement, but become a consultant in your field. (Many people claim they're going to do this, but never follow through. Are you different?)

CAUTION: Finding a way to stretch your transition can be difficult, but it increases your financial security. Finding a way to cut short your transition can be easy, but it decreases your financial security. Always look before you leap.

Transitions and the Three Boxes of Life

Changing the way we transition to a stage of life is an important issue. There's an even more important one, though. What are the life stages themselves? Could you make up your own life stages, if you wanted to?

Let's start with the standard-issue life stages, and transitions, the way most of us were brought up to think of them. The retirement event has been the doorway from the life stage of work into the life stage of retirement. And much earlier, another event—graduation—was the doorway from the life stage of education into the life stage of work. These transitions divided life into three stages: education, work, and retirement. These have been so rigid, and so closed off from each other, that we could even think of them as *boxes*. (This idea was first put forth by Richard N. Bolles in his book *The Three Boxes of Life*.) They look like this:

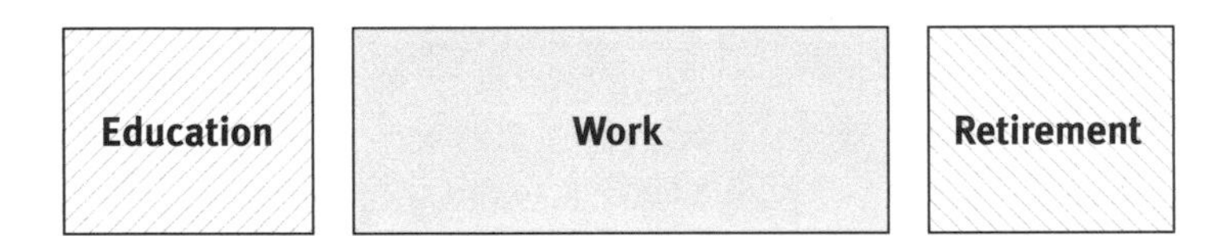

For most of human history, these boxes didn't exist for most people. Children farmed and fished and crafted with their families from an early age. Then, when the Industrial Revolution happened, children went to work in factories instead. (It sounds appalling to you now, doesn't it?) When economic prosperity increased enough, society was able to create the education box. There was a cost to doing that, but it was an investment in the future. The education box directed the people in it toward the activities of learning and self-development. That meant that only adults would be in the box called work. They were the ones directed toward the activities of working and being productive. Finally, when prosperity had increased enough again, we created the box called retirement. There was a cost to society for creating that box, too.

The retirement box was unique in one way, though. Instead of being defined by what the people in it could and should do, it was defined by what they couldn't and shouldn't do! Specifically, they shouldn't be learning and developing. And they shouldn't be working and productive, either. You know the story of how the old retirement was born: It was created for older workers who were too worn-out to learn anything or produce anything new. There's a name for what they could do—it's called *leisure*.

So, across the life course, we were supposed to first focus on self-development (the first box), then on being productive (the second box), and then on leisure. So the *contents* of the three boxes look like this:

When young people are in the box of education, their parents, teachers, and peers create an environment that pretty much tells them what to do. They may think they're "doing their own thing." But if they get off course, others in the education box usually straighten them out—in a well-meaning way—and put them back on the standardized path. So when it comes down to it, the first box doesn't allow much freedom. Society in general, and families in particular, must provide support for that box, so they run the show.

Likewise, when people are in the box of work, the supervisors, coworkers, and their own professional expectations keep them in line. Although they're adults, the environment pretty much tells them what they should be doing. They definitely have more freedom and more choices. But society needs people in the second box to support the ones in the first and third boxes, so they pretty much keep their noses to the grindstone.

The Old Retirement Was the Final Box of Life

What about the retirement box? When the old retirement was created, the people in it were retiring from old-fashioned factories or other demanding work, and typically in declining health. Most of them were going to live only a few years in retirement. They were retiring to a life of leisure, because that's all they were capable of. And unlike the earlier boxes, there weren't many societal expectations. No parents, teachers, or supervisors to keep retirees in line. They were left alone, to do whatever they wanted, with the short time they had left. Society and employers provided significant economic support for this nonproductive life stage through Social Security and retirement pensions.

This was a major achievement of modern society. All three boxes were in place, and supported by societal institutions. Everyone knew what they were supposed to be doing, and when they were supposed to be doing it. The structure and funding for education was in place, and working pretty well. The structure and funding for retirement was in place, and working pretty well, too. After thousands of years of gradual life-stage transitions, the human life course had been changed forever. It was now neatly divided into three well-defined boxes. Society was great!

Breaking Down the Boxes

Then, as time went on, something amazing happened. The retirees didn't die. Well, they died, but not as soon as expected. For a variety of reasons, they kept living longer. Each group of retirees lived longer than the previous groups had. And they weren't just living longer, they were healthier and more active, too. The leisure box extended, and the Three Boxes of Life changed to look like this:

At the same time, workers were looking at the old retirement and deciding that they'd like to get there as early as possible. With personal savings, employer pensions, and Social Security, the average age for retirement became younger. The productivity box shortened a bit, and the leisure box was even longer. The three boxes looked like this:

Development	Productivity	Leisure

The retirement stage of life had been transformed. Instead of being worn-out and sick for much of their retirement, people were healthy and vital. Instead of lasting just a few years, retirement stretched out to a decade or more. And because no one was telling them what to do, retirees could do whatever they wanted. Some decided that an entire life stage based on leisure didn't make sense. They forgot (or never knew) that productivity and development were supposed to be off-limits. They took up formal and informal learning, new careers, significant volunteer work—you name it, they did it. They mixed up development, productivity, and leisure all in one box! They made the earlier, healthier part of retirement into a completely different stage of life than the old retirement was supposed to be. Only the later part of retirement looked like the original idea, as people became frailer and were winding down their lives. It looked like this:

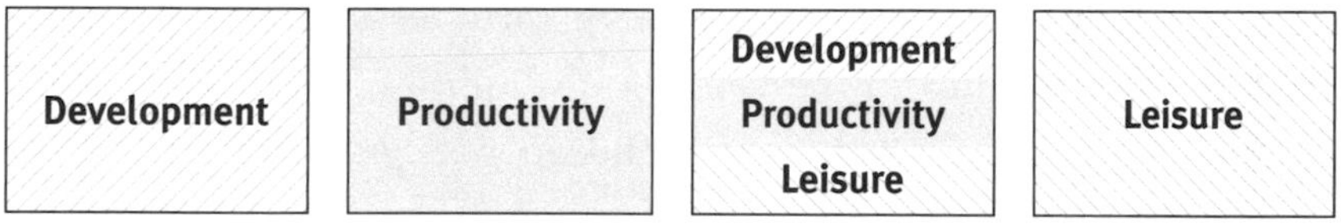

Development	Productivity	Development Productivity Leisure	Leisure

From the Three Boxes to the Four Ages

In the 1980s, a historian at Cambridge University by the name of Peter Laslett had anticipated what would happen. He knew that the original idea of retirement—the old retirement—couldn't stretch enough to fit what was happening in the world. He saw that the healthy, active, early part of retirement wasn't very much like the frail, inactive, later part. They were altogether different ages of life. At the same time, the last years of the second box were becoming more and more varied. Some workers were retiring, or semi-retiring, in their fifties. They were still supposed to be in the second box but were living more like the healthy, active early part of the third box. Laslett realized that to understand what was going on, and to make plans for ourselves, we needed a fresh map of life. It looks like this:

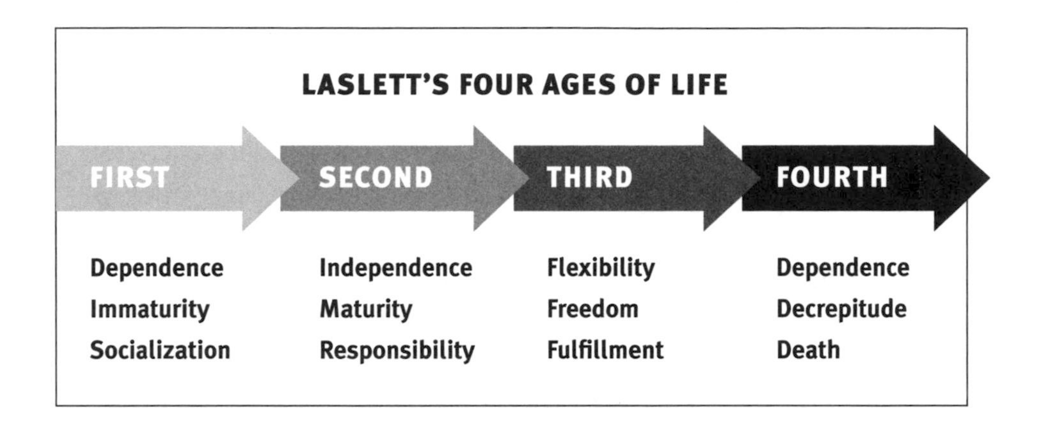

Laslett's description of the First and Second Ages are equivalent to the first and second boxes. His description of the Fourth Age has similarities to the original industrial-age retirement—sickly and short. But his concept for the Third Age is something else altogether. He recognized that for the first time in human history, we were creating a life stage that had significantly reduced responsibilities—but also continuing health and vitality. As people at midlife were gradually freed from child care and work, what would they do with that freedom? He suggested that this newfound opportunity could be the peak of human achievement. Rather than being *over the hill*, people could be *climbing the summit* of life. They could develop themselves to their full capacity and attain their greatest degree of life fulfillment. He even referred to it as the "crown" of life! Rather than defining it by specific ages, he suggested that the Third Age is defined by an orientation toward life. Laslett was a good role model, as his book on this subject was published when he was seventy-four. For many of us, the Third Age is most likely to occur between the ages of fifty and seventy-five. We may be working, retired, or somewhere in between. But that's less of a factor than our commitment to fully explore, develop, and express ourselves. The fact that you're reading this book right now is an indication that the idea of the Third Age probably appeals to you.

You Could Have a Third Age of Life—Whether or Not You're Retired

What interesting new combination of work, learning, and leisure would you like to create? The more creative you are, the less retirement income you may need. In our consumer culture, advertising tries to convince us that happiness can be found mostly with a credit card. It can take tons of money to fund a retirement that's based on all leisure all the time. You could be saving up forever to afford such a retirement.

In contrast, learning is pretty inexpensive. Public universities and community colleges often provide courses at nominal cost for retirees. Many faith communities sponsor programs for both self-exploration and socializing. Nonprofit entities such as Elderhostel sponsor low-cost opportunities to explore and learn about the world. Senior-level athletic events are also becoming more common. On a more individual level, you're free to explore hobbies or activities that are based on self-development rather than entertainment. Self-development can be a bargain.

Productivity can be even better than a bargain. It can cost as little or as much as you're willing and able to spend, and the result is often making money rather than spending money. One form of productivity is paid employment, which might help make ends meet. Or if you can afford to, you may choose to be productive as a volunteer, for no pay. And you may even find something in the middle—such as a job that pays less than you'd normally accept—so you can do something more important to you than just earn a paycheck.

For each of us, the right kinds of self-development and productivity can be just as satisfying as leisure—or even more satisfying. Add all this up and it's clear that a life stage based on three types of activities—leisure, self-development, and productivity—may allow you to live on less money than a leisure-based retirement would cost.

OK, You've Got the Job. When Can You Start?

If you're thinking this new Third Age approach to retirement might work for you, then the next question is, when can you start? If you're not going to be "over the hill" at any particular age, but will still be climbing the summit, then you don't need to retire based on some arbitrary calculation of how many years you've been on earth. After all, chronological age is only one way to think about where you are in your life's journey. (Biological age is another way—but we'll get to that in chapter six.) You may retire "early" for your age, or you may retire "late" for your age. So instead of thinking about chronological age, try thinking in terms of your life stage—what's actually going on in your life.

If you're still carrying the heavy burdens of raising children (or paying their expenses), pushing to keep going strong in your career, or paddling to keep your financial head above water, you're squarely in the Second Age, no matter how old you are. (Keep going—you'll get there!) On the other hand, if your children have flown the coop, if you have the choice at work of pushing hard or easing off, and if you've salted away enough money to make a paycheck optional, you may be ready for the Third Age, even though you're not ready to retire. Instead of the all-or-nothing old retirement approach, perhaps you can make a more gradual transition—as humans once did, naturally, for millennia. You can withdraw from work on your own schedule, and mix and match it with learning and leisure, however you want!

Just to get your Third Age imagination going, here are some questions to ask yourself about the three types of activities:

1. **Self-Development.** What do you really want to learn about, or how have you dreamed of investing in your ongoing development? Can you imagine exploring career options that would allow you to somehow get paid to learn or develop in this way?
2. **Productivity.** If you were determined to work at something that you absolutely love, what might that be? Could you afford to earn less money doing it—or even do it without pay—solely for fulfillment

and satisfaction? Can you imagine exploring career options that would allow you to get paid to work at something you love?

3. **Leisure.** What have you wanted to do, just for the sheer pleasure of it, but productivity and self-development seemed always to take precedence? As crazy as it may sound, can you imagine exploring career options that would allow you to somehow get paid to play?

If the Third Age sounds like crazy talk to you, and you just want to think about the old retirement and taking it easy, don't feel guilty. It's OK if you just want all leisure, all the time. You could be, like the original workers, just plain worn-out from all the work of the second box. You may really need to do absolutely nothing but enjoy yourself—without trying to be productive or self-developing—for a while after you retire. Farmers know that a field that's allowed to lie fallow for a year will yield a better crop the following year. That may be the case with your retirement; you may find you want to do something else later, after you're fully rested and recharged. In fact, you may surprise yourself.

What Should We Call This New Stage of Life?

This new way of thinking about the stages of life has folks in a lexical quandary. Because it's so different from the original idea of retirement, some people don't even want to call this new life stage *retirement*. They've come up with labels to try to articulate what a huge shift it represents. Here are some terms that you might see:

- The New Retirement
- Re-Firement
- Re-Wirement
- Rest-of-Life
- Second Half of Life
- Unretirement

- Renewment
- Re-Engagement
- Second Adolescence
- The Bonus Years

The change that's happening may ultimately be as profound as the creation of the original old retirement was. But we think that in terminology, a strange thing is likely to happen. As more and more people take this new approach—of greatest freedom, mixing it all up, development and productivity and leisure—it won't seem so unusual anymore. It will eventually become the normal thing to do. People will ask, "Wasn't retirement always about development and productivity and leisure?" The original idea of retirement of all leisure, all the time will have faded away, and this revolutionary new approach won't even need an alternative name. This radical new life stage will eventually come to be called, simply, *retirement*.

Retirement is dead—long live retirement!

PRINCIPLES OF RETIREMENT

Retirement is changing in many ways, and for many reasons. What was true in the past may not be true in the future. With so much uncertainty, how can you design the life you want to live?

Before making the big decisions about your retirement, think through these fundamental principles. Keep them in mind as you develop your specific strategies and tactics, and you'll be building on a firm foundation. Forgetting about them could lead to a shaky retirement!

1. **Retirement is a career transition.**

   Your transition may be away from work completely or from one career to another. The transition can be all at once or happen gradually over time.

2. **Retirement can be voluntary or involuntary.**

   You could choose the timing, or you might be terminated even though you want to keep working. You may think you're temporarily unemployed, but discover later that you're retired.

3. **Retirement is a stage of life.**

   Your retirement is not only an event, but a life change that occurs over a period of time. Your experience is unique, and yet it also has much in common with many other adults.

4. **Retirement includes biological aging.**

   Your body ages over the course of retirement, which results in decline and death at an unknown future time.

5. **Retirement requires economic support for an unknown time.**

   For you to remain retired, sources of material support must continue for as long as you live.

6. **Retirement changes your level of engagement.**

   Retirement increases or decreases your psychological engagement, and increases or decreases your social engagement with others. Both tend to decrease over the course of your retirement.

7. **Retirement is shaped by earlier life stages.**

   All the domains of your life prior to retirement will affect your life during retirement.

8. **Retirement well-being includes prosperity, health, and happiness.**

   Your well-being doesn't come from economic security, physical health, or life satisfaction, but from all three in combination.

"Without ignoring the importance of economic growth, we must look well beyond it."

—Amartya Sen, winner of the 1998 Nobel Prize in economics

Chapter TWO

The Retirement You've Always Wanted but Forgot About

Because the old retirement is dying, and no one is sure what this new life stage will be like—doesn't that mean we get to design it ourselves? Isn't this our chance to have what we've always wanted in life?

Yes! But designing a new stage of life is a big responsibility, and it doesn't come along very often. (Look how long the old retirement lasted.) So we're doing this not only for ourselves but also for those who will follow in our footsteps. We want to get it right.

Designing the old retirement was much simpler. The conceptual process went something like this: "I'll get retirement income and won't need to do that dirty, dangerous, boring, back-breaking work anymore!" That was enough. The organizing concept that guided the old retirement was simply *not working*.

According to Peter Laslett, we've now moved well beyond that simple original goal. For the new retirement, we've moved on to the idea that it should be the "crown" of our life. But to actually make that happen, we need a new organizing concept. What we choose is important, because it guides our thoughts and actions. It's what we use to imagine the future, set goals, and motivate ourselves. It drives how we gather information, make decisions, and take action. *The organizing concept we choose ultimately determines what we get.*

For the new retirement, we need a concept that's big enough to get the job done. A concept that describes what we really want in retirement. A concept based on human experience.

What We All Want in Life

We've always known what we wanted in retirement. But we learned it so long ago, we usually don't remember. To understand it, we need to go back to the beginning.

At the start of our human existence, we didn't know anything, really. We didn't even know we existed. And the way we learned anything was through our senses. That's how we made the fundamental distinction between our environment and ourselves. That distinction is embedded in our nervous system at such a deep level that we've forgotten how we even learned it!

Try this simple experiment right now, to remember how you did it. Tap your finger on this book, and then tap your finger on your cheek. How do you know which is you and which is the book? Here's how. When you tap the book, you feel it in only *one place*—on your finger. When you tap your cheek, you feel it in *two places at the same time*—on your finger and on your cheek, too. It's called the double touch. That, my friend, is how you learned that *you exist*, and that *the world exists*, too. (Had you forgotten how you learned this?)

To make sense of reality, we had to make a fundamental distinction: "Is it ME, or is it NOT ME?" We were a physical self, in a physical world.

We interacted with the world, and so the NOT ME expanded and differentiated. It was soft or smooth or rough or hard. (The one thing became ten thousand things.) At the same time, the self expanded and differentiated, too. It had physical sensations such as hunger, fullness, cold, warmth, pain, and pleasure. Then *a leap in consciousness* occurred. A new experience. It was definitely coming from the self. Except it wasn't like hunger or fullness. It wasn't *physical*—it was *nonphysical*.

So to make sense of reality, the first fundamental distinction had been: "Is it ME or NOT ME?" And now the second fundamental distinction became: "Is it *physical* or *nonphysical*?" We created a map with three dimensions:

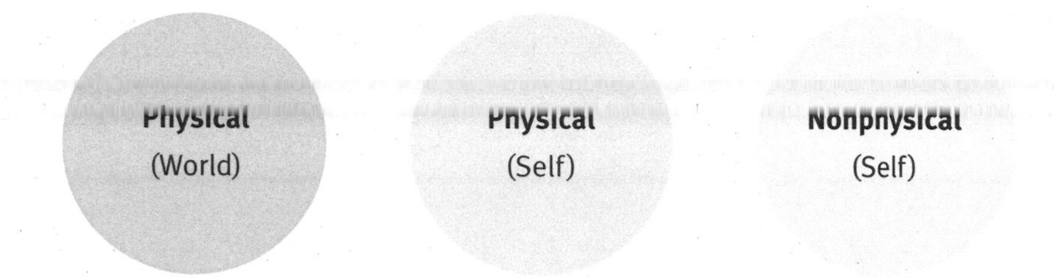

What Do You Want in Your Three Dimensions?

It was in our nature to need or want something for each of the three dimensions. You might say we're motivated to control them, or manage them, or be in balance with them. And it's not enough to just *survive*. We want to *thrive*. We don't just want each dimension to be OK; we want it to be positive.

This process didn't start with you and me, of course. We've been making these distinctions, and working to create this map, for eons. Since humans use language to think and communicate, we invented a word to describe what we want for each dimension:

- In our physical world, we want prosperity.
- In our physical self, we want health.
- In our nonphysical self, we want happiness.

The map looks like this:

Prosperity
(Physical World)

Health
(Physical Self)

Happiness
(Nonphysical Self)

We took thousands of years to split reality into these parts and invent words to describe what we want. Now, we're finally putting it all back together again! About four hundred years ago, we invented a single word—a unifying concept—that integrates all three experiences. The word is *well-being.*

Well-being is a state characterized by prosperity, health, and happiness. It's an ideal organizing structure for the new retirement, don't you think? After all, we've been working on it for a very, very long time. So we probably won't outgrow it. It describes what we want much better than *not working* ever did!

Conduct this thought experiment, to try it out:

1. Imagine, on the one hand, that you could choose *not working*. But if you did, you wouldn't get prosperity, health, and happiness. That is, you wouldn't be working—but you might be poor, sick, and sad.

2. Imagine, on the other hand, that you could choose prosperity, health, and happiness. But if you did, you wouldn't get *not working*. That is, you'd have well-being—but you might also be working.

Which option did you choose? (Or did you cheat, by imagining an option that had both? Good—you'll need that creativity for later in the book.) It's just a thought experiment, and you may never need to choose between them. But there is a possibility that you may need to keep working, in one form or another, to have the well-being that you want. Who knows what tough decisions you may need to make in the future? But if you ever need to make this one, at least now you've had some practice!

The New Retirement Is about Well-Being

Your goal, and the goal of this book, is to figure out how to have the *not working* of the old retirement and the *well-being* of the new retirement, too. You'll notice that most of this book is structured around well-being. Here's a quick description.

PART ONE. Prosperity is about creating a state of well-being for our physical environment. That includes the environment itself, and in the modern world, it includes the system we invented to support that environment—finance! (Prosperity existed as goats and cattle, long before there was anything called money.) It's the community where we're located, the house we live in, the furniture we sit on, the car we drive, the clothes we wear, and the trips we take. And it's also the paycheck, the 401(k), the IRA, and the Social Security benefits that give us control over the physical environment.

PART TWO. Health is about creating a state of well-being for our physical body. That includes our body itself, and in the modern world, it includes the system we created to support our body—medicine! (Health existed long before there were any doctors.) It's our vitality, energy, strength, flexibility, and endurance. And it's also the family physician, the cholesterol-lowering drug, the alternative medicine practitioner, and the insurance plan that provides access to treatment to support our physical health.

PART THREE. Happiness is about creating a state of well-being in our nonphysical self. That includes our inner happiness itself, and it includes the system we invented to support our happiness—our social system. (Happiness exists in two places: in our relationship with ourselves and in our relationship with others.) It's our fun and enjoyment, our blissful engagement, and our sense of meaning. It's also our family connections, our loving relationships, our true friendships, and our larger networks, which are the social side of our happiness.

These dimensions of life have been *philosophized* about for a long time. But now we're actually doing hard-nosed scientific research into them. We've learned a lot and have new insights into how they work. Knowing about each one individually, and how to make it a part of retirement, is a good idea. Each one stands alone just fine. But if we're going to base a new stage of life on them, there's something else you'll want to know. You'll want to know how they work together.

A RECIPE FOR RETIREMENT WELL-BEING

Here's an analogy for how the dimensions of well-being combine. If you want to bake a dessert, many recipes call for four basic ingredients: flour, sugar, eggs, and butter. It's amazing how many varied and delightful desserts you can create by using those four ingredients in different amounts and proportions. But no one of these ingredients can completely take the place of any of the others in the recipe. Not only does each contribute a different sensory pleasure to the eating experience, but each also plays an essential, irreplaceable chemical role in the transformation from dough or batter to baked dessert. If you don't have any eggs, you can't add more butter and expect the recipe to work. If you're out of sugar, no amount of flour can compensate. When you choose a recipe, you need to make sure you have enough of each ingredient on hand—no substitutions!

When you create your own recipe for Retirement Well-Being, you'll be doing the same thing. Think of prosperity, health, and happiness as your essential baking ingredients. Remember that you can compensate only so far! You can't add more money and expect it will turn into happiness. If you're short on health, you can't compensate with happiness. Sometimes you can't waffle, and you'll need to get more of the ingredient you're short on. Demand your just desserts.

Well-Being Has a Structure

Now that we've actually been studying prosperity, health, and happiness, it's possible to make a few observations about how they fit together in our lives.

It's obvious that all three dimensions affect each other. Positive effects in one dimension almost always have positive effects in the others. And negative effects in one can easily have negative effects in the others, too. But there's an important distinction between the dimensions. Prosperity and health are often seen as an *intermediate* goal, and happiness as an *ultimate* goal. That is, prosperity and health are the means, and happiness is the end. If you ask someone why they want to be prosperous or healthy, they often answer, "To be happy." But if you ask them why they want to be happy, they probably won't answer, "To be healthier" or "To be more prosperous." And yet, research shows that happy people are more likely to stay healthy and possibly be more prosperous, too.

Some amounts of prosperity and health are probably *necessary*, but not *sufficient*, to produce happiness. If you don't have much prosperity (you're poor), you probably won't be happy. If you don't have much health (you're sick), you probably won't be happy, either. But no amount of prosperity or health, either alone or in combination, can *produce* happiness. They make it more likely, but they can't create it. You need to create happiness directly. Also, remember that prosperity and health are physical states and happiness is a nonphysical state. For all these reasons and more, there's an actual structure to well-being. When you look at the diagram, you'll see that prosperity and health are the *foundation*, and happiness rests upon them.

RETIREMENT WELL-BEING

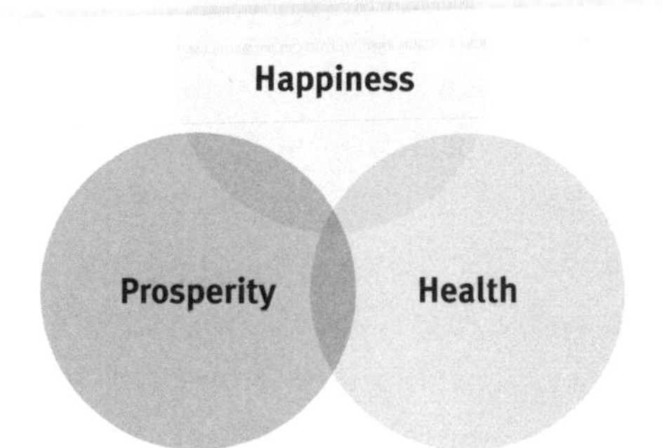

But it's also true that no dimension is more important than any other. Just like political parties and sports teams, each dimension has fans and opponents. There will always be people who argue that *their* dimension trumps the others (and they probably believe it). They have an emotional investment in the relative importance of that one dimension. They almost always know more about that one dimension than the others. So it's like the old saying, "If you're not up on it, you're down on it."

Four Truths about the Interaction of Prosperity, Health, and Happiness in Your Life

So we can see that the structure of well-being has implications for how we go about designing Retirement Well-Being. Beyond the basic structure, we've learned some important things about how the dimensions interact with each other and about how we interact with them, too.

Four basic truths about that interaction:

1. The Truth of Diminishing Returns. When we're low in a given dimension, an increase in that dimension will have a *big* effect on our total well-being. But when we're already high in a given dimension, an increase in that dimension will only have a *small* effect on our well-being.

Let's take prosperity as an example. You might remember a time when you were first living on your own and didn't have much in the way of material possessions or money. A small increase of $100 per month would have improved your well-being in all three dimensions. It would have raised your material standard of living. It would have made you instantly happier (ecstatic, possibly). And by decreasing your stress level or letting you eat better, it would have made you healthier. That increase in prosperity produced a big effect on your total well-being, because your prosperity was low. How about now? How much of an increase would you need to get the same impact on your total well-being?

The same is true for health, too. You might remember a time when you were really sick and couldn't even climb out of bed. Getting just a little increase in strength and energy could have improved your well-being in all three dimensions. It would have improved your health directly and allowed you to make yourself a good meal, perhaps. It would have improved your happiness directly, and also allowed you to rejoin the world of people. And it would have improved your prosperity by allowing you to go back to work. But what about when you're already healthy? You don't even notice taking those first few steps out of bed each morning.

The same is somewhat true for happiness. You may remember a time when you were working too hard and not taking time off. You hadn't done anything for ages! Then a friend or loved one forced you into an evening out or a social gathering. You were surprised how much fun you had. You realized your happiness had run a bit low, and that single event made a difference. We know that happiness has a measurable effect on physical health, too. It even has a demonstrated effect on productivity, which will help your prosperity. But what about when you're already happy? You hardly notice when one more day is added to a two-week vacation.

The truth of diminishing returns makes it very difficult to create retirement well-being by increasing only one dimension. But we tend not to notice that. We notice the times when increasing a low dimension had a big impact, and it sticks with us. When that dimension is high, we still think an increase will make a difference. Because it worked so well at one time, we think it will always be the key. However, just because prosperity—or health or happiness—was the solution *then*, doesn't mean it's the solution *now*. For designing your next stage of life, you need to take stock of where you really are in each dimension. Otherwise, it's like the old saying, "You can never get enough of what you don't need."

QUESTION: Across most of your life, which dimension has consistently been your highest? Your lowest?

2. The Truth of Specialization. For one reason or another, most of us specialize in one of the dimensions—*at the expense of the others*. One of the dimensions interests us more, so we learn about it, talk about it, hang out with others who are interested in it, and more or less become an expert in it. We might even end up with degrees or careers related to it. If we're more interested in prosperity, we might be drawn to finance or real estate or consumer goods. If we're more interested in health, we might be drawn to medicine or fitness or organic foods. If we're more interested in happiness, we might be drawn to psychology or education or social services.

Specialization is good, because we become experts in that dimension. But it also tends to make us view our well-being through that one perspective, rather than seeing all three dimensions clearly. For designing your next stage of life, you'll want to get the perspective of specialists from other dimensions, whether they are professionals or friends. Otherwise, you won't see your own blind spots. As the saying goes, "If your only tool is a hammer, everything looks like a nail."

QUESTION: For most of your life, which dimension have you specialized in?

3. The Truth of Compensation. We use the dimensions that are high, or that we're specialists in, to compensate for those dimensions that are low. Many things we want to accomplish, and many problems we need to solve, can be addressed from more than one dimension. Each dimension represents an *accumulation of resources*. For any given task, we get to choose which dimension—which resource—to use.

This applies to tasks large and small. Let's use a small task to illustrate. Three elderly people live in the same neighborhood, and each has a lawn to maintain. The task of lawn maintenance is exactly the same for all three. However, each person addresses it from a different dimension. They use a high dimension to compensate for a low dimension.

The first person has lived their life from the dimension of prosperity, and without hesitation, hires a lawn service to do the work. The second person has lived their life from the dimension of health, and without hesitation, does the work as a form of exercise. The third person has lived their life from the dimension of happiness, and without hesitation, asks one of their many friends for help. In this example, all three dimensions worked just fine! *However, there is usually one dimension that's easier, or more efficient, than the others.* But if you're low in the dimension, you can get creative. For designing your next stage of life, keep all your dimensions in mind when thinking about how to get what you want.

QUESTION: Across your life, what has been your most consistent pattern of compensation?

4. The Truth of Decline. Most of this book is about the Third Age of Life, rather than the Fourth. (There are already good books that focus on challenges of the Fourth Age.) Our focus here is on freedom and opportunity, which is why we're looking at Retirement Well-Being! But once we acknowledge the *trajectory* of decline, we can use the structure of well-being to anticipate and compensate. Might it be in our finances, or physical surroundings? In our body, or access to medical treatment? In our thoughts and feelings, or social connections? Decline often begins in a narrow part of life but then has a *cascading effect* into all the dimensions. Looking at specific trajectories in our lives helps us manage risks.

QUESTION: When you think about the trajectory of your life, which dimension holds a risk that you need to address in advance?

The Well-Being Model Organizes the Sea of Information

Organizing the sea of information for the old retirement was much easier, for two reasons. First, the information we needed was just related to finding ways of *not working*, so that was a narrower topic. Second, the sea of information itself was much smaller and calmer in the era of the old retirement. The information we need for designing the new retirement is much broader, and fortunately, we can use the Retirement Well-Being Model to do it.

Also, the practical tools developed for planning the old retirement were almost completely related to prosperity—things like savings calculators, risk tolerance questionnaires, and asset allocation models. Those financial tools are still very important and easy to find. But now we need to develop practical tools for the other dimensions because they're not easy to find. The first edition of this book introduced some of the earliest tools for planning your health and happiness, too. This edition expands on those, but we're still just getting started!

We're fortunate, at least, that we've slowly been getting closer to retirement life planning. Researchers have been studying a variety of topics that, one way or another, relate to retirement. We can turn some of these scientific findings into tools and guidance that will help us plan for our well-being. That's what we call progress!

We know that the dimensions of Retirement Well-Being interact dynamically in real life. We couldn't separate them, even if we wanted to. But most researchers, journalists, and professional practitioners pretty much still look at them one at a time and separately. They need to split things into parts—and into further subparts—to be better able to learn about them, communicate them, and work on them. Science usually needs to break things down into smaller chunks to get a better look. After all, you can't fit an elephant under a microscope, can you? Remember the old riddle "How do you eat an elephant?" Answer: "One bite at a time."

So most of our sources of information—scientists, journalists, and practitioners—tend to focus on one dimension (and usually one aspect of that one dimension). Medicine, for example. Or psychology. Researchers in each field develop theories, conduct research, and create useful knowledge, but usually only within the boundaries of their own field. Journalists write articles about new discoveries, but usually from the perspective of one field. Practitioners work to keep up with new developments but only in their own field. Even when this system works well, it means that most knowledge is *field-centered* rather than *you-centered*. It's from the perspective of that field rather than from the perspective of your real life, in the real world. You're the only one who can pull these fields together to design your next stage of life.

So if we're going to organize information about all three dimensions of well-being, how can we do that? The good news is that organizing information is built into the concept for the Retirement Well-Being Model. Each of the three dimensions is directly connected to two fields of research and practice, as shown in the figure. Without the model, the sea of information would swamp us. But the organizing concept of well-being keeps us afloat!

THE RETIREMENT WELL-BEING MODEL

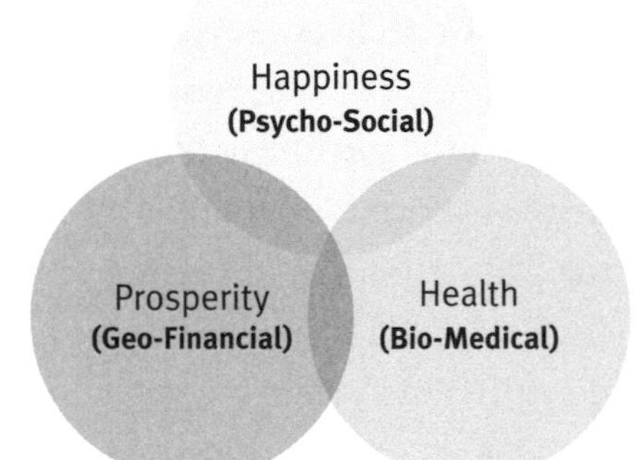

To design your retirement health, you'll benefit from Bio-Medical information; to design your retirement happiness, you'll benefit from Psycho-Social information. And for prosperity, there's a new term for information: Geo-Financial. These labels identify two fields you'll use for making key decisions in each dimension. They play essential roles and are full of good ideas for your retirement planning. That's why this entire book, chapter by chapter, is organized according to the Well-Being

Model and these fields of knowledge. Each chapter focuses on that one part of your life, and offers exercises that help you design your retirement. By the end of the book, you will have created a picture of your Ideal Retirement, chapter by chapter. In addition to envisioning what you want, the model is also valuable for evaluating how you're doing. It gives you a way to see all the parts of your life clearly, to see where you're on track and where you may be headed for trouble. The evaluation tool is the Retirement Well-Being Profile, and you'll find it in the Appendix section at the end of the book. You could even take that assessment right now if you'd like, although it will make more sense to you after you read the supporting chapters.

Geo-Financial

The Geo-Financial dimension—prosperity—is based on geography and finance. The original scope of retirement planning was finance, all finance, and nothing but finance, and of course that remains a key component. Now why, you may ask, is geography included? First, because the *relative* value of your money is greatly affected by where you happen to be on the face of the earth. (If you live in Manhattan, you couldn't afford to retire on a million dollars. But if you live in Manhattan, Kansas, you might live like royalty!) That is, your geography has an enormous impact on your cost of living. Second, your geography impacts your ability to earn an income, if you need to, or want to. Third, your home is traditionally one of your most important retirement assets. Figuring out how to use your home equity and still have a place to live is both an opportunity and a challenge for the prosperity dimension of retirement. To have the money you want for retirement, you need to be able to think both financially (see chapters four and five) and geographically (see chapter six).

Bio-Medical

The Bio-Medical dimension—health—is made up of biology and medicine. Medicine, of course, studies diseases and how to treat them. Where would you be in retirement without access to medicine? However, quite apart from the necessity of treating disease, it's helpful to understand the basic biological processes of your body. Health means not just the absence of disease but also *biological vitality*. You'll see it called other things, such as optimum health. To support that for yourself, you need to understand how your body works, how that changes as you age, and how you can support your body through those changes. Whether you're healthy or sick, knowledge from biology and medicine can help you achieve optimum health, which translates to greater well-being. The sooner you start acting on your Bio-Medical knowledge, the more health (strength, stamina, flexibility, good habits, you name it) you'll establish for your retirement. And the more health you build up, the longer it's likely to last. Remember, *health is an accumulated resource*, like prosperity. (You'll find more on this in chapters seven and eight.)

Psycho-Social

The Psycho-Social dimension—happiness—is made up of psychology and sociology. Psychology has often studied *un*happiness rather than happiness—similar to the way that medicine has studied disease rather than health. That means when most of us hear the word *psychology*, we think of mental illness and psychotherapy. But visionary psychologists are now doing research into how happiness actually works, and how we can build it into our lives. How's that for useful? On the social side, psychology has studied interpersonal relationships, and sociologists have studied retirement within society and among groups of people. We can use findings from these fields to come up with specific plans for our personal happiness and our happiness with other people. That's the kind of planning that can pay off now as well as later. After all, happiness is an *accumulated resource*, like prosperity and health. (More on this in chapters nine and ten.)

Well-Being Is Like an Elephant

Due to the specialization of the modern world, even the word *well-being* has a very different meaning depending on who is using it! Within each field, well-being has a specific, narrow meaning—not the overall, real-world, total life meaning that we want for the new retirement. Because these fields don't talk with each other very much, it doesn't matter that they have different definitions. But in the real world, seeing an article with the word *well-being* can be confusing, because it's usually just referring to one of the dimensions of well-being. You'll discover that medicine has one understanding of what it means, psychology has another, economics has yet another, and so on.

THE SIX FIELDS OF KNOWLEDGE FOR WELL-BEING

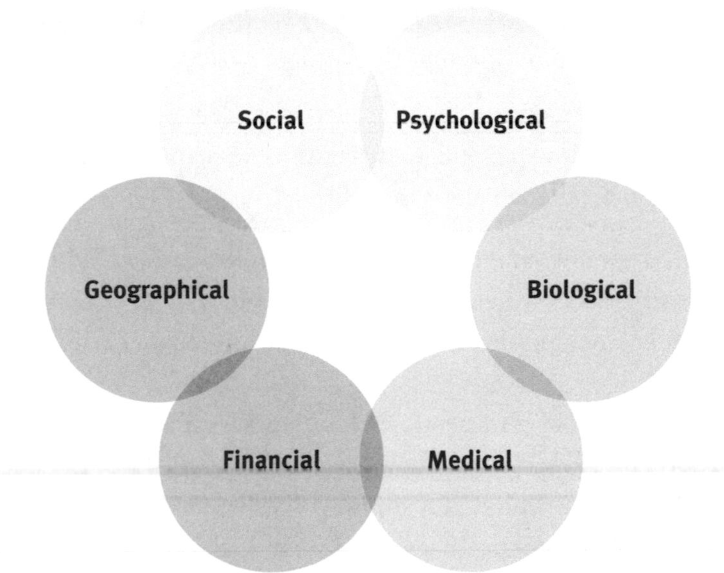

This means that there are medical researchers who spend their time studying "health and well-being." They've learned a lot about how to keep our bodies healthy as we approach retirement and progress through it. And there are research psychologists who spend their time studying "subjective well-being." They've learned a lot about how to conduct our lives in order to be happier as we travel along our journey. And, yes, there are economists who spend their time studying "economic well-being." They've learned a lot about how we can more easily accumulate money for retirement and how we can make it last as long as we need it to.

Earlier in this chapter, we looked at the structure and interactions of the three dimensions of well-being. To design the new retirement, that's the kind of information that we'll all need. But connecting one field's version of well-being with another field's version of well-being just isn't easy! It's a bit like the story of three blind wanderers who encounter an elephant. They don't know what an elephant is, but they want to learn about it. Because they can't see it, they have no way to know what the whole thing is like. So they split up, and each one takes a part to explore:

- The first one encounters the side of the elephant. He slides his hands back and forth across the elephant's hide. He stretches his arms out as far as possible but doesn't find anything else. He concludes that an elephant is like a wall.
- The second one encounters the elephant's leg. She puts her arms around it, but it won't budge. It seems to be planted in the ground. She concludes that an elephant is like a tree.
- The third one encounters the elephant's trunk. It coils around his arm, and he can feel how long and flexible it is. He reaches out but doesn't encounter anything else. He concludes that an elephant is like a snake.

That's the story of well-being. Economics sees it one way, medicine sees it another way, and psychology sees it a third way. Each field knows a lot about the dimension that it studies, but it doesn't have an easy way to connect with the others. That's true for your advisors, too. How often do financial planners, medical doctors, and counselors or coaches get together to help clients plan for retirement? (In a word, never.)

Using the Well-Being Model to Design Your Next Stage of Life

Now, because you know about the Well-Being Model, you have a new perspective. You have a conceptual structure for designing the new retirement. *Only you, dear reader, can see the whole elephant!*

The Well-Being Model isn't an esoteric theory or hypothesis. It's a practical, down-to-earth planning tool. You might think of it as a literature organizer, collecting information from different fields all in one place. Or as a puzzle, showing you where and how the different parts of your retirement can fit together. Or as a checklist, helping you make sure you've taken care of everything you were supposed to. Or even as a Swiss Army knife—you may not know which tool you'll need to use, or when, but you'll be glad it's in your pocket.

THE ELEMENTS OF YOUR IDEAL RETIREMENT

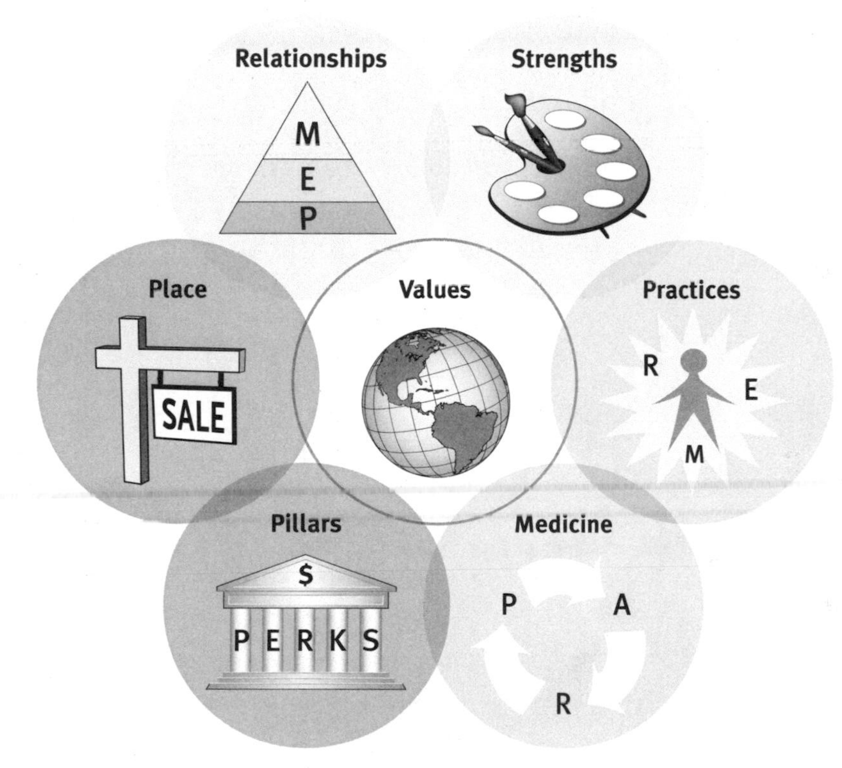

As an organizing concept, well-being is really a new way of seeing your life. The remainder of this book provides information about the different parts of retirement. Just as important, it provides you with a *process* for designing, and integrating, all those parts of your life. Your personal information and knowledge become the essential *content*. In each chapter, make sure to actually complete the exercise. That way, at the end of the book, you'll be able to assemble all those parts of your well-being into a picture of the life you want to live.

So keep going!

"Tell them I've had a wonderful life."

—Ludwig Wittgenstein, eminent philosopher

"I think I did a pretty good job."

—Julia Nelson, John Nelson's mom

Chapter THREE

The Life You Can Live (Right Now)

HOW will you know you've had a wonderful life? How will you know you did a good job?

Midlife is a time when we're asking ourselves those questions. Asking whether we're getting what we really want from life—and whether we're making the contribution we want to make. We're evaluating, and reevaluating, what it is we're here for.

It's the perfect time to be asking those questions, too. That's because we're far enough along the journey to have experience and perspective. But, thankfully, there's plenty of the journey yet ahead. We're wrapping up the Second Age, or exploring the Third. We're making plans for what's next and can see the forks in the road. Or we may be at a crossroads and need to make some decisions right away. We may even have thought it was all figured out—and then things changed. But one way or another, we're facing *high-stakes decisions*. Some of those have good and bad choices, and a little research will help us choose. Need a mutual fund? We'll check out the stats from Morningstar. Deciding on a cholesterol-lowering drug? We'll read the articles on WebMD.

But there are plenty of things that can't be resolved through research and analysis alone. Questions that have no right or wrong answers. Decisions that would deadlock a jury or stump a blue-ribbon panel. These are choices that ultimately come down to what's most important to us.

For example, should someone keep their head down for a few more years at a job they hate, or take a pay cut to work at something they could love forever? Should someone stay in the family homestead where all their possessions (and memories) fit comfortably, or downsize to move closer to kids and grandkids? Although questions like these don't have clear-cut answers, they do have enormous consequences. At some point down the road, we'll look back and see that some choices would have served us better than others.

One of life's great truths is this: The questions that don't have right or wrong answers are the ones we use to evaluate our lives. The decisions we need to base on *internal values*—not *external data*—are the ones we judge ourselves by. When we look back, those are the ones that let us say, "I've lived a wonderful life" and "I've done a good job."

Or not.

The What, How, and Why of Making Decisions about the Life We Want to Live

This chapter won't provide answers to these values-based dilemmas. (How could it? After all, they're *your* values.) Instead, it will help you see the structure you use to make decisions, when you're at your decision-making best. You'll crystallize what motivates you at the deepest level, and clarify how you want to live the rest of your life. You may even decide to live a bit differently than you had thought. Heaven forbid!

What We Want

When we think about making choices among all the things we might want to do, it's often expressed in terms of interests, preferences, and attitudes. This is the WHAT of decision making. As in, "What interests you more: A or B?" Or, "Do you prefer X or Y?" We go through life having to pick things, one after the other, in the endless stream that comes our way. Likes and dislikes, one after the other. As though life were one long menu.

"Let's see . . . I'll choose this major . . . take that internship . . . go to work in that other industry . . . live in the city . . . vacation at the seashore . . . drive a Honda . . . because they're *interesting*. And, I'll marry that cute one with the brown hair and brown eyes . . . because, I *prefer* them." (Just kidding. True love is more than a preference. Isn't it?) And so on. Decisions, small and large, can all be made on preferences and interests. One thing to note, however. These may not be very deep parts of us, and they often shift as we go along. Who knows why? Yours have probably shifted many times as you've grown older and wiser. As you move from one life stage to the next, when you look back, you can see that they've shifted a lot. (Can you believe you actually wore that outfit?) Making decisions at the mall, or about a hobby, and sometimes even a job, based purely on interests is fine. But this level isn't sufficient for designing your next stage of life. You wouldn't want to use Second Age preferences for your Third Age. Who knows how unfashionable and out-of-date they might be? Instead, by connecting them to other deeper levels, you're more likely to find your *enduring* interests and preferences.

This is, admittedly, an oversimplification in order to shed some light on the subject. But it's useful to see that there are multiple levels of yourself that you can also bring into decision making. The next level is HOW, and it includes both how you approach the world and how you get things done.

How We Want to Do It

HOW we approach the world is our personality, or temperament. It's the pattern of how we *consistently* think, feel, and act. It's a set of traits that we express over and over (and over and over) in life. For example, one common personality trait is a dichotomy between extroversion and introversion. Extroversion means you tend toward being more outgoing and action oriented, with a focus on your outer world. Introversion means you tend toward being more reserved and thoughtful, with a focus on your inner world. It's not that you're exclusively one or the other, or that you are that way 100 percent of the time. Rather, it's that you consistently tend to think, feel, and act in that way. It's natural and automatic. You can exhibit the other behavior, of course, but it usually requires conscious effort to do so. (Stop right now to check whether you're more of an extrovert or more of an introvert. Got it? Good.)

Personality traits have been studied for decades now, so we know a lot about them. One thing we know is that unlike preferences, traits are quite stable over time. People pretty much keep the same underlying traits for an entire lifetime, regardless of circumstances. Walk into any kindergarten class and look for the strong extroverts. (They'll be easy to spot.) Now follow them for seventy years. They're likely to be extroverts in college, extroverts at work, extroverts in the retirement community, and even extroverts on their deathbed. The old adage "A leopard doesn't change its spots" was probably a reference to human personality traits. They shape our decisions without us even having to think about them. And as we get to know ourselves better and better, we actually *do* think about them. We may consciously make decisions that support and align with our traits. How about you? Do you know whether your tendency is to attend a big party or a small get-together? Book a lively holiday on a cruise ship or seek out a quiet vacation retreat? Do you make choices to consciously *reinforce* your traits or to *compensate* for them? Both approaches can be useful, depending on the situation.

The other HOW relates to our strengths and skills. These are HOW we accomplish things in the world. You might also think of these as abilities, gifts, or talents. (Did you already know that you are gifted and talented?) Strengths are a relatively new idea, with a focus on the deep underlying positive traits that we use to get things done. Persistence and creativity are good examples. Although strengths can be thought of as natural gifts or talents, we can also choose to develop them. They are the fundamental "HOW" behind our specific capabilities and competencies. We can use them across *all the contexts* of our lives—work, family, and leisure. Making decisions and designing our lives to align with our greatest strengths is probably a good idea. In fact, it's a great idea!

Skills are similar to strengths. Skills are HOW we accomplish things in the world, too. But although strengths are deep elements of our character, skills are learned behaviors. Skills are *specific abilities* that we might need to acquire to do a specific job, such as drive a forklift, design a website, or teach reading. When we learn a particular skill easily and well, it's probably because it's aligned with one of our more fundamental, underlying strengths. Because we acquire skills to do specific things, they're narrower than strengths are. They're often related to work. (Although we have specific nonjob skills, too, such as parenting or cooking.) Transferable skills relate to more than one job, though, and thus more than one context. That's why they're especially valuable when changing jobs or careers. We can certainly look for opportunities to put our skills to use in the Third Age. It's just that skills learned in our career may or may not be useful for other contexts. Our last day on a particular job may well be the last time we ever use a particular set of skills. (We may not miss using them, either.) Even though you've listed them on your resume for years, you may or may not be able to keep using your "skill set." On the other hand, your traits and strengths can always be put to use.

This level of HOW—your traits, strengths, and skills—doesn't tell the whole story, though. There's another level you can bring into designing your life: the WHY.

And Most Importantly, Why

Reflecting on WHY a person, place, or thing is important to us is fundamental to who we are. We can tell that something is important because it stirs up emotion. We feel good or bad about what happens or might happen. But we don't ask WHY very often, and truth be told, we don't need to. Most of the time we can just accept that our values and beliefs are doing their job. They're working just fine, and we let it go at that.

That is, until—and sooner or later this always happens—life changes. When internal or external forces bring us to a major crossroads, we want to be conscious of our values. When we transition to another stage of life, we want to be conscious. When we make those once-in-a-decade (or once-in-a-lifetime) decisions, we most definitely want to be conscious.

We want to be fully conscious at these key points, because if we aren't, we'll do things that we wish we hadn't. And we won't do the things that we wish we could have. (That is, we'll be sorry later.)

Remember the Retirement Well-Being Model?

Our values are at the center of our lives, and so they're at the center of the Well-Being Model, too. The three dimensions of well-being—prosperity, health, and happiness—are all tied to what's going on in the outer world. But our inner values drive our own personal definitions of prosperity, health, and happiness. We get to decide what our well-being is, regardless of what our friends or "the experts" might say.

The world and the media are filled with experts these days. There's not a shortage of information or advice—there's an overload. Remember, those three dimensions have six aspects: geographical, financial, biological, medical, psychological, and social. Those fields all have their own experts, with their own way of looking at you and at your life. To make decisions for our retirement well-being, we'll want to gather objective data, become informed, and get good advice from that external world of knowledge. But then, for the WHY, we need to look inward.

For example, what if you developed a serious disease? (Based on your family history or some other factor, you've already thought about some diseases you might get as you age. But for heaven's sake, don't imagine it too vividly! Also, make sure to de-imagine it, right after this example.) As you learn more, you realize that you might not pull through. You might not make it. There are multiple treatment options and no clear-cut, right, or wrong answer. There are simply options, trade-offs, and compromises. Which treatment you choose will not only affect whether you survive, it will affect your ongoing health, your finances, your future success, you opportunities for enjoyment, your independence, your ability to help others, and your place in your family and in society.

First, you'd gather *objective* data from the world. You need to get information from hospitals, insurance companies, drug makers, research studies, survivability rates, and so on. There is a lot of hard data and a lot of science out there. You also want the perspective of trusted advisors. What does your family doctor think you should do? What does the specialist think you should do?

But then you need the *subjective* part, too. You need to know your underlying motivations. You need to know what you most value in life.

After all, that's how you evaluate your options. Which option gets you closer to the life you want to live?

In the end, the WHY of the choice you make goes by many names. You might call it your:

Belief System
Definition of "The Good Life"
Guiding Principles
Life Goals
Life Purpose
Meaning in Life
Perceptual Filters
Perspective on Life
Philosophy of Life
Point of View
Value System
Way to Live
Weltanschauung
Worldview

For simplicity, going forward, let's use the term *core values*.

Core Values Are Subjective

Sometimes we think of them as our *deepest* values, because they provide us with a foundation and we are grounded by them. We're motivated to hold them tightly, and we find comfort in them. At other times we think of them as our *highest* values, because they are what we aspire to and are inspired by. We're motivated to rise toward them and are elevated in the process. Deepest and highest are both useful ways of thinking about our values, and they fit with the concept of core values. Your core values are somehow comforting and motivating at the same time. They are both grounding and inspiring, simultaneously. That's pretty amazing, isn't it? Your values are so powerful that it seems like a good idea to design your next life stage around them, don't you think?

Where do our values come from? You could say they develop organically, in the interplay between us and the world. The dynamic interaction of many factors—our genes, gender, upbringing, education, religion, ethnic group, income level, social roles, work environment, and political involvement would only be a partial list. As we encounter new circumstances, people, and ideas, our values change. Remember how the extroverted kindergartener is probably an extrovert for life? That's not true with values; they don't stay the same for one's whole life. It's ironic that while values are a deep part of us—like traits—our values are much more changeable. That's a good thing, though. Becoming a more fully developed adult often includes shifts in our values.

As you moved across the stages of life you assumed new roles, took on new responsibilities, and met with new opportunities and barriers. You held multiple roles at the same time, transitioning from child to young adult to citizen to worker to spouse to parent to whatever you're going to be next. In the same way that your interests and preferences shifted, so did your values. But your values are probably more important to you. That's why it's crucial to see that in addition to these *organic* sources of values, there are *synthetic* sources, too. In the modern world, we're bombarded with commercial messages from cradle to grave. They're synthesized in order to motivate us to consume something. After a lifetime of this, how do we know where our values really came from? Did they grow out of our own real-life experiences, or did we just absorb them from the commercial media? In order to really get down to our core values, first we need to take a good, hard look at what it means to live in a consumer society.

Bombarded with Consumer Values

As a consumer, you're a target. If you're a member of the baby boom generation, you're part of the most targeted market that has ever existed. Marketers came up with the term *target market* to describe a group of people they have determined have enough in common to need or want the same things. Businesses use those similarities to design new products and services, then sell them to that target market.

On the one hand, target marketing by businesses is good. It means they're thinking of us when they decide what to offer. And it's nice to be thought of. On the other hand, no one really enjoys being thought of as a target. It sounds too much like *warfare*. Maybe it really is a type of warfare. Marketers talk about *penetrating* a market and, they hope, *dominating* it. They think in terms of dividing and conquering—*segmenting* markets into smaller slices to more effectively target them.

Not that the products and services they are marketing to us aren't valuable; many of them are. Some of the stuff they're selling we truly want. Some of it we even truly need. It's just that we'd like to decide consciously, based on what's best for us. What's best for them is always more and more and more sales. They are, in a word, insatiable.

Marketers Know All about the Four Ages

While we think of the Four Ages as stages of life, marketers see them as target markets. When the baby boomers were kids, marketers realized how many of them there were and that it was a huge business opportunity. A gold mine. It's as though they asked themselves, "What can we pitch to kids and young people who are in the First Age?" The answer, of course, was kid cereals and toys and dolls and tennis shoes and fast food. They carefully researched how to package products and where to place them in retail stores to be more attractive to children.

Television arrived with the boomer generation, and marketers studied how to make TV commercials that would be most persuasive to kids, first during Saturday morning cartoons and much later on the cable channels oriented toward children and families. They figured out how to use the youngest members of the family to shake the money tree and generate sales. They mined the psychology of persuasion, the emotion in children, and the dynamics of power between children and their parents. They knew that kids—being the least skeptical members of any family—were the exposed flank in marketing warfare. They learned the importance of establishing the little consumers' brand loyalty at an impressionable age. In short, the marketers became experts at penetrating the child market. (How did they sleep at night?)

As the boomers became teenagers, marketers became experts at penetrating the teen market. Even though those in the First Age usually don't have a lot of their own money, they have high discretionary spending because they don't yet have financial obligations. And of course, young people in the First Age have influence, beyond their own small piggy banks, on the much larger family piggy bank.

We've been especially targeted in the Second Age because those are our peak earning and spending years. Marketers know what we're doing in that age—starting careers, getting married, buying cars, then buying homes, furnishing them, and taking vacations to get away from them. They know we need clothes, groceries, dinners out, and lots and lots of coffee.

Some very clever people have made a science and a billion-dollar industry out of studying how to get us to buy more stuff. They learned that educating us on the features and benefits of their product works, to a point. But getting us to associate an *experience* with their product is more effective. And when they can get us to connect the consumer experience with our *values*—bingo!

Consuming to Infinity

Where are these marketing geniuses turning their attention now? Just as they followed the baby boomers from the First Age to the Second, they've been making war plans and strategies for the Third. Millions of people and trillions of dollars are in *transition*. It's when our lives are changing and we're moving through life transitions that we particularly need new products and services.

It's also true that, in general, we may be at a financial high point when we're in the Third Age. We may still be pulling down a full-time salary and be at the peak of our earning power, but (ideally) finished with the financial obligations of raising children. We're cashing out of employer retirement plans and perhaps moving to a new house. Even if our investment accounts and home equity have taken a beating, if we're transitioning, we have a lot of money to deal with. Access to cash can even make us a bit impulsive. Marketers, of course, have been studying all this. And making battle plans.

Their plans *don't* have anything to do with optimizing our well-being. Or making our retirement engaging or meaningful. Or making sure we're socially connected or live in a vital community. Or keeping us truly healthy or physically active. Not that they don't want us to have these things—they just don't particularly care one way or the other. What they do care about is that we keep buying their products and services and experiences. And when we reflect back upon our lives, marketers won't care whether we lived a good life and did a good job. They'll just care whether we kept consuming—to infinity and beyond!

Their Secret Weapon Is Values-Based Marketing

Marketing has changed over the years. One thing you may have noticed is less use of the so-called hard sell—a pushy, obvious, obnoxious approach. Particularly in the branding of companies and products, you may have noticed more use of the so-called soft sell—a gentle, subtle, even witty approach. This didn't happen because the billion-dollar advertising industry decided to be nice and give consumers a break. It didn't happen because companies decided it was OK to sell fewer of their products and make a smaller profit. Just the opposite: Marketers figured out how to sell us just as much, or even more, with a breakthrough concept: *psychographics*.

We're all familiar with marketing *demographics*—the practice of profiling us by age, gender, income level, and other external characteristics. The idea is that those of us who are similar in those respects will be similar in the products and services that we need and buy. More to the point, the idea is that we'll also be susceptible to the same marketing approach. Marketing based on demographics works, of course, and is still widely used. However, researchers have discovered that beyond our external characteristics, our internal characteristics—based on psychological research—are the most effective way to profile us. We're actually more likely to fall for a given pitch based on our psychographics than our demographics. After all, we make decisions, including buying decisions, from the *inside*, not the outside. So they use psychographics to skim the surface of our preferences and to plumb the depths of our values.

Psychographics results in what most of us would call *lifestyle* marketing. We've all seen it, over and over. A company positions itself and its products (cars, coffee, clothes, condos, you name it) as a gateway to a certain lifestyle. The marketing message to consumers is that when we purchase that company's products, we automatically get the lifestyle that's implied. Research tells the companies about the values we aspire to live by (party animal, cultured connoisseur, loving caretaker), then they project those values onto their products. Instead of using a hard sell to push the features and benefits of specific products, they use the soft sell to get us to buy a lifestyle. It works because the lifestyles they invite us into are based on our deepest and highest values. Psychographics and lifestyle marketing may seem subtle, but don't be lulled by that subtlety—this is powerful stuff.

Buying a "Lifestyle" or Creating a Life?

Until recently, marketers have tended to use a simple attack to sell retirement-oriented products and services—a carefree, leisure-based lifestyle. The "Sun City"–inspired image that was appealing to your parents is an example. However, just as they knew about the Three Boxes of Life, they know all about the Four Ages, too. They've carefully researched the consumer values of boomers, which are different than those of earlier generations. Now they're creating products—and pitches—that appeal to those values. They're showcasing a variety of Third Age lifestyles (lifelong learner, youthful athlete, wise elder, and so on) to dangle in front of you, attached to their products, services, and experiences. The almost subliminal message is this: If these are your values, and this is the lifestyle you want, you can have it. Just get out your credit card.

The marketers want to define your retirement for you. Instead of building a life, they want you to buy a lifestyle. Instead of reflecting on your values, they want you to value consuming the right investments, the right insurance, the right real estate, the right travel, the right retail goods, and the right antiaging products. Instead of discovering your identity, they want you to simply identify yourself as a consumer. They want images of products and services dancing in your head so that you make acquiring them the goal and the purpose of your retirement. They want consuming to be your highest priority. They want you to believe that if you buy all the right stuff, you'll live the right lifestyle, have "the good life," and have their idea of a good retirement. And if you don't buy all the right stuff, you'll have a bad retirement—an impoverished retirement, an unsafe retirement, a nowhere retirement, a boring retirement, a nobody retirement, an old person's retirement! That's no one's idea of "the good life." In short, they want you to believe that you'll be in pain if you don't buy into *their* concept of what the new retirement should be. In fact, more ingeniously, they want you to believe you're in pain already if you haven't yet acquired all the stuff they want you to buy.

The businesses serving the "Third Age market" aren't bad or evil, any more than a predator like a wolf or a shark is bad or evil. Marketing and selling are just in their DNA. But that doesn't mean that you want to get gobbled up by them, either. Do you want to be *sold a lifestyle* dreamed up by an advertising agency? Or do you want to *design a life* based on your own core values? (With your own values, at least you know you're buying the right stuff!)

The reason these issues are so important right now is because we're designing a new stage of life for ourselves, and for others who will follow. We have the opportunity to define it as a life stage when people have freedom to live life according to their core values. But the challenge is that we're doing all this in an environment that promotes consumer values, instead of core values. *Caveat emptor*. (Or in English: Let the buyer beware.)

Activate Your Core Values Before You Design Your Next Stage of Life

Now that we've identified the consumer values that bombard us, let's move on to a process for identifying our own deepest core values. For each of the chapters that follow, you'll be looking at one aspect of well-being. An important part of each chapter is considering the objective information that plays a role in good and bad decisions. But it's also important to use your core values for all the subjective decisions you need to make. *Activating* your values means that you're conscious of them and motivated to use them in your everyday life.

When you activate your values, you're more likely to act according to them. Living in alignment with your core values allows you to say, "I lived a wonderful life" and "I did a good job!"

The Universe of Values

Many people—from prophets to philosophers to poets—have advanced the idea that a set of universal values exist. That some values are so important that they've been held by all people, at all times, in all places. There is certainly some truth to this idea. Most people would say they value a basic level of prosperity, health, and happiness, for example. Everyone wants well-being.

But there are probably other specific values that are more motivating to you. Values that you feel so strongly about, they guide your actions across most situations of your life. Even though those specific values may be very important to you, they may be only somewhat important to your spouse, and hardly important at all to your best friend. It's the *difference* in our values that we're most likely to notice. The difference in our values is what causes us to set different goals and choose different groups of people and situations. Our values often drive our actions. But as individuals we often hold many values and don't know which are most important until we're forced to choose between them. The following exercises will give you an opportunity to do exactly that. They're based on the Values Theory of Shalom Schwartz, of Hebrew University. More than twenty years ago he, too, wondered if there was a set of universal values and began searching for them. He discovered that while everyone doesn't *have* the same values, everyone *recognizes* the same values. That is, each person acknowledges the same range of values that may be held by others—whether they personally hold those same values, or not. Rather than universal values, you might think of them as a universe *of* values. A values universe!

After asking more than one hundred thousand people in sixty countries about their values, Schwartz has analyzed the data many different ways to confirm that human values actually have a structure. You'll be able to see that structure in the values universe on page 57. If you already know your three most important core values, enter them in the Life Circle on the following page. If you'd like to explore your values more deeply, continue to the Values Universe exercise that follows on page 56.

LIFE CIRCLES EXERCISE

What are your three most important core values, or guiding principles? Enter them in this Life Circle. If you'd like some help deciding what to enter, use the Values Universe exercise beginning on the next page. You'll also use them for your One Piece of Paper in chapter eleven.

My Ideal Retirement includes living by these core values:

______________________________________,

______________________________________,

and ____________________________.

THE VALUES UNIVERSE

From the Values Theory of Shalom Schwartz

Our core values guide us on life's journey. We look to them for navigation and inspiration, as ancient travelers looked to the stars. We use them to orient our lives, decide if we're headed in the right direction, and determine if we're making progress. The Values Universe is a diagram (see opposite) that helps us find our way. It reveals the integrated structure of value systems, and the relationships between our values. The values in the center are a small sample drawn from the many specific values important to individuals and groups. The ten values around the edge are the comprehensive set of basic values that people in all cultures recognize. These ten basic value orientations are in conflict or congruence, as shown by their relative position around the circle. Closer together means they're more compatible; farther apart means more in opposition. The outer arrows show the broad underlying motivations that create the organizing structure.

Three Options for Activating Your Values

Depending upon how deeply you've explored your values and how much time you have, choose from the three options below.

1. The best option is to use the forty-item questionnaire (there are both female and male versions, beginning on pages 62 and 65, respectively). You identify what you value most, and also what you value *least*—which can be almost as important. See "Ten Steps to Your Values" on page 61 to get started. This option takes thirty to sixty minutes.
2. The second option is to use the diagram and descriptions on pages 57 to 60. Mark the values that most resonate with you, and personalize them with your own words. Then use the Core Values Activator on page 70 to see how active they are in your life. This option takes about fifteen minutes.
3. The third option—if you're convinced you already know your core values—is to use the Core Values Activator on page 70 as a reality check. This option takes less than ten minutes.

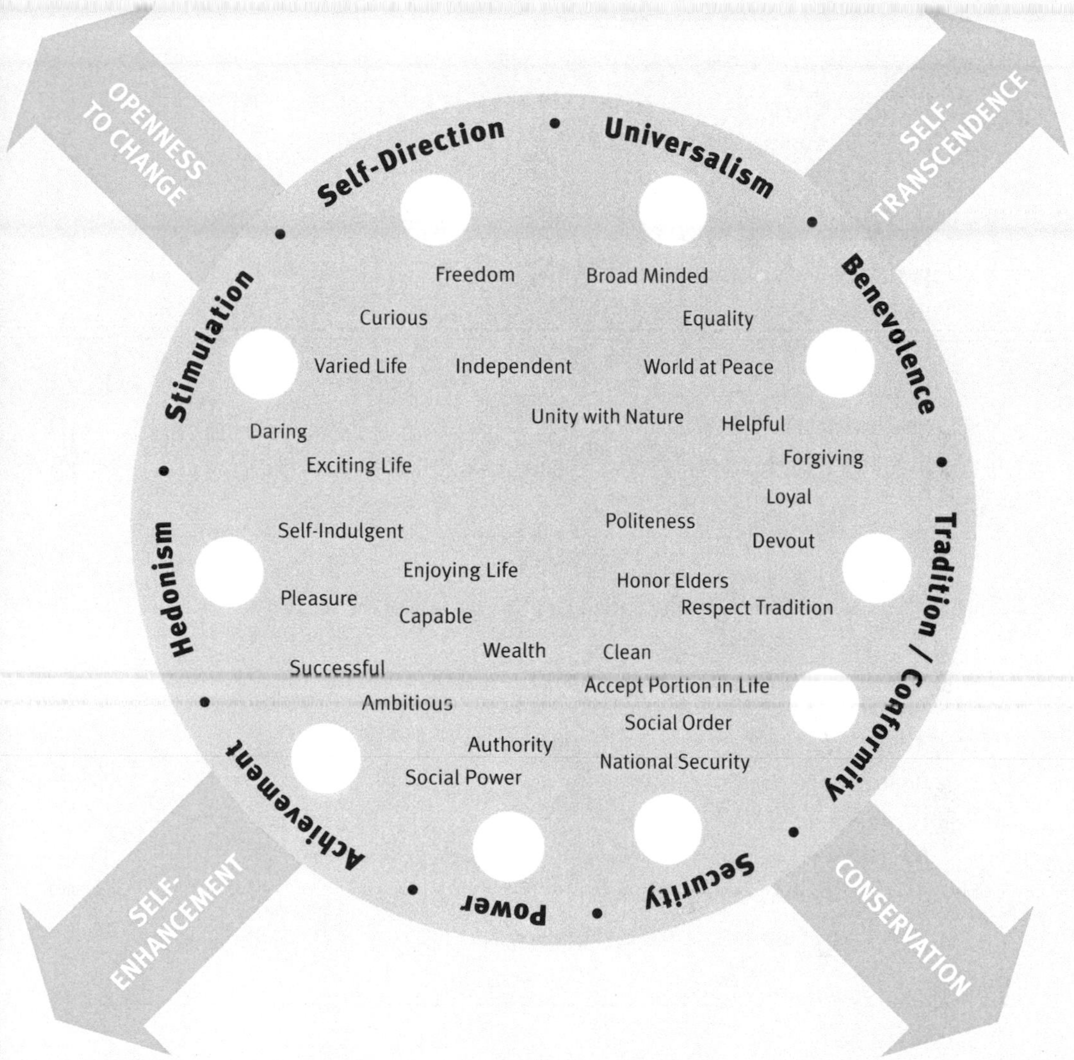

OPENNESS TO CHANGE

SELF-TRANSCENDENCE

SELF-ENHANCEMENT

CONSERVATION

Self-Direction • Universalism • Benevolence • Tradition / Conformity • Security • Power • Achievement • Hedonism • Stimulation •

Freedom

Broad Minded

Curious

Equality

Varied Life

Independent

World at Peace

Unity with Nature

Helpful

Daring

Forgiving

Exciting Life

Loyal

Self-Indulgent

Politeness

Devout

Enjoying Life

Honor Elders

Pleasure

Respect Tradition

Capable

Wealth

Clean

Successful

Accept Portion in Life

Ambitious

Social Order

Authority

National Security

Social Power

Exercise based on the Values Theory of Shalom Schwartz, Hebrew University. Used with permission.

THE TEN BASIC VALUES ORIENTATIONS WITH A SAMPLE OF SPECIFIC VALUES

From the Values Theory of Shalom Schwartz

UNIVERSALISM: Understanding, appreciation, tolerance, and protection for the welfare of all people and for nature.

Broad-minded: Tolerant of different ideas and beliefs.
Equality: Equal opportunity for all.
Protecting the environment: Preserving nature.
Social justice: Correcting injustice, care for the weak.
Unity with nature: Fitting into nature.
Wisdom: A mature understanding of life.
World at peace: Free of war and conflict.
World of beauty: Beauty of nature and the arts.

Your own value words? ____

BENEVOLENCE: Preserving and enhancing the welfare of those with whom one is in frequent personal contact.

Forgiving: Willing to pardon others.
Helpful: Working for the welfare of others.
Honest: Genuine, sincere.
Loyal: Faithful to my friends, group.
Mature love: Deep emotional and spiritual intimacy.
Responsible: Dependable, reliable.
True friendship: Close, supportive friends.

Your own value words? ____

TRADITION: Respect, commitment, and acceptance of the customs and ideas that one's culture or religion provides.

Accepting portion in life: Submitting to life's circumstances.
Devout: Holding to religious faith and belief.
Humble: Modest, self-effacing.
Respect for tradition: Preservation of time-honored customs.

Your own value words? ____

CONFORMITY: Restraint of actions, inclinations, and impulses likely to upset or harm others and violate social expectations or norms.

Honoring parents and elders: Showing respect.
Obedient: Dutiful, meeting obligations.
Politeness: Courtesy, good manners.
Self-discipline: Self-restraint, resistance to temptation.

Your own value words? ________________________________

SECURITY: Safety, harmony, and stability of society, of relationships, and of self.

Clean: Neat, tidy.
Family security: Safety for loved ones.
National security: Protection of my nation from enemies.
Reciprocation of favors: Avoidance of indebtedness.
Social order: Stability of society.

Your own value words? ________________________________

POWER: Social status and prestige, control or dominance over people and resources.

Authority: The right to lead or command.
Social power: Control over others, dominance.
Wealth: Material possessions, money.

Your own value words? ________________________________

ACHIEVEMENT: Personal success through demonstrating competence according to social standards.

Ambitious: Hard working, aspiring.
Capable: Competent, effective, efficient.
Influential: Having an impact on people and events.
Successful: Achieving goals.

Your own value words? ________________________________

HEDONISM: Pleasure or sensuous gratification for oneself.

Enjoying life: Enjoying food, sex, leisure, etc.
Pleasure: Gratification of desires.
Self-Indulgent: Doing pleasant things.

Your own value words? ______________________________

STIMULATION: Excitement, novelty, and challenge in life.

Daring: Seeking adventure, risk.
Exciting life: Stimulating experiences.
Varied life: Filled with challenge, novelty, and change.

Your own value words? ______________________________

SELF-DIRECTION: Independent thought and action—choosing, creating, exploring.

Choosing own goals: Selecting own purposes.
Creativity: Uniqueness, imagination.
Curious: Interested in everything, exploring.
Freedom: Freedom of action and thought.
Independent: Self-reliant, self-sufficient.

Your own value words? ______________________________

TEN STEPS TO YOUR VALUES

This looks more complicated than it really is. Just have a basic calculator handy, and take it one step at a time. You'll be glad you did!

1. Note whether you're female or male, and answer the forty-item questionnaire starting on page 62 or 65.
2. Copy all of your scores from the questionnaire into the appropriate value columns of the Values Universe Scoring Sheet on pages 68–69.
3. Add your scores within each of the value columns, to fill in all ten of the "Total" boxes.
4. Add your ten Totals together, and put that number in the single "PVQ TOT" box on the far right.
5. Divide your PVQ TOT box by 40, and put that number in the "PVQ AVG" box right below it.
6. Divide each of your ten Total boxes by the number printed below each one, to fill in your ten "Average" boxes.
7. Divide each of your ten Average boxes by the single PVQ AVG, to fill in your ten "Quotient" circles. Round to two decimal places (for example, 0.99).
8. Copy your ten Quotients into the ten corresponding circles of the Values Universe on page 57.
9. Identify which of your basic values are highest, and which are lowest. More importantly, what *pattern* do you see around your circle?
10. Read the descriptions on pages 58–60 to confirm which basic and specific values resonate most with you. Choose your own words to describe your own core values, and write them in your Life Circle on page 55.

To confirm how active they really are in your everyday life, use the Core Values Activator on page 70.

NOTE: This exercise prioritizes your values—but doesn't compare you with other people. A value that is not your highest could still be "higher than average." That's especially true for values on the Self-Enhancement and Openness to Change side of the universe. For example, if Hedonism is your second or third highest value, it's probably higher than for most people.

FEMALE QUESTIONNAIRE

Here are brief descriptions of some people. Please read each description and think about how much each person is or is not like you. Circle the number that shows how much the person in the description is like you.

How Much Like You Is This Person?	***Not like me at all***	***Not like me***	***A little like me***	***Somewhat like me***	***Like me***	***Very much like me***
1. Thinking up new ideas and being creative is important to her. She likes to do things in her own original way.	1	2	3	4	5	6
2. It is important to her to be rich. She wants to have a lot of money and expensive things.	1	2	3	4	5	6
3. She thinks it is important that every person in the world be treated equally. She believes everyone should have equal opportunities in life.	1	2	3	4	5	6
4. It's very important to her to show her abilities. She wants people to admire what she does.	1	2	3	4	5	6
5. It is important to her to live in secure surroundings. She avoids anything that might endanger her safety.	1	2	3	4	5	6
6. She thinks it is important to do lots of different things in life. She always looks for new things to try.	1	2	3	4	5	6
7. She believes that people should do what they're told. She thinks people should follow rules at all times, even when no-one is watching.	1	2	3	4	5	6
8. It is important to her to listen to people who are different from her. Even when she disagrees with them, she still wants to understand them.	1	2	3	4	5	6
9. She thinks it's important not to ask for more than what you have. She believes that people should be satisfied with what they have.	1	2	3	4	5	6
10. She seeks every chance she can to have fun. It is important to her to do things that give her pleasure.	1	2	3	4	5	6

11. It is important to her to make her own decisions about what she does. She likes to be free to plan and to choose her activities for herself.	1	2	3	4	5	6
12. It's very important to her to help the people around her. She wants to care for their well-being.	1	2	3	4	5	6
13. Being very successful is important to her. She likes to impress other people.	1	2	3	4	5	6
14. It is very important to her that her country be safe. She thinks the state must be on watch against threats from within and without.	1	2	3	4	5	6
15. She likes to take risks. She is always looking for adventures.	1	2	3	4	5	6
16. It is important to her always to behave properly. She wants to avoid doing anything people would say is wrong.	1	2	3	4	5	6
17. It is important to her to be in charge and tell others what to do. She wants people to do what she says.	1	2	3	4	5	6
18. It is important to her to be loyal to her friends. She wants to devote herself to people close to her.	1	2	3	4	5	6
19. She strongly believes that people should care for nature. Looking after the environment is important to her.	1	2	3	4	5	6
20. Religious belief is important to her. She tries hard to do what her religion requires.	1	2	3	4	5	6
21. It is important to her that things be organized and clean. She really does not like things to be a mess.	1	2	3	4	5	6
22. She thinks it's important to be interested in things. She likes to be curious and to try to understand all sorts of things.	1	2	3	4	5	6
23. She believes all the worlds' people should live in harmony. Promoting peace among all groups in the world is important to her.	1	2	3	4	5	6
24. She thinks it is important to be ambitious. She wants to show how capable she is.	1	2	3	4	5	6
25. She thinks it is best to do things in traditional ways. It is important to her to keep up the customs she has learned.	1	2	3	4	5	6
26. Enjoying life's pleasures is important to her. She likes to 'spoil' herself.	1	2	3	4	5	6
27. It is important to her to respond to the needs of others. She tries to support those she knows.	1	2	3	4	5	6

28. She believes she should always show respect to her parents and to older people. It is important to her to be obedient.	1	2	3	4	5	6
29. She wants everyone to be treated justly, even people she doesn't know. It is important to her to protect the weak in society.	1	2	3	4	5	6
30. She likes surprises. It is important to her to have an exciting life.	1	2	3	4	5	6
31. She tries hard to avoid getting sick. Staying healthy is very important to her.	1	2	3	4	5	6
32. Getting ahead in life is important to her. She strives to do better than others.	1	2	3	4	5	6
33. Forgiving people who have hurt her is important to her. She tries to see what is good in them and not to hold a grudge.	1	2	3	4	5	6
34. It is important to her to be independent. She likes to rely on herself.	1	2	3	4	5	6
35. Having a stable government is important to her. She is concerned that the social order be protected.	1	2	3	4	5	6
36. It is important to her to be polite to other people all the time. She tries never to disturb or irritate others.	1	2	3	4	5	6
37. She really wants to enjoy life. Having a good time is very important to her.	1	2	3	4	5	6
38. It is important to her to be humble and modest. She tries not to draw attention to herself.	1	2	3	4	5	6
39. She always wants to be the one who makes the decisions. She likes to be the leader.	1	2	3	4	5	6
40. It is important to her to adapt to nature and to fit into it. She believes that people should not change nature.	1	2	3	4	5	6

Now turn to the Values Universe Scoring Sheet on pages 68–69.

MALE QUESTIONNAIRE

Here are brief descriptions of some people. Please read each description and think about how much each person is or is not like you. Circle the number that shows how much the person in the description is like you.

How Much Like You Is This Person?	*Not like me at all*	*Not like me*	*A little like me*	*Somewhat like me*	*Like me*	*Very much like me*
1. Thinking up new ideas and being creative is important to him. He likes to do things in his own original way.	1	2	3	4	5	6
2. It is important to him to be rich. He wants to have a lot of money and expensive things.	1	2	3	4	5	6
3. He thinks it is important that every person in the world be treated equally. He believes everyone should have equal opportunities in life.	1	2	3	4	5	6
4. It's very important to him to show his abilities. He wants people to admire what he does.	1	2	3	4	5	6
5. It is important to him to live in secure surroundings. He avoids anything that might endanger his safety.	1	2	3	4	5	6
6. He thinks it is important to do lots of different things in life. He always looks for new things to try.	1	2	3	4	5	6
7. He believes that people should do what they're told. He thinks people should follow rules at all times, even when no one is watching.	1	2	3	4	5	6
8. It is important to him to listen to people who are different from him. Even when he disagrees with them, he still wants to understand them.	1	2	3	4	5	6
9. He thinks it's important not to ask for more than what you have. He believes that people should be satisfied with what they have.	1	2	3	4	5	6
10. He seeks every chance he can to have fun. It is important to him to do things that give him pleasure.	1	2	3	4	5	6

11. It is important to him to make his own decisions about what he does. He likes to be free to plan and to choose his activities for himself.	1	2	3	4	5	6
12. It's very important to him to help the people around him. He wants to care for their well-being.	1	2	3	4	5	6
13. Being very successful is important to him. He likes to impress other people.	1	2	3	4	5	6
14. It is very important to him that his country be safe. He thinks the state must be on watch against threats from within and without.	1	2	3	4	5	6
15. He likes to take risks. He is always looking for adventures.	1	2	3	4	5	6
16. It is important to him always to behave properly. He wants to avoid doing anything people would say is wrong.	1	2	3	4	5	6
17. It is important to him to be in charge and tell others what to do. He wants people to do what he says.	1	2	3	4	5	6
18. It is important to him to be loyal to his friends. He wants to devote himself to people close to him.	1	2	3	4	5	6
19. He strongly believes that people should care for nature. Looking after the environment is important to him.	1	2	3	4	5	6
20. Religious belief is important to him. He tries hard to do what his religion requires.	1	2	3	4	5	6
21. It is important to him that things be organized and clean. He really does not like things to be a mess.	1	2	3	4	5	6
22. He thinks it's important to be interested in things. He likes to be curious and to try to understand all sorts of things.	1	2	3	4	5	6
23. He believes all the worlds' people should live in harmony. Promoting peace among all groups in the world is important to him.	1	2	3	4	5	6
24. He thinks it is important to be ambitious. He wants to show how capable he is.	1	2	3	4	5	6
25. He thinks it is best to do things in traditional ways. It is important to him to keep up the customs he has learned.	1	2	3	4	5	6
26. Enjoying life's pleasures is important to him. He likes to 'spoil' himself.	1	2	3	4	5	6

27. It is important to him to respond to the needs of others. He tries to support those he knows.	1	2	3	4	5	6
28. He believes he should always show respect to his parents and to older people. It is important to him to be obedient.	1	2	3	4	5	6
29. He wants everyone to be treated justly, even people he doesn't know. It is important to him to protect the weak in society.	1	2	3	4	5	6
30. He likes surprises. It is important to him to have an exciting life.	1	2	3	4	5	6
31. He tries hard to avoid getting sick. Staying healthy is very important to him.	1	2	3	4	5	6
32. Getting ahead in life is important to him. He strives to do better than others.	1	2	3	4	5	6
33. Forgiving people who have hurt him is important to him. He tries to see what is good in them and not to hold a grudge.	1	2	3	4	5	6
34. It is important to him to be independent. He likes to rely on himself.	1	2	3	4	5	6
35. Having a stable government is important to him. He is concerned that the social order be protected.	1	2	3	4	5	6
36. It is important to him to be polite to other people all the time. He tries never to disturb or irritate others.	1	2	3	4	5	6
37. He really wants to enjoy life. Having a good time is very important to him.	1	2	3	4	5	6
38. It is important to him to be humble and modest. He tries not to draw attention to himself.	1	2	3	4	5	6
39. He always wants to be the one who makes the decisions. He likes to be the leader.	1	2	3	4	5	6
40. It is important to him to adapt to nature and to fit into it. He believes that people should not change nature.	1	2	3	4	5	6

Now turn to the Values Universe Scoring Sheet on pages 68–69.

VALUES UNIVERSE SCORING SHEET

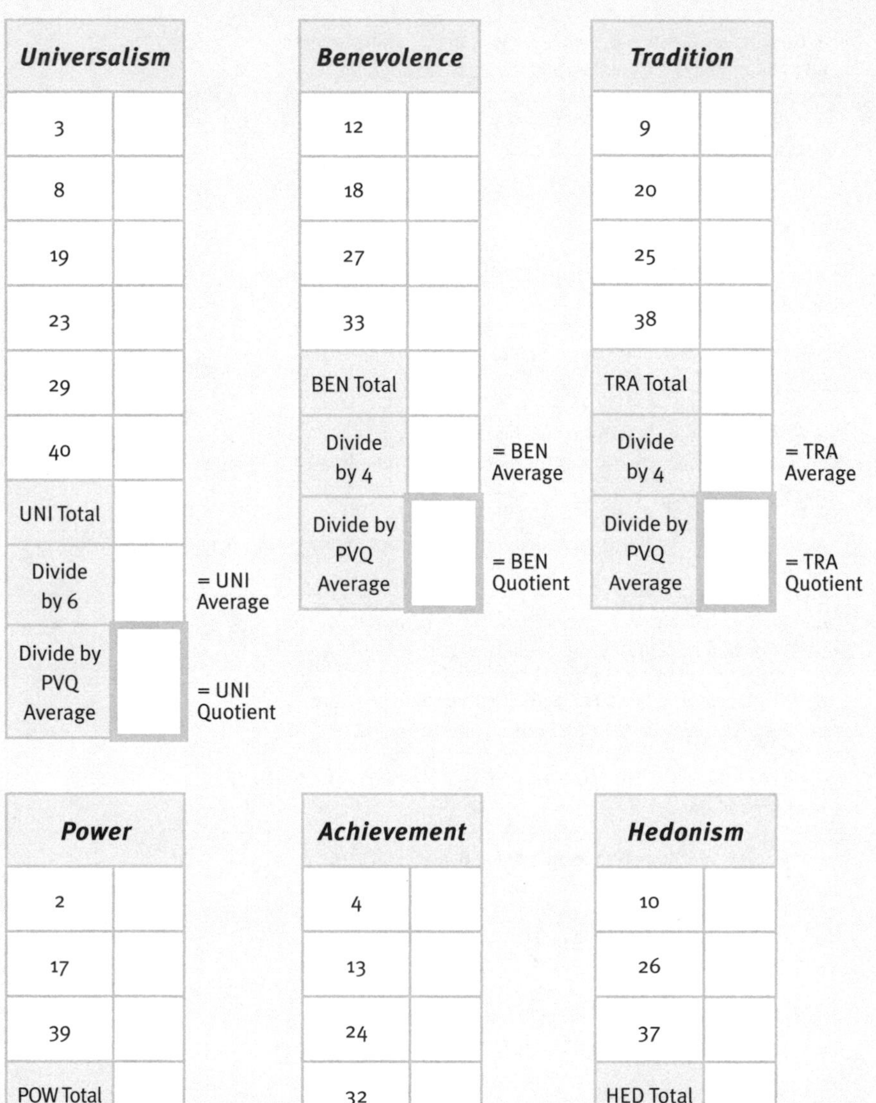

Universalism		
3		
8		
19		
23		
29		
40		
UNI Total		
Divide by 6		= UNI Average
Divide by PVQ Average		= UNI Quotient

Benevolence		
12		
18		
27		
33		
BEN Total		
Divide by 4		= BEN Average
Divide by PVQ Average		= BEN Quotient

Tradition		
9		
20		
25		
38		
TRA Total		
Divide by 4		= TRA Average
Divide by PVQ Average		= TRA Quotient

Power		
2		
17		
39		
POW Total		
Divide by 3		= POW Average
Divide by PVQ Average		= POW Quotient

Achievement		
4		
13		
24		
32		
ACH Total		
Divide by 4		= ACH Average
Divide by PVQ Average		= ACH Quotient

Hedonism		
10		
26		
37		
HED Total		
Divide by 3		= HED Average
Divide by PVQ Average		= HED Quotient

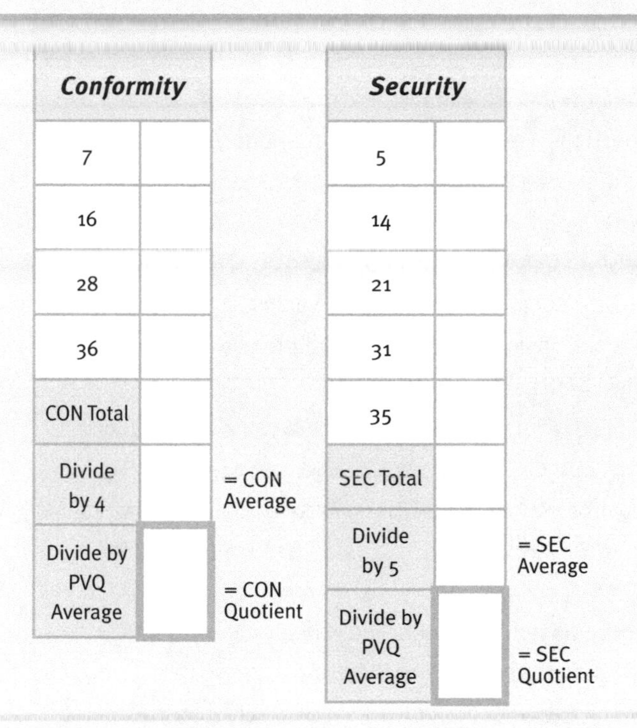

Conformity		
7		
16		
28		
36		
CON Total		
Divide by 4		= CON Average
Divide by PVQ Average		= CON Quotient

Security		
5		
14		
21		
31		
35		
SEC Total		
Divide by 5		= SEC Average
Divide by PVQ Average		= SEC Quotient

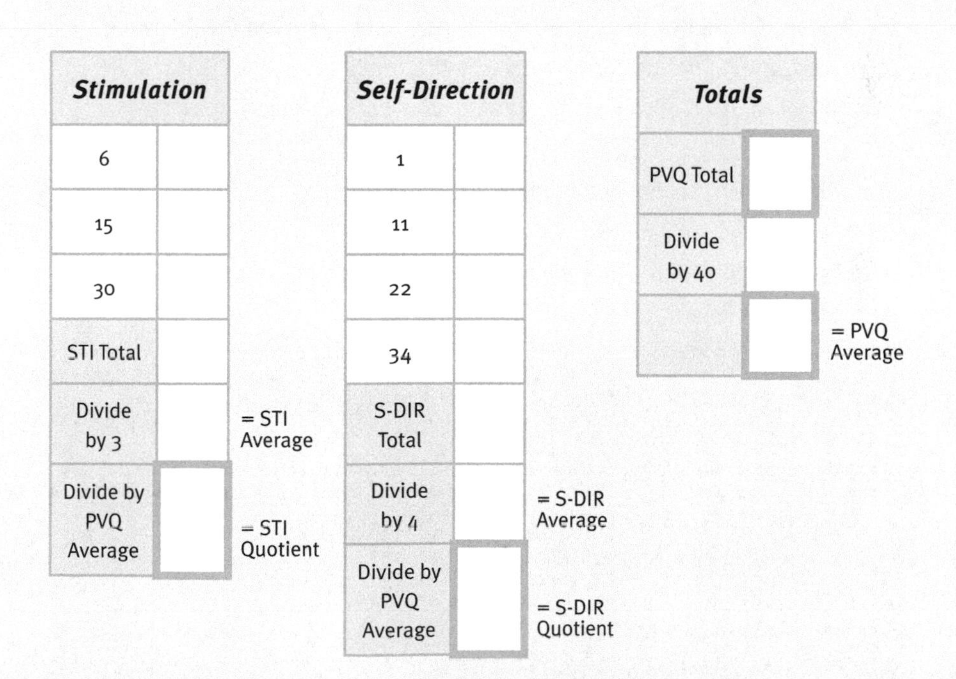

Stimulation		
6		
15		
30		
STI Total		
Divide by 3		= STI Average
Divide by PVQ Average		= STI Quotient

Self-Direction		
1		
11		
22		
34		
S-DIR Total		
Divide by 4		= S-DIR Average
Divide by PVQ Average		= S-DIR Quotient

Totals		
PVQ Total		
Divide by 40		
		= PVQ Average

CORE VALUES ACTIVATOR

Are your core values active in your daily life? If not—are they *really* your core values? Values are beliefs about what is desirable and undesirable, good and bad, or right and wrong. Some of the values we hold are situational, and apply to specific times, contexts, or people. Other values are much more core to who we are and transcend any specific situation. They guide us across all the domains of our lives. These core values determine the people and opportunities we seek out, and the ones we avoid. They shape the goals we set in life, and then motivate us to move toward those goals. Ultimately, they're the criteria we use to evaluate our own actions and the actions of others.

How can you tell if one of your values is really a core value? One good test is to see how *active* it is in your daily life. Do you hold it on a theoretical level—but it doesn't find its way into your daily life? Or is it active in only one domain of your life, but not in others? Or was it once a core value, but isn't anymore—and you didn't realize it? Or perhaps a new core value has emerged? Use this worksheet to see how active a value really is in your life. Or compare two or more values by completing a copy of the worksheet for each one.

The more active a value is in your life, the higher it's likely to score across the four areas below. You can remember the four areas with the acronym CORE, for Choose, Orient, Respond, and Express. As you ask yourself the following questions, and reflect on this value in your life, you'll come to a clearer understanding of what's really most important to you. Follow these steps:

Step One. Write the name of this value: ______________________________.

Step Two. For this value, rate each statement on page 71 from strongly disagree (1) to strongly agree (5).

Step Three. Subtotal and total your scores to compare this value with your other values.

C	CHOOSE	Score	Subtotal
1	I choose this consciously.	1 2 3 4 5	
2	I know how this became important to me.	1 2 3 4 5	
3	This is more important than any particular situation.	1 2 3 4 5	
4	This is a central part of my identity.	1 2 3 4 5	
5	I would be a different person without this.	1 2 3 4 5	
O	**ORIENT**		
6	I orient my whole life toward this.	1 2 3 4 5	
7	I make plans for how to have this.	1 2 3 4 5	
8	This is like other values that are important to me.	1 2 3 4 5	
9	The opposite of this isn't important to me.	1 2 3 4 5	
10	I would trade almost anything else for this.	1 2 3 4 5	

R	RESPOND	Score	Subtotal
11	I respond emotionally to this.	1 2 3 4 5	
12	I automatically notice this in the world.	1 2 3 4 5	
13	I feel strongly motivated to have this.	1 2 3 4 5	
14	When this is threatened, I feel bad.	1 2 3 4 5	
15	When I pursue this, I feel good.	1 2 3 4 5	
E	**EXPRESS**		
16	I express this every day in some way.	1 2 3 4 5	
17	I have worked toward this over time.	1 2 3 4 5	
18	I have sacrificed other things to uphold this.	1 2 3 4 5	
19	I evaluate people and situations according to this.	1 2 3 4 5	
20	I'm drawn to people and situations that have this.	1 2 3 4 5	
		Total Score	

"Our nation's system of retirement security is imperiled, headed for a serious train wreck."

—John Bogle, founder of the Vanguard Funds

Chapter FOUR

Retirement Economics Is More Than Personal Finance

Does the topic of *personal finance* attract you or repel you?

No doubt you're attracted to all the wonderful things personal finance can do for you—having a nice place to live, going shopping, doing fun things with your friends and family. But the question here is about the nuts and bolts of personal finance, as a topic in itself. Are you interested in delving into money's inner secrets? How to get it, make it grow, protect it, and so on?

If your answer is yes, then the prosperity dimension of well-being may be an area of *specialization* for you. You may have a job working with money, or it might be your hobby. You read financial books, articles, and e-newsletters. You're curious about your retirement accounts and check on them. You enjoy swapping money stories with other financial specialists.

If that's not like you *at all*, then it's probably not an area of specialization. The subject may bore you, frustrate you, or even scare you a little. But it doesn't interest you one bit. You don't have a job working with money, and it isn't your hobby, either. You check your accounts from of a sense of obligation (or not at all). When the topic of finance comes up at a social gathering, you either change the subject or tune it out.

No matter which end of that specialization spectrum you're closer to, you'll discover this chapter isn't what you might have thought. Most retirement books are personal finance–oriented and offer variations of the same nuts and bolts information. If you expected an explanation of qualified plan types, advice on mutual funds, or tips on cutting your taxes, you won't find that here. You can get that stuff from the sea of information.

Instead of being stuck at the surface layer of personal finance, we'll take a deeper look at the economics that drive your retirement stage of life. In this chapter, you'll:

- See how the evolution of retirement relates to today's financial problems
- Identify practical strategies that your financial advisor doesn't know about
- Tap into resources that you probably wouldn't have thought of

The Retirement Crisis

You may be worried about your retirement finances or feeling pretty good about them. Regardless of your personal situation, you know from ongoing media coverage that many workers are concerned about being adequately financially prepared for retirement. Many are facing a similar set of challenges. The same themes keep coming up, over and over. They're less optimistic about their employer's retirement plan. They haven't been saving enough personally and are carrying too much debt. They weren't that confident about how to invest their savings, and now they have ridden the roller-coaster ride of a lifetime. They believed home equity was the foundation of financial security, but aren't so sure anymore. They know that Social Security and Medicare are underfunded, and are worried about what will happen to them.

There are so many theories about what has gone wrong that it's like a multiple-choice question. How did we all get into such a pickle?

a) Lack of personal responsibility

b) Greedy financial companies

c) Not enough government control

d) Too much government intervention

e) Globalization and outsourcing

f) All of the above

Even if we could pick the right answer, it wouldn't be relevant to your personal planning. The high visibility news stories seldom provide insight or ideas for how to approach your next stage of life. (They do get attention and sell advertising, though.)

Rather, we'll look at the most important stories that aren't in the news. These are more relevant because they're more likely to prompt your own creative ideas for designing a new stage of life. We'll start by reviewing approaches that people have used for support as they stopped working in later life. Our task isn't just to design the new retirement—we need to design a new way to pay for it, too. Due to a changing demographic and economic environment, we'll need to weave together elements from many approaches to make it work.

The Family Approach to Retirement Economics

Workers have had the old retirement available for a century or so, but people have always gotten old. What did they do for the fifty centuries before retirement was invented? There are some important clues here for us.

After all, the need to support older people has always existed. How did we meet that need? At the *family level*. But it wasn't called retirement, and it didn't require money. Even after money was invented, working people could live their whole lives with little need for coins or currency. People grew their own food, built their own houses, made their own clothes, and taught their own children. Parents had an economic relationship with their children, in addition to the social one. There was an understanding between them. A family contract of sorts. Here's a simplified version.

Parents raised their children by teaching them how to become productive in the world. Children learned by working alongside their parents to gain the skills for a particular way of life. It could have been farming or fishing or herding or a craft or trade. These multiple generations may have lived together as an extended family or as nuclear families that were geographically close to each other (probably right next door!). Siblings had an economic relationship, too. Children pooled their risks with their siblings, so that if one had a catastrophe such as a fire, the others helped rebuild. They pooled their opportunities too, such as building or buying new equipment. It wasn't just brotherly (and sisterly) love—it was a reciprocal economic arrangement. Insurance companies and banks weren't available, so they used the family contract instead.

The family contract addressed the aging of the older generation, too. We already know that aging and withdrawing from work had always been a gradual process, and that's what happened. The children took up the slack, but the parents didn't slack off! They contributed to the family's welfare in important ways. They helped maintain the household or cared for and taught their grandchildren. From their long experience, they provided practical knowledge on many topics. They offered connections to the community for the benefit of the family. Both genders made contributions, and both were valuable.

This original approach to retirement economics was based on a reciprocal relationship between the generations. It wasn't a one-way deal, with the children (and grandchildren) supporting the older parents. There was reciprocity between the generations, as they all contributed to the family's welfare. The reciprocation was also across an entire life span, with children paying parents back for teaching them a way of life. Property, in the form of land or tools of the trade, was part of the deal, too. Underneath the social relationship, there was this reciprocal economic exchange.

This is how "retirement" operated for thousands of years, and it still does in some places and situations. Even in modern times, it's the basic economic principle behind the *family business*! Although it phased out as societies became industrialized, it was still common just a few generations ago. Do you remember the television show that was famous for the closing line of every episode, "Good night, John Boy?" That was *The Waltons*—a multigenerational family operating on this principle. It was set in the 1930s.

As societies industrialized, people left traditional ways of working to become employees, because the hard cash increased their material standard of living. They could buy things they couldn't produce themselves. They migrated to cities and towns, where the jobs were. There, life wasn't about making the stuff they needed for daily life, but about making the money to buy the stuff they needed for daily life. It shifted from making their daily bread to "Another day, another dollar." Economics shifted from the multigenerational family contract to an individual and nuclear family cycle of earning and spending money.

For designing the new retirement, here's the sixty-four-thousand-dollar question: When the younger generation went to the factory, what happened to the older generation? The pattern of life they had planned on, and worked for, didn't happen. Forces beyond their control changed the way they had planned to retire. *They all needed to design their own solution to retirement.* (That's what you'll need to do.) Some of these parents probably worked themselves to death, without having another generation to reciprocate with. Some were able to sell their holdings and get money to retire in the modern sense. Others needed to live with their children and grandchildren in the city, even though they couldn't contribute to the family in the way they had anticipated. Societal transitions force changes in individual's plans, whether they anticipate them or not.

That's not to say the family approach isn't alive and well today, even in the era of personal finance. When folks sell the family farm or business to have money to retire, that's using the family approach. When someone receives an inheritance and it allows her to retire, that's the family approach. And when a single person who can't afford to retire somehow finds and marries his true love (who can afford to support two retirements), that's the family approach, too. You'll notice immigrants from developing nations using it, regardless of their educational or socioeconomic level.

There are (at least) three strategies you can take from the family approach that may be useful in making the new retirement work for you:

Practical Strategy #1: Reciprocal Exchange. The multigenerational family can be a powerful economic unit. How might you create a new form of *reciprocal exchange* (not a one-way street) that would harness your family's power?

THE ORIGINAL PYRAMID SCHEME

A pyramid scheme is a financial arrangement in which a small number of early members receive payment from a larger number of later members. The schemes collapse, because they can't recruit enough new members at the bottom to make payments to the old members at the top. They're unsustainable.

Human societies were the original pyramid schemes—except they're actually population pyramids. A small number of old people were like the early members at the top, and a large number of workers were like the later members at the bottom. The younger ones helped the older ones with food, shelter, personal care, or money. It was positive, because honoring parents and elders is one element of a just society. It was also sustainable, because most people didn't live to be that old and they had plenty of children. The family approach to retirement economics worked this way.

The population pyramid still stacked up like that when retirement was invented. There were many more workers than retirees, so the societal approach to retirement economics (Social Security, Medicare, and employer pensions) was relatively inexpensive, per worker. But as people live longer and have fewer children, the top of the pyramid gets broader compared to the bottom. This isn't a onetime effect of the baby boom generation; it's a permanent shift. This has never happened before, and it will profoundly change society. One inescapable change is that the societal approach to retirement will become more expensive, per worker.

Personal investments for retirement may be affected, too. Will home values and stock prices become depressed as a relatively large number of retirees try to sell out to a relatively small number of workers? No one knows for sure, because this has never happened before. But one thing is certain—retirement is changing!

U.S. Census Bureau: U.S Population Trends, www.census.gov/mso/www/pres_lib/trends2050/textmostly/index.html

AGE DISTRIBUTION OF THE U.S. POPULATION, BY SEX: 1950

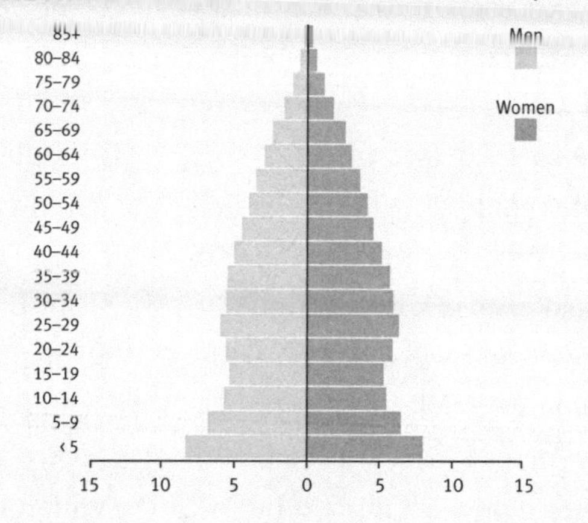

AGE DISTRIBUTION OF THE U.S. POPULATION, BY SEX: 2000

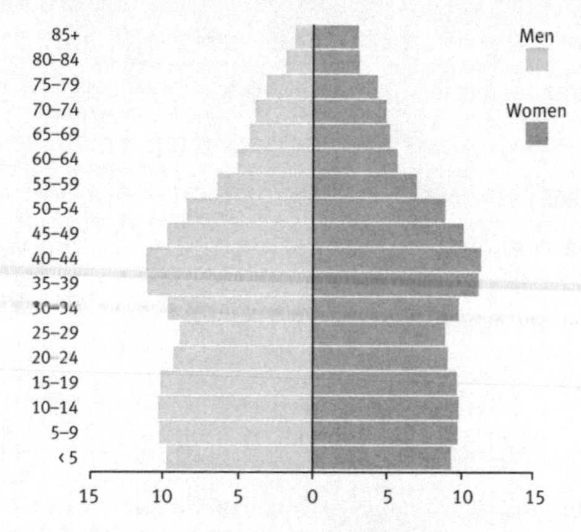

AGE DISTRIBUTION OF THE U.S. POPULATION, BY SEX: 2050

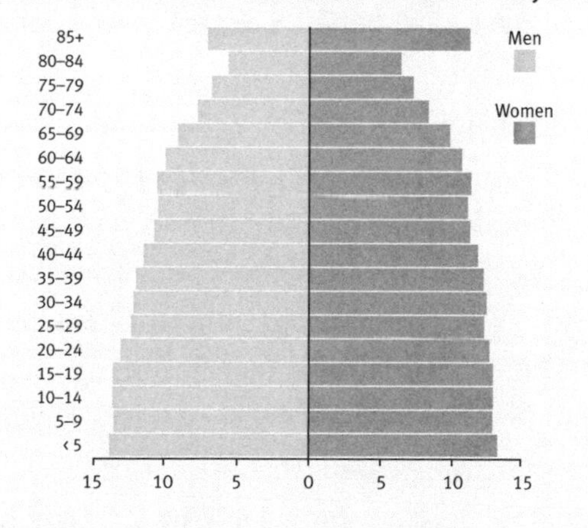

This is close to the spirit that animates a family business. It's about identifying the unique resources and abilities each could contribute and the unique needs each may have. It's about creating a synergy that benefits the entire family.

To scratch the surface, let's imagine some possibilities. Who needs elder care, and who could provide it? Who needs child care, and who could provide that? Who has unused land, or extra space in her home? Who could put that to use? Who might benefit from owning a two-family residence, with family living in both units? Who might benefit from sharing a vacation home? Who might be able to start a family business together? Who has money, time, or expertise? (Third Age entrepreneurship needs to be very tight with money, but it can be generous with time.)

This is a way of thinking that families have traditionally employed but that has disappeared from most Americans' thought patterns. It's still common in much of the world and among families that immigrate to the United States. There is much that Americans can relearn!

Practical Strategy #2: Adopt a "Family." The benefits of reciprocal exchange aren't reserved for biological families. Especially if you don't have access to a family of your own, how else could you become part of a supportive community?

Although families are multigenerational communities, that's not an easy relationship to find outside of your biological kin. The most common form is the old-fashioned neighborhood. (See chapter six.) Living in close proximity to First, Second, and Third Agers creates more opportunities for informal reciprocal benefits. In true neighborhoods, people look out for each other, remember?

It's relatively easy to find single-generation communities, where most people are in the Third Age. The most individual version is considering being a long-term roommate. This is easiest to do if you're single, of course! But remember that many people enter the Third Age as part of a couple and then, for a variety of reasons, become single. If that were to happen, rather than being a family of one, consider becoming a roommate. The next version is more formal and usually referred to as cohousing. This is a creative legal-financial arrangement that creates common ownership of property among people at the same life stage. The most common version is choosing to live in a "retirement community." However, most of the developments that go by that name are just places to live, and they don't create reciprocal exchange. (To look for a true community, see chapter six.)

Practical Strategy #3: Improvisation. In times of great transformation, when established practices break down, families need to improvise. How might you explore creative ways that your family can improvise *together*?

In modern society, most people are tight-lipped about their finances and personal affairs, even within their family. Not until someone needs help or leaves an inheritance do the others know what his or her situation was. Openly communicating about the subjects in family strategies #1 and #2 might seem a little . . . unconventional. But times of transformation mean that conventions are breaking down and not working as well. That's why you need to be *un*conventional! The place to start is by opening up communication with family, friends, and others you're in community with. Only then can you explore ways of improvising as an economic "family."

The Societal Approach to Retirement Economics

This is the original old retirement, and the approach we grew up under. It's been around our whole lives, so it's deeply embedded in the way we think. Just like the family approach, it will always exist, but will now need to change in order to accommodate the enormous shift in our demographics. It came about as the family contract was replaced by the employment contract, and a new way had to be found to economically support people as they aged.

Workers were being paid in money, of course. They knew they needed to save for a future time when they couldn't work anymore, and no doubt they did their best. But moving from tangible prosperity (land, animals, equipment) to intangible prosperity (savings accounts and investments) requires an enormous conceptual shift. People struggled with it. Many people still struggle with it today, don't they?

Personal savings wasn't enough to provide retirement security, and the need could no longer be addressed at the family level. So instead it was addressed at the societal level, through the government and organizations. In the words of President Franklin Roosevelt:

"Because it has become increasingly difficult for individuals to build their own security single-handed, government must now step in and help them lay the foundation stones."

In 1935, the Social Security Act created a system for providing old-age benefits for Americans. The goal wasn't to reward retiring workers with a lengthy period of leisure. Rather, the goal was to provide a safety net for a few years to those workers who managed to live past the age of sixty-five. A generation later, in 1965, the Social Security Act was expanded to provide medical benefits under Medicare. Both of these plans are funded by equal contributions from workers and their employers, out of everyone's paychecks.

Society also created the environment where it became common for employers to provide pensions for retiring workers. The number of plans increased steadily over the decades of the twentieth century. In 1940, about four million workers were covered by pension plans. By 1960, that number had grown to more than twenty-three million! The federal government created an incentive through the tax structure for organizations to create and maintain retirement plans for employees.

By the mid-twentieth century, these three separate approaches for providing retirement income—Social Security, employer pensions, and personal savings—had acquired a name. They were called the three-legged stool of retirement security. Although the origins of this metaphor aren't completely known, the concept of the three-legged stool has become very well known (at least among retirement geeks).

Taken as a whole, this three-part financial retirement system is a marvel of engineering. Or, more accurately, social engineering. Before it was developed, retirement as leisure was relatively uncommon. Afterward, retirement became taken for granted. Of course, each person didn't necessarily have all three sources, or the same income from all three. Rather, the three-legged stool created a system of retirement income that provided support and stability for society in general.

Society had succeeded in *institutionalizing* the Three Boxes of Life. Along with public education for the first box of life, the three-legged stool for the third box of life became one of the most profound achievements of the twentieth century.

But Now the Three-Legged Stool Is Wobbly

In general, this system worked well for our parents and grandparents. But now it's creaking and cracking and beginning to wobble. No one knows what will happen with Social Security, employer pensions, and personal savings, but here are a few reasons why we can't depend on the three-legged stool like we could in the past.

The First Leg: Social Security

Social Security has been a popular favorite for more than seventy-five years now. The happiest day of the month, for many millions of people, has been the day the envelope from Social Security arrives in their mailbox. (A few even wait to greet the mailman.) For some, it has added to the total wealth that will be passed on to their heirs. For others, it has provided the extras in life that they couldn't afford otherwise. And, for millions, it has been their *largest source of income* and keeping them afloat. But all feel entitled to their monthly payment and look forward to it. Future recipients of that monthly payment feel just as *entitled*!

That's why Social Security's wobble is high profile; it has made headlines for years and will continue to do so. Where do all those payments come from? It was designed primarily to be a pay-as-you-go plan, meaning that the current workers' contributions that are going in are used to pay the retired workers' benefits that are going out. But the ratio of workers paying into the system has fallen in comparison to the number of retirees collecting benefits. This is mostly due to a decreasing birth rate in the United States, because families don't need to have as many children as they did in the era of the family contract. A lower birthrate means fewer workers paying in. (Workers emigrating to the United States bolster that number, though.) The other factor is an increasing life span, as people have taken longer and longer to kick the bucket. That increases how many years of payments each retiree receives and also how many are still living and receiving payments. Not surprisingly, this means that the total contributions coming in are shrinking in proportion to the total payments going out. On the current trajectory, there won't be enough money to pay all the benefits. Social Security will run short of money. Medicare is on an even more precarious trajectory.

We'll need to either increase the contributions coming from workers and employers or reduce the benefits, or some combination of the two. The sooner that course corrections are made, the less drastic they'll need to be. The *mathematical* resolution of this problem isn't that big of a deal. There are people endowed with very powerful, very warped minds—economists and actuaries—who actually love puzzles like this. Unfortunately, the *political* resolution is a very big deal. Lawmakers tried—and failed—to find a middle ground for fixing the problem when economic times were good and the federal deficit was in much better shape. Who knows whether they'll work together better in bad times? As with every political issue, there are those who claim that the problem is nearly insurmountable, and others who claim that it's not really a problem at all.

SOCIAL SECURITY: AN URGENT CRISIS, DECADES IN THE MAKING

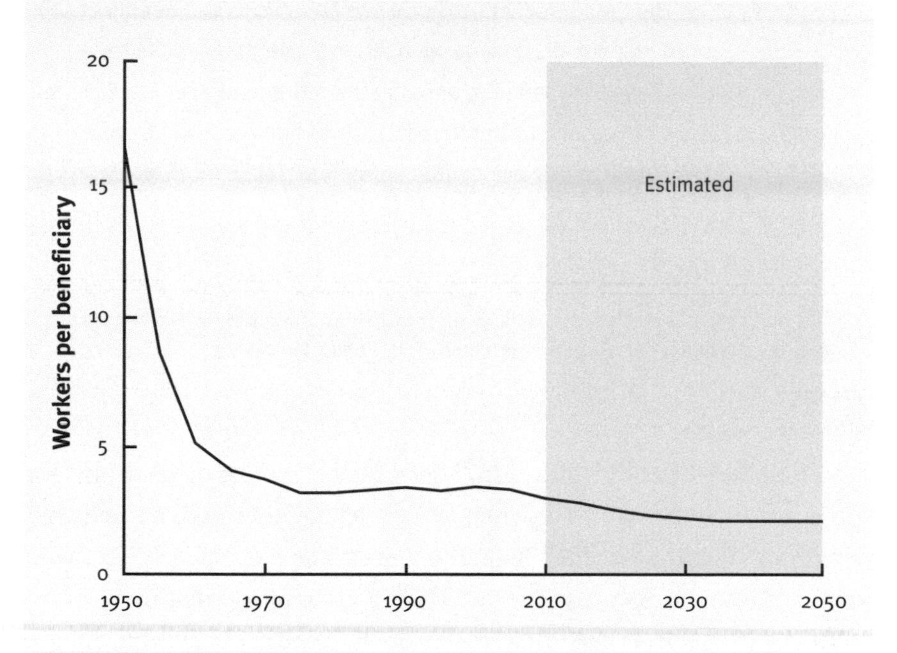

The Social Security funding crisis is like an accident in slow motion. Demographically, it's been unfolding for *decades*. The challenge is that the system operates on a fundamental premise; incoming payroll taxes from workers must be sufficient to pay outgoing benefits to retirees (and other beneficiaries). Because you understand the changes in the population pyramid, you already know we're headed for trouble.

The graph above shows how the number of workers per beneficiary has fallen over time. In 1955 there were more than eight workers for each beneficiary, although the ratio was dropping quickly. But since the 1970s, there have been more than *three* workers for each beneficiary. Now the ratio is dropping again and may end up at only *two* workers for each beneficiary. That may not sound like much, but it's a 33 percent reduction!

When incoming payroll taxes were greater than outgoing benefits, the system built up a surplus for the future. But starting in 2010, payroll taxes coming in fell below the benefits being paid out. The surplus will only cover the difference until 2037. Then benefits would need to be cut by about 25 percent! How do we fix it? We need to increase the payroll tax, carefully trim benefits, or delay the retirement age. *Maybe all three*. If we do it sooner, rather than later, the changes won't be as drastic. So even though this accident is unfolding in slow motion, it's urgent!

SOURCE: 2009 Annual Report of the Board of Trustees of the Federal Old-Age and Survivors Insurance and Disability Insurance Trust Funds, Table IV.B2.

There's another complication. Social Security built up a surplus for the future, in anticipation of when benefit payments would exceed contributions. But the broader federal government has actually *borrowed* against the Social Security surplus. There's no question that the government is good for it. It's just that, to pay Social Security back, they'll have to raise taxes or cut spending elsewhere. Only time and the prevailing political winds will determine how much, and how soon, we should be worried. Even if the first leg isn't wobbling yet, we can hear it creaking loudly. It's crying out for repair.

The Second Leg: Employer Pensions

Pensions have been a popular favorite, too. They haven't provided a monthly mailbox smile to as many people as Social Security has. But they have transformed retirement for many millions of Americans. The *monthly* aspect is important, because the term *pension* is used to refer to many different types of retirement plans these days. However, employer pension actually refers to a very specific type of plan. A pension was the original type of plan that an employer *promises to pay for* and accumulates a benefit for only one purpose: retirement. A profit-sharing plan that an employer may or may not contribute to isn't a pension plan. A salary savings plan that an employee may or may not contribute to, such as a 401(k), isn't a pension plan, either. It's only a pension plan if there's a requirement to provide a *defined benefit* at retirement or a *defined contribution each year*. It's only a pension if there's a *commitment*.

There's another feature that most pensions share. At retirement, pensions provide a *monthly income for life*. So no matter how long the employee lives, they can't outlive their money, as they might in the case of an investment account. This is the type of plan that formed the original leg of the three-legged stool. You can see why it provided a solid foundation for retirement—a pension was something you could count on. A happy mailbox every month, for as long as you lived!

However, a smaller and smaller proportion of workers will ever receive benefits from this type of plan because of two trends in the U.S. workplace. One trend is from the employee side. Because employees tend to move from company to company more than they used to, they are less likely to stick around long enough to earn this type of pension. It takes many years of service to build up a benefit. Unlike times past, few employees consider themselves to be lifers at a given job, and so they don't reap the benefits of this type of long-term benefit structure.

The other trend is from the employer side. The number of employers still willing to foot the bill for a traditional employer-funded pension is steadily decreasing. Government employers at all levels have generally stayed with this traditional approach, and they are still likely to maintain pension plans. (Although some of these plans are facing the same type of funding problems as Social Security is.) At the opposite end of the spectrum, smaller companies have rarely provided them. Large companies are somewhere in between, historically sponsoring pension plans, but many have now terminated or frozen them. The total number of traditional pension plans reached a peak of more than 114,000 in 1985, but well over two-thirds of those are now gone. In recent years, the news has been filled with stories of well-known employers reducing or eliminating these benefits.

Why are employers doing away with pensions? First, the regulatory compliance for these plans became so complex that some employers decided it wasn't worth the bother. Second, and probably more important, plans designed to reward long-term service were simply out of touch with the need to attract and retain new talent. Third, employees themselves seemed to have a better understanding of, and appreciation for, profit-sharing and 401(k)-type plans. Another reason—one that's less cited but pretty obvious—is that many employers who have eliminated their traditional defined-benefit pensions were simply looking to reduce costs. Employers who replaced pensions with profit-sharing and 401(k) plans almost always were able to cut their costs significantly. (This is echoed in the emerging trend of employers eliminating or reducing medical insurance coverage for retirees.) In any case, the combined result of these two broad trends (employee and employer) is that fewer people can look forward to getting a monthly pension for as long as they live. For U.S. workers, the second leg is definitely shorter.

You may ask, "Aren't 401(k) plans the 'modern' replacement for the second leg?" That's a good question. These hybrid employer-employee savings accounts go by a variety of names, often the section of the Internal Revenue Code that made them possible. Depending on where you work, it could instead be a 403(b), 457, SIMPLE, Thrift Plan, or some other type of payroll savings plan. Although the details vary, all of these plans, in all these environments, are essentially the same thing: Your employer provides an easy way for you (*you, you, you!*) to save for your own retirement. The cornerstone of these plans isn't an employer contribution, like in a traditional pension. No, the cornerstone is your own savings. Technically, these plans are salary-reduction plans. (Guess whose salary gets the reduction to fund them? You get only one guess.)

If you're fortunate, your employer may match part of your contribution or make other types of contributions. However, in general, there are no required employer contributions in these salary savings plans. If your employer is *generous*, you could be on the receiving end of some hefty contributions—every bit as valuable as anything you might get from a traditional pension. But if your employer is *stingy*, you could be carrying the ball all by yourself, with no contributions at all from your employer. (Do you know how generous or stingy your employer is?) A 401(k)-type plan simply provides a framework for you and your employer to make contributions into your retirement account, and each of you decides whether to put in a little or a lot. So if your employer only puts in a little, you'd better put in a lot!

To rephrase the question at hand: "Are these plans part of the second leg or part of the third leg?" The answer is . . . yes. They don't fully measure up to the original concept of the second leg, because they don't have the level of commitment of a traditional pension. But they are like an employer pension in that they're maintained by the employer, who does have significant responsibility to make sure everything is on the up-and-up and who may make some contribution. But they're like personal savings in that you're the one who needs to save the significant money (through payroll deductions) to create a retirement benefit. For an increasing number of workers, 401(k)-type plans are the only second leg they'll have. Any way we look at it, the second leg is wobbling.

The Third Leg: Personal Savings

One reason the first and second legs worked so well is that they were automatic. People didn't need to do anything in particular to build up benefits in those legs, other than work for a paycheck. The workers paid attention to the week-to-week, month-to-month money. And Social Security and the employer pension paid attention to the age-sixty-five-until-you-die money.

Workers do pretty well with month-to-month money. After all, most people don't spend their entire paycheck on the same day they get it. If they get paid on Fridays, they don't live like royalty on Friday night and like paupers by the next Thursday. No, they try to level things out so that they don't have such drastic peaks and valleys in spending. Most people, even if they're not financial specialists, get pretty good at leveling it out. Week-to-week, month-to-month, and over a whole year or longer, people more or less level out their spending. Through trial and error, they learn how much to spend right away and how much to save so that they have something left to spend later. It's a skill that people acquire over time, because they get many weeks, months, and years to practice.

But shifting modes to think about age-sixty-five-until-you-die money isn't natural for most people. It wasn't needed back in the era of family retirement economics. People had always saved, of course. They saved for a new piece of equipment. They saved for years to buy a piece of property. People were accustomed to doing that. But the third leg of the stool was a new idea. Saving, saving, saving for decades in order to then s-l-o-w-l-y spend over more decades. How would that work?

Franco Modigliani won a Nobel Prize in economics for coming up with an explanation for how people are thought to save, which he called the Life Cycle Hypothesis. (Milton Friedman advanced a similar concept

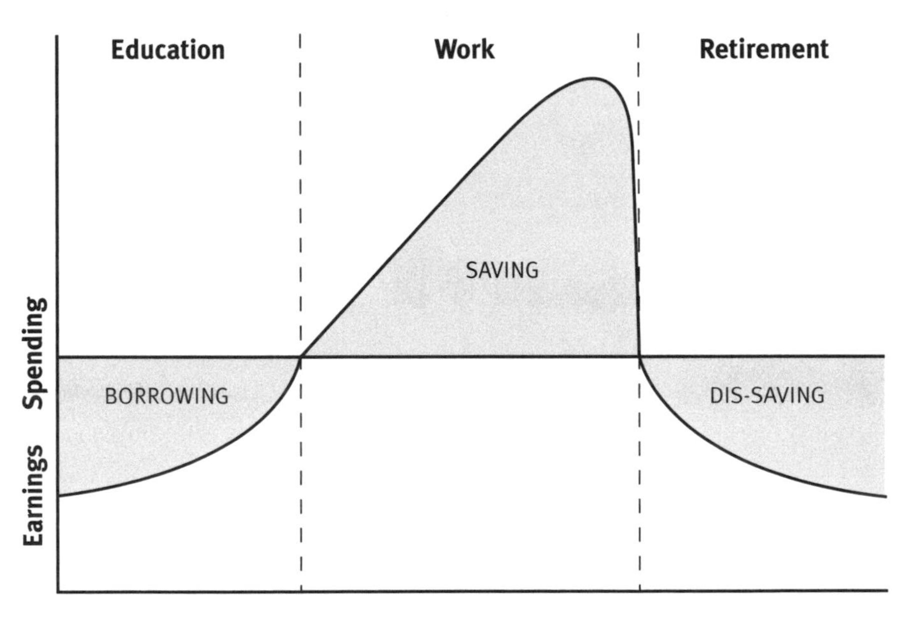

called the Permanent Income Hypothesis.) Modigliani assumed that people are *rational agents*. That means they anticipate what's going to happen in the future, figure out the right course of action, and then use willpower to follow through. He said that people don't spend based on their *current* level of income but on the level they *expect to average over their lifetime*. When we expect to have a higher income in the future, we're more likely to dip into savings—or borrow money—to spend more than our current income. That's because we expect to make plenty of money later, and we'll catch up to our spending over time. So in the *early* part of our lives, we tend to spend more than we earn, through *borrowing*.

On the other hand, when we expect to have a lower income in the future, we're more likely to put money into savings and spend less than our current income. Instead of continuing to borrow like when we were younger, we flip-flop over to saving. That's the kind of long-term retirement saving envisioned as the third leg of the three-legged stool. Modigliani suggested that even if we overspend in the early part of our life cycle, we make up for it by underspending in the middle part. Similar to leveling out our spending from paycheck to paycheck, the Life Cycle Hypothesis says we try to level out our spending over our entire lifetime. That's how the third leg of the stool—personal savings—would be able to work. Because we're rational agents!

In general, though, it hasn't worked out that way. Many (most?) workers apparently aren't rational. Over the past twenty-five years, the aggregate percentage of our income that we've set aside as personal savings has steadily declined. When you look at the graph on page 92 you might even say it has plummeted—from a peak of about 11 percent in the early 1980s to almost nothing by the year 2005. Saving was so low that it was initially calculated as negative! It would have been the first year since the Great Depression that we collectively spent more than we earned. For the rate to fall that low, some Americans had to spend from their savings; others had to borrow from credit cards, mortgages, car loans, college loans, or home equity loans. The true opposite of saving isn't spending—it's borrowing. In 2009, the savings rate rose sharply. But given the tough state of the economy and the high rate of unemployment, it's probably not that

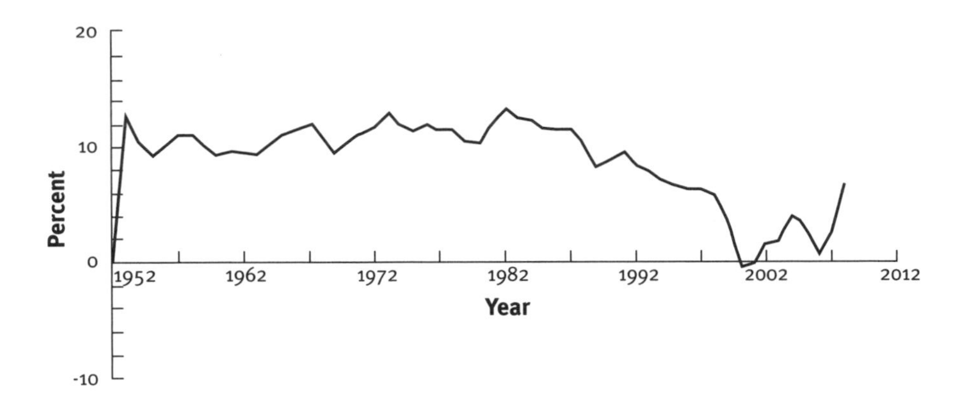

Americans suddenly decided to sock away tons of money. Maybe they just stopped borrowing so much. In any case, there is nothing to suggest that Americans are now committed—over the long term—to building a solid and secure third leg. (We can always hope.)

Maximizing the Societal Approach

The societal approach (like the family approach) is still very much alive. For some workers, it's the way that they'll be able to afford to retire, even if the three-legged stool is wobbling. Thanks to years of service under pensions and Social Security, millions will still have a happy mailbox (or e-deposit) every month, for as long as they live. However, if you missed out on getting a full employer pension, there are still (at least) two strategies you can use to maximize your retirement savings.

Practical Strategy #1: Maximize Social Security. Your Social Security benefits represent our collective society's commitment to help support you in retirement, and these benefits are more valuable than you realize. How might you *maximize* the benefits you receive?

This isn't about gaming the system, but about making smart decisions for accruing your benefits and for collecting them. We're willing to pay for professional services to maintain other valuable assets such as our home or investment accounts. But we don't think about getting advice for Social Security benefits. With boomers becoming eligible to apply for benefits, more advisors will turn their attention to strategies for maximizing benefits.

For example, gaining just a few more years of credited service may help those who were in and out of the workforce over their career. With today's blended families, couples that live together but haven't married should see how tying the knot could affect their benefits. And everyone—*everyone*—should double and triple think the age at which they apply for benefits. How much earned income you'll have and your biomedical prospects for living shorter, or longer, than the average retiree are both important factors. They should shape your decision about taking a smaller benefit at age sixty-two, or a larger benefit later. (See chapter eight regarding your personal life expectancy.) There are now strategies for beginning benefits at age sixty-two, and then *paying them back* to Social Security later, to trade up to a higher monthly benefit. Have you ever heard of such a thing?

Practical Strategy #2: Tap into a Pension. Benefits from a traditional employer pension can provide peace of mind for life, but they are becoming harder and harder to get. Can you tap into one of these plans for a partial benefit?

If you already work for an employer that provides a traditional pension, you know you want to accrue the maximum benefit you can. But be savvy when choosing your payout option, too. (By the way, the joint-and-survivor monthly benefit for your spouse may have a lower payment but probably a larger total payout over your lifetimes.) If you worked for one of these employers years ago, you may have the opportunity to accrue more benefits by working there again, or you may even be able to buy back benefits from the first time around. These plans are so complicated that they can make a CPA's eyes glaze over. Get expert advice.

If you have never been in a traditional pension, you should know that older workers typically accrue benefits faster than younger workers do. So if you're looking for a job, strongly consider finding one of these hidden gems. Look at government employers, schools, large corporations, and smaller companies that have been around for a long time. Even five years of plan participation at the end of your career can produce a significant benefit. In some cases, you can even earn pension benefits for part-time work after you retire from your primary career. But you'll need to do your detective work to find these diamonds in the rough.

The Rational Agent Approach to Retirement Economics

This approach sprang up as the societal approach passed its high point. It's based on the belief that people are *rational agents*. That means, given enough information and choices, workers will automatically save however much they need in order to retire.

When the three-legged stool was created, saving was pretty simple. It was downright boring, to be more accurate. People were content to save in plain old bank accounts and earn interest. One reason is because a decade earlier, many Americans had begun investing in stocks, and they rode a market bubble all the way up to the stock market crash. (The one in 1929, not 2009.) Having been burned, they resolved to stick with guaranteed, low-yielding investments in the solid banks that had weathered the crash and the Great Depression. Only a few rich or courageous (or foolish) souls invested in individual stocks and bonds.

But decades later, when 401(k) plans were supplementing and then replacing traditional pensions, personal saving became much more exciting. Within 401(k) plans, participants could choose different investment strategies, which they couldn't do inside employer pensions. And outside the 401(k), new types of accounts such as IRAs were passed into law. Financial instruments such as mutual funds and variable annuities proliferated and multiplied. In a few decades, personal saving for retirement went from boring to bewildering! And it was being marketed to the max. There were armies of stockbrokers and mutual fund salespeople marching out every day, loaded with investment products, reminding workers of their need to save for retirement. There were also the more recent "no-load" providers, offering products wholesale, via mail and telephone (and eventually the Internet). In addition to the products themselves, more and more investment *information* began pouring in, too. Although it was only a river of information in those days, and not yet a sea.

This environment was no problem for the rational agents of the Life Cycle Hypothesis. These workers would recognize that employer pensions were weakening and would embrace the 401(k) plan as a worthy successor. They would sign up for their employer salary savings plans, learn about the investment options, carefully determine which were appropriate for them, and follow through with ever-increasing plan contributions, as they monitored and managed their investments. They would carefully shore up the second leg, as traditional pensions disappeared.

But they wouldn't stop with the second leg; these rational agents would shore up the third leg, too. They would also invest in IRA accounts, Roth IRA accounts, tax-deferred annuities, variable life insurance policies, and just for good measure, section 529 college savings plans for the kids. (And of course, they would remember to read the prospectus before investing money.) That would take care of the third leg!

All the retirement geeks—employee benefit managers, 401(k) providers, mutual fund companies, insurance companies, investment representatives, and even the government—shared a set of common beliefs. They all believed that people *really were rational agents*, just as Franco Modigliani and other economists had theorized. They all believed that if people simply had *access to financial information*, they would come to the right conclusions. They all believed that if people simply had *enough choices*, they would choose good ones. And most important, they all believed that if people simply understood the need for *personal responsibility*, they would become responsible and save enough for retirement.

We already know how all that turned out. If you've forgotten, peek back at the personal savings graph on page 92. However, in retrospect, it makes complete sense. Under the rational agent approach, the workers who actually *are* rational agents did just fine. They anticipated the future, made good decisions, and used willpower to follow through. They compensated for the wobbly stool just fine. (That is, until the stock market and real estate crash of 2009. But that's related to a different concept in economics, about *rational markets*. Hmmmm.)

Nonrational Agents in the Rational Agent Approach

What about all the other workers—the ones who weren't rational agents? The *nonrational* agents? What could they possibly have been thinking? (You'll want to know what they were thinking, so you can avoid it!) Let's examine the fundamental decision of how much to consume. Should they spend all their income, or should they save a bunch of it?

Because economists are fond of the idea that things are in equilibrium, or in balance, we'll use an example called the *Spending-Saving Seesaw*. You can see that spending is on the left side of the seesaw, and saving on the right. First we'll look at the consumption economics of a rational agent and then at three nonrational agents. For the rational agents, the seesaw is in balance. They adjust their spending and saving according to the Life Cycle Hypothesis, of course.

RATIONAL ECONOMICS

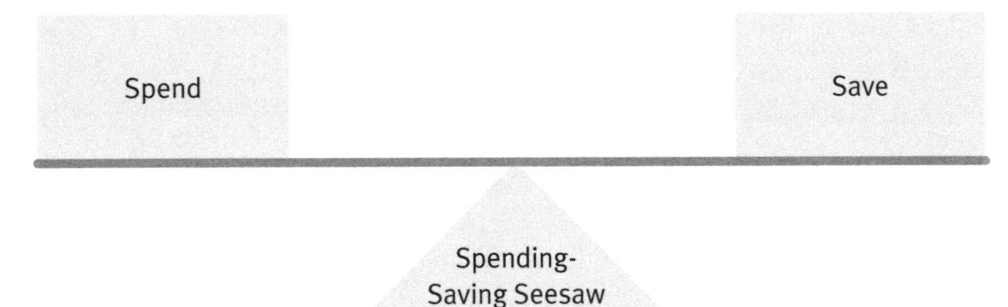

However, for most people—the nonrational agents—it isn't easy to balance the seesaw. The first reason has to do with temptation. If they're going to save their income, they only get one chance to save it, and then it's gone forever. That's because the only income they can save is today's income.

But spending doesn't work that way. If they're going to spend their income, they get *three chances* to spend it. That's because they can spend *today's* income, obviously. They can also spend *yesterday's* income, by taking money from savings. And they can also spend *tomorrow's* income, by borrowing. (It's paid back from tomorrow's income.) You can see what that does to the seesaw. It's a lot of temptation!

TEMPTATION ECONOMICS

Spend
TOMORROW'S
Money
Spend
YESTERDAY'S
Money
Spend
TODAY'S
Money
Save
TODAY'S
Money
Spending-
Saving Seesaw

The second reason has to do with how people perceive today's money versus tomorrow's money. When people save, they give up spending the money today in order to spend it (plus interest) tomorrow. We know from behavioral economics that people perceive spending today's money as *much more* valuable that it really is. And they perceive spending tomorrow's money as *much less* valuable than it really is. It's like they're looking through the wrong end of a telescope. You can see what that does to the seesaw. It makes tomorrow seem too small and dim compared to today.

BEHAVIORAL ECONOMICS

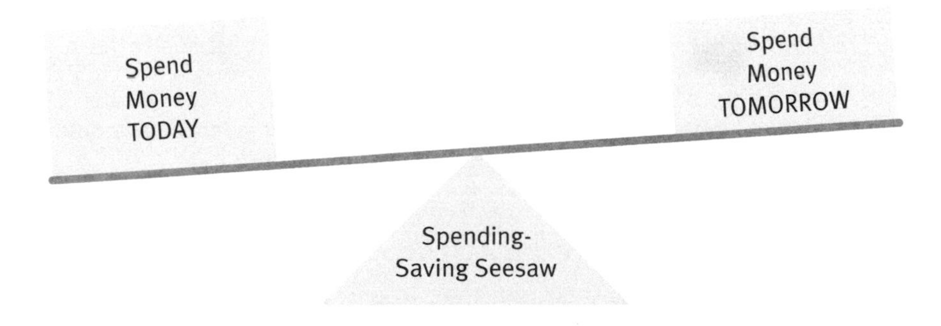

The third reason has to do with the market economy. We know that businesses are driven to earn a profit through satisfying the needs and desires of consumers. So to understand market forces, we need to ask two questions: "How much profit can businesses earn by getting people to save?" as opposed to "How much profit can businesses earn by getting people to spend?" The answers determine how much outside pressure will be applied to consumers.

It turns out that a good profit can be made by businesses that get people to save via their CDs, mutual funds, and other products. But there's more profit to be made in getting people to spend, for two reasons. The first is the profit to be made on the goods and services consumers spend money on. The second is the profit to be made in loaning consumers money to spend. The saving end of the seesaw loses again.

MARKET ECONOMICS

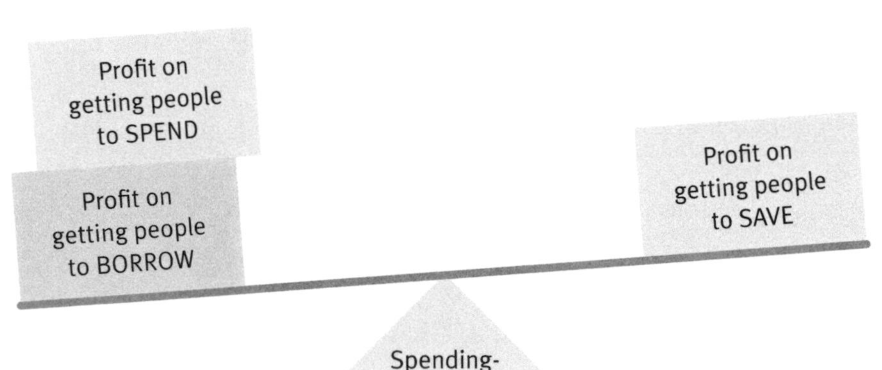

Here are two practical examples.

Which do you see more of in the newspaper: colorful ads for consumer goods or colorful ads for investment accounts?

Which do you receive more of in your mailbox: offers for snazzy new savings plans or offers for snazzy new credit cards?

To estimate how profitable an activity is, see how much the business spends on trying to influence you. It's obvious that much more is spent on getting us to spend and borrow than in getting us to save. So workers have to contend not only with their *inner* forces but also with *outer* forces. It's enough to tempt a rational agent!

However, that's not to say the rational agent approach doesn't work. In the most general sense, it works better for workers with more formal education than those with less. It works better for workers with higher incomes than those with lower incomes. It works better for workers who receive a lot of financial education than those who receive little or none. (And if you're a financial specialist, it's probably been working for you.) But we're looking for a new approach that will work for as many people as possible. What's the answer? If the rational agent approach is where our society is headed, how can we make it work for as many workers as possible? The answer, dear reader, is in the next chapter.

"I would rather spend my time enjoying my income than bothering about my investments."

—Clive Granger, winner of the 2003 Nobel Prize in economics

Chapter FIVE

A New Approach to Retirement Security

In the last chapter, we reviewed a variety of approaches to retirement economics, and gathered clues for how to approach the new retirement. Now, it's time to draw on the best elements of each!

We saw that the family approach was a very strong life cycle system, because it worked for millennia. It was so strong that it stifled personal initiative. When a young person aspired to be a farmer but was from a family of fishermen, leaving the family occupation was a huge gamble. But an older farmer or fisherman who had a family didn't need to worry about how to get along in later life. It had been natural for them to have children, and it didn't matter whether they were consciously planning their own "retirement." Instead, the system was *automatically* oriented toward that goal. They still had to exercise personal responsibility by working from dawn till dusk. But their work focused on the months and years, while the family economic *system* took care of their life cycle.

We saw that the societal approach was a strong life cycle system too, because it worked for generations. It allowed for more personal initiative in choosing an occupation. And after workers did choose, it was natural for them to focus on their occupation over the months and years ahead, not on a retirement decades in the future. Yet, the system was automatically building their retirement benefits *even before they realized how important it was.* They still had to exercise personal responsibility by staying with an employer long enough to earn a pension. But they were working with a system *oriented toward their life cycle goal.* A worker didn't need to worry about how to get along in later life.

We saw that the rational agent approach worked well for the few rational agents, but not for the rest of us. Instead of an external system, it assumes there's an *internal* life cycle system within each person. If we provide information and choice, the internal system will supposedly do the rest. It's clear that our internal system attends to the months and years of earning, spending, and saving, of course. But the rational agent approach also assumes our internal system correctly anticipates financial needs *decades in the future*, properly calculates savings needed *to the end of life*, and exercises sufficient discipline to follow through, *both before and after we retire.* The Life Cycle Hypothesis is an elegant theory, but we can't count on it. Humans have never lived like that before, and we only get one chance at the life cycle. The stakes are just too high! But this approach offers an important breakthrough: *Information and choices are good.* Educating people on personal finance is absolutely essential as daily life becomes ever more financial.

The New Retirement Economics: Autopilot

For designing the new approach, we've learned (at least) two things that are essential. First, when we have *automatic external systems* oriented toward our goal, we're more likely to get there. Second, when we have *freedom and knowledge* (or access to knowledge), we're more likely to get there, too. This new approach is called retirement autopilot, because we need to take control but also use intelligent external systems.

Retirement has been like traveling by airplane. In the family approach, we knew we'd get there but couldn't even choose the destination. In the societal approach, we could choose a destination but were mostly like a passenger. In the rational agent approach, we were put in the pilot's seat and could choose any destination we wanted. Except some of us actually were pilots, while many of us crashed and burned. The retirement autopilot approach is the next stage. We must choose a destination and course. But instead of needing to do everything manually, we turn the myriad details over to automatic external systems that keep us on course. We can still take the controls, of course. But if we become distracted, forget the destination, or even fall asleep, we're still making progress toward our goal. The autopilot frees us up to do something else. If we truly are a pilot (a financial specialist), the autopilot allows us to consider other destinations, plot alternate courses, check the weather report, and chat with other pilots about flying. It takes over the mundane tasks of flying and frees pilots up for *higher level* pilot activities. But if we're like most people and we're *not* good pilots (or financial specialists), we have peace of mind knowing the systems keep us on course.

The key elements of the retirement autopilot approach look like this:

1. **Sources of Income.** Five pillars, or PERKS, provide more stability than the old three-legged stool.
2. **Financial Education.** Both rational agents and nonrational agents make better decisions when they know more.
3. **Automatic Systems.** Automatic systems for saving, investing, and distributing money are more reliable and efficient than humans are.
4. **Fiduciary Advice.** Experts free from conflict of interest can improve decisions at key points in time.

Let's take a peek at each of the four elements.

The First Element of Retirement Autopilot: PERKS

It turns out the three-legged stool wasn't a good reflection of what people have been doing in the *real world*. When we look at the sources of retirement income that you're most likely to actually use, we can see there are five of them. Five pillars of retirement income. It's time to recognize what they are, be more conscious of them, and make specific plans. You'll want to take really good care of your *largest* pillars. At the same time, building up *additional* pillars would give you more stability, wouldn't it? Later, you'll learn about making the pillars more *automatic*, too.

The acronym for the five sources is PERKS. Perks used to be perquisites, or special privileges that go to bigwigs. But retirement security isn't just for bigwigs—we all need PERKS.

P Is for Personal Savings

This pillar is just like the personal savings leg from the old retirement. It's the pillar that offers us the most freedom and choice, which also means it *demands* the most of us. It doesn't even exist unless you take the initiative. You can take the initiative to set up automatic savings programs, however.

E Is for Employer Plans

For most of us, this pillar will *not* be like the employer pension from the old retirement. It will refer to 401(k)-type employee savings plans, with some employers kicking in a little, others a lot. Although sponsored by employers, they require much more of us than the original employer pension did. As with personal savings, this pillar may not even exist unless you take the initiative. Employers will increasingly offer automatic features for you to take advantage of.

R Is for Real Estate

This wasn't recognized as part of the three-legged stool, even though it's been around for a long time. For most of us, real estate is simply the American dream of owning our own home. (Unless you're a real estate investor, too.) Workers have always used homes for retirement security; they paid off the mortgage and had a free place to live. But in the new retirement, many people imagine using home equity as a source of income, too. That's asking for double duty; a place to live and a stream of income at the same time. If that's your goal, you'd better plan extra carefully. The good news is that all by itself, paying down your mortgage is the essence of an autopilot program.

K Is for Keep Working

Continuing to work in some form was once the *only pillar* of retirement income! During the societal era, it was supposed to disappear. Doesn't the metaphor of a three-legged stool suggest sitting on our duff? But in the new retirement, many of us can't afford to do that. We'll need to work, at least a little. All the other pillars are your *financial capital*, because they're measured in accumulated dollars. This pillar is your *human capital*, because it's measured in your future value as a worker. In the old retirement, your human capital dropped to *zero* when you reached retirement. You were worthless! But in the new retirement, you may not be worthless. If you have biological health, psychological strengths, and social connections, you still have human capital. But we haven't figured out automatic ways to make sure you can keep working. Because of these unknowns, this pillar is the *least dependable*. Take good care of your human capital, but don't depend on it!

THE FIVE PILLARS

S Is for Social Security

In the old retirement, Social Security was intended as a safety net for people who lived long enough to become too old to work. Then, as people lived longer and longer, it became a key source of retirement income for nearly everyone. It's the most automatic of the pillars. At the same time, it's the pillar you have the *least control* over. Your strategy is to maximize the benefits you're entitled to, and then hope that society keeps its promise.

So there you have them: the five pillars of retirement income. Even if you're not a bigwig, you can still have PERKS!

The Second Element of Retirement Autopilot: Financial Education

As it became obvious the rational agent approach wasn't working, a new term emerged: *financial literacy*. (You'll be hearing about it, a lot.) Coined by well-intentioned thinkers in education, government, and nonprofit organizations, the idea is to finally get serious about increasing peoples' *knowledge* to make good decisions. It's about using education to turn nonrational agents into rational agents. It's a great idea. In the coming years, you'll see more efforts and programs from many entities on a variety of financial topics, including preparing for retirement.

However, you know it's only *part* of the solution. If financial literacy is just knowledge on financial topics, it isn't enough. Financial literacy needs to include knowledge on how to use autopilot systems and how to get good advice. Instead of just trying to make people into rational agents, we need to connect them with systems that support them over time.

So even you, dear reader, should polish up on the nuts and bolts of finance after you finish this book. It's painful, I know. But you're going to be bombarded with programs designed to increase your financial knowledge anyway. They emerge from three basic philosophies. Which is most likely to resonate with you?

"Facts of Life" Financial Education

The philosophy here is to provide us with the financial "facts of life." Like teaching us about the birds and the bees, the assumption is that we're naturally curious about the subject and eager to know all the intimate details. Sort of like a variation on a best-selling book of the 1970s: *Everything You Always Wanted to Know About* Money *(But Were Afraid to Ask).*

Because the people creating these programs *actually do* find money that interesting, they imagine others will, too. It doesn't occur to them that we're already living in a sea of financial information. It doesn't occur to them that if the curiosity is there, people will seek out the information. But if people aren't curious, the existence of another fact-filled website, publication, or curriculum won't attract much interest.

Financial education like this can work in a mandatory or compulsory setting, though, like an employer-sponsored retirement plan or a school. But just because they make us learn this financial stuff doesn't mean we're interested. Or that we'll remember to practice "safe spending" in the moment of passion.

"Scare and Scold" Financial Education

The philosophy here is that the "facts of life" aren't sufficient, because people are naturally complacent. Probably even lazy. At the very least, they're somewhat clueless. Anyway, the well-intentioned folks behind this approach tend to believe that people are motivated only by doom and gloom. That only a potential catastrophe will awaken them from their stupor. So the core theme of the "scare and scold" scenario warns people that they're probably doing something wrong and urges them to take action to avoid disaster.

The "scare and scold" approach makes surface statements like these (*which have these underlying messages*):

- "Most people aren't saving enough for retirement." (*Translation: You aren't saving enough for retirement.*)

- "You need to plan ahead." (*Translation: You haven't planned ahead, have you?*)
- "Building retirement security takes time." (*Translation: It may be too late for you, anyway.*)
- "Saving is easier than you think." (*Translation: Can't you at least try?*)
- "Start today!" (*Translation: Or you'll be living in a tar-paper shack and eating dog food.*)

If this motivates you to learn, it's not because you suddenly love finance. No, it's probably because dire warnings tend to grab your attention and get you to *imagine nasty outcomes that you don't want*. If you're the type of person who imagines what could go wrong, and then takes steps to safeguard against it, this could be exactly what you need. (It's called defensive pessimism.) Although not an especially enjoyable way to get motivated, it can sometimes be just the ticket. It may be good to scare the dickens out of ourselves now and then.

"Motivational" Financial Education

One underlying assumption here is the same as "scare and scold": that information by itself isn't sufficient. It knows that people tune out when information seems irrelevant to them (like high school algebra). It works best when offered in the context of people's lives. The educators behind this approach think humans are good at accomplishing things. But they need a motivating positive vision of what they want. The "scare and scold" will startle people initially, but then they grow accustomed to it and it ceases to motivate them. On the other hand, a positive goal can keep us motivated forever. That's why this book helps you create a vision of the life you want to live. If you get the vision right, you'll learn what you need to know and take the actions you need to take to get there. Aren't humans great?

The Third Element of Retirement Autopilot: Automatic Systems

Autopilot systems are available to help us accomplish the three essential tasks of financial retirement: saving, investing, and distributing our retirement money. We'll look at these tasks and how the automatic systems might work. However, the systems are in the form of products, services, and arrangements that will vary and even go by different names. Autopilot systems are catching on, though, and multiplying in type and number. The details will change, but once you start thinking this way, you'll be able to spot them.

Autopilot Saving

Autopilot saving is about getting around the spending-saving seesaw. It's about replacing willpower with systems power. It's about saving the money before you even get it, or turning it into that phone bill you need to pay. But your goal is to make it not only automatic but also as *painless* as possible.

Your Social Security pillar is the epitome of autopilot, because your FICA is deducted from your pay, whether you ask for it or not. But your employer plan pillar may be a problem. In the world of 401(k)-type plans, doing the wrong thing (not saving) has been automatic. And doing the right thing (saving) has required a manual override of the system.

When you change to a new job, the *default* contribution for your retirement savings is *zero*, which is definitely the wrong amount. It's not taking you in the direction of your retirement destination. Doing the right thing requires a manual override. You need to overcome your own internal inertia (the tendency to keep things as they are) and also the external inertia of your new employer's payroll and benefits department. You must complete the enrollment forms, choose a contribution percentage, and select a beneficiary. Later, when you're able to afford a higher contribution percentage, you have to overcome the same inertia to increase your contribution. For you and your employer, *it's easier to do nothing*. And yet that keeps you headed in the wrong direction!

What if we made all the *right things* into defaults? That way, even if we did nothing, we'd be headed in the right direction!

Some employers are catching on and implementing an arrangement called auto-enrollment. When you start a new job, a moderate percentage of your pay is automatically withheld and contributed to your retirement. There's no inertia to overcome. Your employer needs to tell you, and you typically have ninety days to opt out (if you're determined to do the wrong thing). An even cooler arrangement is called auto-escalation. You agree to allow your contribution percentage to increase at specific dates in the future. (It's painless today, right?) Those future increases are when you get raises, so the increases aren't even painful when they happen! You can always manually decrease, but you probably won't, because of your inertia. However, your inertia now keeps you on the right course instead of the wrong course. By doing nothing, you're doing the right thing. Doesn't that make life easier?

If you're not starting a new job, march into your payroll and benefits department and demand these savings arrangements. If they're implemented, it's usually only for new hires, not for existing employees.

For your personal savings, are you getting some creative ideas? It will take a little more legwork to find options. The beauty is that it takes initiative only *one time*—when you put it into place. It doesn't require ongoing initiative and willpower to keep saving. Explore what new options may be available from your investment providers. At the very least, they should offer an *automatic monthly transfer* from your bank account into a longer-term retirement account.

If you have debt, paying that down is as good as personal savings. Especially for credit cards, not paying those high interest rates are an excellent return on your money. So don't make a manual payment each month, especially one for just the minimum amount. Instead, set up an automatic payment for a larger amount. You'll need to get up your gumption only once, instead of over and over.

That's like your real estate pillar. You have an automatic saving arrangement called a mortgage payment. Instead of coming out of your pay before you see it, like a 401(k), it *turns saving into a bill* that you must pay. You can improve it, though, by setting up partial mortgage payments based on your paycheck cycle, instead of monthly. It will be less painful, and you'll actually build up equity faster, too.

Autopilot Investing

Unless you specialize in financial well-being, you probably dislike making investment decisions. Most people don't like saving because it's simple and boring. But they don't like investing because it's complicated and volatile. Some people have so much trepidation that they allocate their portfolio just *one time*, and then don't change it for years or even decades. That's inertia at work again. Unfortunately, portfolio management means not just selecting appropriate investments initially but also *rebalancing* them as they fluctuate in value. Over the long term, it means *reallocating* them to be more conservative as you approach retirement. If your trepidation and inertia keep you from making these changes, you're in deep trouble.

Autopilot investing is now probably available for your employer plan and your personal savings, too. It turns your inertia from a vice into a virtue. Avoiding your investments becomes a good thing instead of a bad thing. An autopilot retirement account does those portfolio tasks you're *supposed* to be doing, but it does it automatically. It also reduces your temptation to make hasty changes when the markets have a big drop.

Until the advent of autopilot investing, it wasn't easy—or cheap—to manage retirement portfolios. It took a lot of investing knowledge and skill to set up an account with the right allocation in the first place. And then it took a lot of boring operational follow-through to keep up with it, rebalance it, and then shift it to become more conservative as you approach retirement.

Before, the choices were either paying significantly higher fees to have this done or taking it on yourself. Understandably, many people opted to have it all done for them, but they paid a huge price, often 1 percent of their account balance every year. (That may not sound like much, but it really cuts into the value of your portfolio.) And workers who *didn't* pay to have it done but opted to do it themselves usually wound up not doing it. They had good intentions, but it was just too complicated. Then they devoted a lot of time and energy worrying about what was happening to their investments because they *weren't* managing them!

But with the autopilot breakthrough, the cost is falling. Instead of an expensive service, it may be available as an automated account or fund, without the extra charges. The terminology for these accounts isn't standardized, and not all providers offer all types. However, for both your employer plan and your personal savings, these are five common types that you'll see:

1. **Balanced Fund.** The most old-fashioned type of automatic investing, this fund generally maintains the account at the same split between stocks and bonds (often sixty-forty). This is more automatic than having to manually split your money between two funds, but it's a one-size-fits-all approach.

2. **Auto Rebalancing.** This automated service periodically shifts your investment allocation back to whatever split you had originally selected. Therefore, if you did a poor job of allocating your investment split in the first place, it keeps replicating that error. It also doesn't get more conservative as you approach retirement.

3. **Lifestyle Funds.** This is like having a range of balanced funds to choose from, instead of just one. There are more aggressive and more conservative versions. Unlike the one-size-fits-all balanced fund, you're more likely to find something off this rack that fits you well. However, it stays the same over time. You might choose an aggressive one early on, but then need to overcome your inertia and trepidation to change to a more conservative one later. It's up to you to remember.

4. **Life Cycle Fund.** This is like a lifestyle fund, except it automatically shifts from aggressive to conservative as you progress through your life cycle toward retirement. This is the most fully automated type of account. Some are called *target* funds, because you choose based on your target date for retirement. As your target retirement date

approaches, the fund automatically shifts into a more conservative split. However, if you don't plan to draw on your investments beginning at your target date, you may actually want a later target date. You might choose based on when you plan to start accessing your retirement account.

5. **Managed Account.** This uses technology to create a more personalized service than a lifestyle or life cycle fund. Instead of a fund whose assets are all managed in the same way, this can be more closely matched to your situation. However, as with a custom-tailored suit rather than one off the rack, you're likely to pay much more. Most people are better off choosing something from the life cycle fund and saving their money.

Whatever your provider offers, consider the most automatic approach that you can. Then you can concentrate on making a really careful decision, knowing you're relieving yourself of the burden of many decisions in the future.

Autopilot Real Estate: Saving and Investing

Real estate, especially your residence, is a unique combination of saving and investing. Home equity results from two distinctly different processes, and most of the time from both. The first process is amortization; the second is appreciation.

Amortization works this way: For an extremely simple example, let's assume you purchase a home for $100,000 with a 10 percent down payment, and you borrow the remaining $90,000. Over the term of the mortgage, let's say fifteen years, you make monthly mortgage payments. As you do, the mortgage balance decreases to $89,000, then $88,000, and so on. Your home equity is building up, slowly and steadily. At the end of fifteen years, even if the house is still only worth $100,000, you now have $100,000 of home equity. Amortization operates a lot like saving does.

But appreciation is more like investing, because you need to ride out market fluctuations. We'll use the same example but ignore the slow, steady amortization process for a moment. Let's say that in the first year, the market value of your home increases from $100,000 to $110,000. Even though that's only a 10 percent appreciation in market value, it *doubled your equity* from $10,000 to $20,000! Appreciation is more exciting than amortization, wouldn't you say? It's actually appreciation combined with *leverage*, but always remember that a lever can move both ways. Instead of increasing, let's say the market value of your home decreased from $100,000 to $90,000 in the first year. Even though that's only a 10 percent depreciation in market value, it *reduced your equity to zero!* Still exciting, but in a different way.

Homes in most real estate markets increase in value over the term of a fifteen-year mortgage. It's the synergy of both factors—the steady saving of amortization and the investing volatility of appreciation—that work together to create home equity. Trying to ride appreciation over shorter periods, without amortization, makes it easy to get burned. Taking home equity loans short-circuits amortization and puts people at the mercy of volatility. Remember, the American dream of home ownership is based on amortization and appreciation over long periods of time.

Autopilot Income Needs to Last As Long As You Do

Finally, the pot of gold at the end of the rainbow—retirement income! But wait a minute. Your transition to retirement income isn't the *end*, it's just a marker along the way, remember? When you finally do retire, you probably have *decades* of retirement life ahead of you. After all, there's no way to know when you're going to kick the bucket. (Check out your retirement biology in chapter eight.) How much income should you take to keep from running out of money?

This wasn't even a question in the family approach. In the societal approach, this only relates to personal savings, because Social Security and traditional employer pensions both pay monthly benefits *for life*. But under the rational agent approach, this is a very important, high-stakes issue. That's because most retirement assets end up as *account balances*, rather than monthly benefits. There's nothing automatic about taking account distributions; it's completely manual. It's a tough question for everyone. Not even a rational agent knows how long they're going to live.

When retirees fly off into the sunset, they typically manage their own account withdrawals. Unfortunately, they often goof it up! They may think they can afford to retire, but they really can't. Retirees are likely to withdraw too much, rather than too little. They tend to generally underestimate what their cost of living will be. They tend to be too optimistic about how well their portfolio has performed and will perform in the future. They tend to find "special circumstances" that justify extra withdrawals, above and beyond what they planned. They use a year-by-year method and can only see a few years into the future. Retirees are trying to do it all by themselves, manually.

Just like autopilot saving or investing, the goal of autopilot income is to combine good decision making with automatic processes that keep you on track. There are two kinds of autopilot, and you might use them in combination: autopilot *products* and autopilot *services*.

Autopilot Income Products

The prototype for automatic income products is the traditional employer pension. Plan participants don't receive an account balance but a monthly payment called a *life annuity*. This isn't a product but a type of plan benefit. Plan actuaries know statistically how long the *average* retiree is likely to live, but half will die later and half will die sooner. You might think the ones who die *later* than average get a better deal, and you'd be right. They collect more payments. But even the ones who die *sooner* get a good deal. That's because the value to them isn't only in the number of payments they receive. There is also value in being able to *plan on living forever*, knowing you'll never run out of payments. After all, when participants retire, there is no way for any of them to know *which group* they will end up in! They can all afford to be optimists. There is real value in security and in peace of mind.

What about people who don't have an employer pension? They can have access to the same kind of security through an insurance product. Insurance companies have actuaries who know how long people are likely to live, too. So they offer a type of insurance policy called an *immediate annuity* that works like the life annuity benefit of the traditional pension plan. The person who buys the annuity knows that half the policyholders will die later than average, and half will die sooner. Part of the value is that personally they can afford to be an optimist.

What about you? Should you consider an immediate annuity? There are two factors to consider. First, how good of a pilot are you? If you're *not a good pilot* and know it, then you're a candidate, and you should research immediate annuities. There's less chance of crashing and burning. But if you manage your financial affairs well, you might easily do better on your own. Second, how long are you likely to live? Health assessments now provide hints about whether you might be in the later or sooner group. If you're in the *later* group, you're also a candidate, and you should research immediate annuities. They can be on just a single life, or a joint and survivor annuity for a couple. But at least with immediate annuities, once you know what you want, you can compare apples to apples from multiple insurance companies. That allows you to shop for a good price and for a highly rated company that's likely to be in business long enough to pay you. Whatever conclusions arise from your research, please remember that an annuity should be only *one part* of your solution.

Be aware that insurance companies, insurance agents, and investment representatives want to sell you a gazillion different products that all go under the broad label of "annuity." Deferred annuities, variable annuities, equity-indexed annuities, and so on. These all have many more moving parts, and are *much more profitable to sell you*, than the simple immediate annuity we've been talking about. If you even breathe the word *annuity* to any of these marketers, visions of BIG commissions will dance in their heads, they'll get dollar signs in their eyes, and you'll hear the sales pitch of a lifetime. On the other hand, the demand for autopilot income products will actually prompt the creation of worthwhile new types of annuities. We'll need to watch for them. Be careful out there!

In addition to immediate annuities, there's a new category of autopilot product emerging. Instead of creating income from your employer plan or personal savings, it taps into a different pillar—your real estate, in the form of your personal residence. It's called a reverse mortgage and creates a monthly stream of income for life. It allows you to access your home equity while still living in your home, without needing to make payments on a home mortgage or home equity line of credit. However, all autopilot income products decrease your flexibility in order to create a lifetime stream of income. So do some serious planning about where you want to live in retirement before investigating a reverse mortgage. At the very least, make sure you do the retirement geography exercises in this book! Also, be as careful about researching a reverse mortgage as you would an immediate annuity. As they become more common, they'll be marketed heavily and subject to some of the same abuses as annuities. That's why, aside from autopilot income products, you should consider autopilot income services.

Autopilot Income Services

The prototype for autopilot income services is the traditional income portfolio. It holds some combination of dividend-paying stocks, corporate or government bonds, and interest-bearing certificates. These instruments all generate income *automatically*, without having to liquidate any principal. This time-honored income philosophy can generate payments for as long as you live, while leaving the principal intact for your heirs.

Unfortunately, most people can't live on just the income from their portfolio and need to liquidate their principal, too. That's where things get complicated. The income portfolio is like cruising along at a level altitude and never needing to worry about hitting the ground. But once you start liquidating principal, you start losing altitude. You've put yourself on a downward sloping trajectory, but it's difficult to tell exactly how steep your descent will be. Who's watching the altimeter? What's your air speed and rate of descent? Other factors come into play, such as wind speed, direction, and even the terrain. If you get into too steep of a dive, you can't even pull up! Thinking about all this makes you stop and wonder—can you really afford to begin your descent at all, or should you work for a few more years?

Even if you've been a good pilot for many years, consider this: *You will land your plane only once.* Autopilot income advice could be an investment representative telling you that the "rule of thumb" for a withdrawal rate is 4 percent per year. But after all of your years of working and saving, are you satisfied with using a rule of thumb?

Instead, an autopilot income service could be as simple as an online calculator provided by your investment company. You enter your portfolio and withdrawal information. It applies historical rates of return and volatility to the asset classes in your portfolio, and tells you your probability of success. Or it could be a review by an investment advisor, who uses a similar computer program combined with real-life experience. The two of you decide which holdings to liquidate in what order, and then set up a system for periodic withdrawals. Or it could even be comprehensive financial planning services, where an ongoing dialogue between you and your financial planner results in changes not only to your investment holdings but also to your lifestyle and spending habits.

Rather than flying the plane all by yourself, shouldn't you explore what types of intelligent, external, automatic systems are available to you?

The Fourth Element of Retirement Autopilot: Fiduciary Advice

Even when you have an autopilot, sometimes it's smart to have a copilot, too! Many decisions related to retirement are complex and only come along once in a lifetime. You don't get to learn by trial and error; you need to make a good decision the first time around. Many of these have high stakes attached to them. For example:

- How much do I need to save to be on track for when I want to retire?
- Are my investments allocated correctly or in the right autopilot fund?
- Should I save more in a pretax account, or an after-tax one, such as a Roth IRA?
- Can I take retirement distributions before age 59½ without a penalty?
- Should I take distributions in order to delay my Social Security for a larger benefit?

WHERE TO FIND A FIDUCIARY ADVISOR

If you want real advice instead of a sales pitch, you need to look for a *fiduciary advisor*. Fiduciary means that they are legally and ethically bound to put your interests first. These professionals are attempting to create a true *financial planning profession* from out of the larger *financial services industry*. It's not an easy task. How can you find a fiduciary advisor? There are three main places you should look. Although you can find a bad apple in any barrel, these are the best barrels!

The first is at www.fpanet.org, the website of the Financial Planning Association, where you can find a member who holds the CFP(r) Certified Financial Planner designation. Some of these advisors earn commissions, but the best approach—for fiduciary advice—is to choose a fee-only planner. Whether they work on commission or fee only, as long as they hold the CFP designation, they've had the proper training and experience. The second place to look is www.napfa.org, the website of the National Association of Personal Financial Advisors. This is a much smaller association and is for financial planners who have sworn off commissions completely and pledged to work on a purely fee-for-service basis. The third place is www.aicpa.org, the website of the American Institute of Certified Public Accountants. Look for "Personal Financial Planning" and "Personal Financial Specialist." Although most CPAs work in business accounting and taxation, a few have taken additional training to become a PFS.

Are there reputable financial advisors who don't belong to any of these three associations? Yes. Are there knowledgeable financial advisors who don't hold the CFP or PFS designations? Definitely. Are there even trustworthy financial advisors who work on a commission-only basis? Absolutely. But your chances of finding a reputable, knowledgeable, and trustworthy financial advisor are much, much greater if you use one of these three websites.

THE RETIREMENT NONCALCULATOR

When you evaluate your sources of retirement income, the most important question is about *quantities*. The question is, "How much?" As a result, retirement calculators have been multiplying like crazy! They're all over the Internet, offering both saving and income calculations.

The second most important question isn't about quantities but *qualities*. The question is, "What kind?" That is, what are the unique qualities and characteristics of your sources of income? How is each source like the others, and how is it different? That's a very different evaluation.

A *quantitative* evaluation helps you see how much your sources decreased in the recession of 2009. But a *qualitative* evaluation helps you see why, and what you might expect in the future. First, use a retirement calculator. Then, use this *Retirement Noncalculator*. It's the qualitative enhancement for your calculator!

Make enough copies of the Retirement Noncalculator worksheet (on page 123) for each one of your *specific* retirement income sources. You may wonder if your specific sources are the same as your pillars, or PERKS. The answer is maybe. Some pillars may be made up of just one source—Social Security, for example. But some pillars are made up of multiple sources. Your Employer Plans pillar might include a traditional pension, a 401(k), and an employee stock plan. If your 401(k) were split between a stock fund and a bond fund, that might be two sources. However, don't bother to complete a worksheet for small sources—just the major ones that will provide the larger parts of your income. For most people, that will be less than ten.

Read through the explanations of the qualities listed on page 121. You'll discover that each of your sources displays some of the qualities to greater or lesser degrees, which you'll be able to note on each worksheet. Retirement calculators obscure these qualities, while the Retirement Noncalculator emphasizes them. If the explanations don't make sense to you, work with a friend or a trusted advisor. Your retirement income may depend upon it.

After you've completed a worksheet for each major source, you'll be able to see the relative quantities and qualities of each one. Which three are most essential for your retirement well-being? Write the names of those three sources on your Life Circle at the end of this chapter.

Explanations of the Qualities

Liquidity. To what degree do you control the timing and amount of income from this source? Can you start, stop, and change at will? Do legal, contractual, tax, or market sale conditions restrict you? What needs to happen to receive your income, or what might prevent you from accessing it?

Examples: Social Security is subject to legal restrictions, annuities to contractual restrictions, IRAs to tax restrictions, and home equity to market sale restrictions.

Volatility. To what degree does this source fluctuate over time? Does the short term go up and down independent of trends in longer-term value? Could there be a "bad time" for you to make a withdrawal?

Examples: Stocks, bonds, and commodities (like gold) and funds that hold them all fluctuate in the short term. Real estate can fluctuate, too.

Market. To what degree is this source tied to some broad market? Is it related to long-term trends? Can the market go down and stay down for years? Could a downturn last longer than your ability to wait?

Examples: Individual stocks can decrease to zero. Stock mutual funds effectively couldn't but are tied to trends by sector, industry, style, and a broader market. Real estate is tied to trends within regions, communities, and neighborhoods.

Issuer. To what degree is this source dependent on a single entity? Could solvency problems prevent them from paying you? How many years into the future are you relying on them? Would anyone take over their obligations?

Examples: Individual bonds can default. Insurance companies can become insolvent, although state guaranty associations cover a portion of the obligations. Traditional pensions are trusts, subject to the Pension Benefit Guaranty Corporation.

Inflation. Will this source lose purchasing power if prices rise over time? Or will it increase with inflation to keep the same standard of living? Is that increase contractual, or dependent on market value?

Examples: Interest from CDs and fixed annuities can lose purchasing power to inflation. Monthly pensions may increase, or not. Inflation-protected bonds increase payments with inflation, contractually. Stocks and home values historically matched inflation, but the future is uncertain.

Interest. To what degree is this source affected by changing interest rates? If rates increase over time, is that good or bad for you? What if rates decrease?

Examples: Rising interest rates decrease bond values, while falling interest rates increase bond values. Interest from CDs rises or falls with rates in general, although not immediately. Fixed annuity interest rates are typically slow to adjust. Reverse mortgage income is based on interest rates initially but typically doesn't change over time. Home equity loans can be very sensitive to changing interest rates.

Political. To what degree is this source dependent on a political process? Would a change in tax laws greatly affect the value? Is the attractiveness dependent on complex regulations? Is continuing government support important?

Examples: Social Security and state programs for older citizens will soon become political tugs-of-war, with unknown outcomes. IRAs, employer plans, insurance products, and long-term capital gains all enjoy tax incentives that could change in the future, due to political pressure.

Foreign. To what degree is this source dependent on a foreign country? What effect might currency exchange rates have?

Examples: Foreign stocks and bonds are subject to even more market forces than domestic securities. Foreign real estate can be subject to complex legal structures.

Management. To what degree does this source require ongoing competent management? Is it a firm that can be evaluated? If you're the manager, how long will you be competent to perform the task?

Examples: Mutual funds are relentlessly analyzed and compared, but other types of funds may not be. Human managers (whether you or a professional) succumb to poor judgment now and then—and ultimately to old age.

THE RETIREMENT NONCALCULATOR WORKSHEET

(Make a copy of this page for each specific source of income.)

Name for this specific source: ____________________________

Which of my PERKS is this source from?

____ P ____ E ____ R ____ K ____ S

The *quantities* of this source, according to my retirement calculator:

Current lump sum $______________ Retirement lump sum $ ______________

Most importantly, the monthly lifetime income from this source $____________

How large a share of my retirement income is this source likely to provide?

___ Small ___ Medium ___ Large ___ Extra-Large ___ Super Size!

The *qualities* of this source, according to my understanding of these characteristics:

Liquidity ____

Volatility ____

Market ____

Issuer ____

Inflation ____

Interest ____

Political ____

Foreign ____

Management ____

Other ____

- Can I really afford to retire now, or when will I be able to?
- Should I take the pension plan monthly benefit or the lump sum option?
- How much part-time income, for how many years, will it take to make a difference?
- Is it more cost-effective to keep the money in my 401(k) or roll over to an IRA?
- Should I take a reverse mortgage or downsize to a less expensive residence?
- Does long-term care insurance make more sense for me or for my spouse?

If you're unsure, good advice is priceless. But even if you're a financial specialist and pretty sure of your decisions, getting feedback can be valuable. Think of it as peer review.

Retirement Autopilot Is Only the Beginning!

Most retirement books are completely dominated by the question of how to manage your retirement finances. But in order to cover all the dimensions of your retirement well-being, it's time for us to move along. That's why you'll find recommendations for additional books that are completely focused on finance and economics in the Resources section on page 257.

LIFE CIRCLES EXERCISE

Now review the information about your financial sources, and consider which three are most important to your well-being. Enter these in the Life Circle to use for your One Piece of Paper in chapter eleven.

My Ideal Retirement
includes managing these
financial pillars:

1. ____

2. ____

3. ____

"We shall not cease from exploration
And the end of all our exploring
Will be to arrive where we started
And know the place for the first time."

—T. S. Eliot, twentieth-century English poet

Chapter SIX

The Nature of Space and Time

When physicists like Einstein and Hawking reference the *nature of space and time,* they're asking questions about the nature of reality itself. But we're only asking questions about where to live in retirement. In comparison, that might seem a bit trivial. But isn't it all relative?

Have you known people who stayed in the same place as they aged, long after they should have moved? They clung to a particular home, neighborhood, or part of the country. They were somehow immobilized, for one reason or another, even when it became more and more difficult to stay there. Living in the *wrong place* came to dominate their life. Then, when they finally relocated (if they ever did), they announced, "I should have moved long ago!"

Or just the opposite—you've known people who couldn't wait to relocate for retirement. They fell in love with a particular home, condo, or apartment. Perhaps they discovered a real estate development, or just a neighborhood, that offered exactly the amenities and activities they had dreamed about. Off they went, with great anticipation and excitement, to inhabit this new place. Then, for one reason or another, it didn't live up to their expectations. They were disappointed. But they stayed in the new place because it was too difficult or too expensive to relocate. Or perhaps they did set off once more, in search of yet another new place. Or, as sometimes happens, they retraced their steps and simply moved back to where they had come from, more or less. They were disillusioned, if not defeated.

Of course, there are stories of success, too. Many people stay in the same place, and it works out perfectly. Or they move somewhere new, and it fulfills their expectations. The question is this: How can you predict, in advance, how well a certain place might work for you?

This chapter answers that question. It offers you a new perspective and a practical approach for understanding the places where you might live in retirement. Equipped with this new perspective and approach, you'll see the pros and cons of moving or staying where you are now.

Most of us at least *daydream* about moving somewhere new. It could be just across town or across the country. Either way, letting go of the place where we live and making a new home somewhere else is one of the most adventurous things we could do. Even the old-fashioned, leisure-oriented approach to retirement was exciting when it included a move to a new location. (Sun City, here we come!) Any move is an adventure, after all.

It's easy to imagine moving, but it's not easy to know whether that move would really support your retirement well-being. Or if you imagine staying where you are, it's not easy to imagine how well your existing place will serve you in the future, as you get older. Geography is an important decision, because it affects almost every aspect of your life—financial, social, psychological, biological, and medical. Let's peek at those connections.

Your geography and finances are linked not only by the cost of your residence itself but also by the general cost of living that goes along with any particular location. If necessary, we can almost always find a place to live that's *cheaper* than where we live now. Or coming from the other direction, if you plan to work in retirement, geography will help or hinder your ability to do that. It's easier to make money in some places than in others. Where you live can affect both sides of your cash flow statement: expenses and income.

Location has an enormous effect on your social relationships, too. As much as you want your social ties to transcend distance, you've probably spent more time with friends and family when it was geographically easier to get together with them. The place where you live affects you psychologically, too. Hopefully it provides you with outlets for exploring your interests and using your skills. In retirement, you'll either be engaged and stimulated by your environment or lulled into boredom.

Finally, geography will affect your health in two key ways. Where you live impacts your healthy living habits, such as being physically active. Retirement offers more free time, and your geography will shape what you do with that time. Will your environment help get you moving and build your biological vitality, or will it shut you down, prematurely aging you? Even if you do take better care of your body, sooner or later you'll seek out more medical services from practitioners and institutions. Will your retirement geography be a help or a barrier to getting the treatment you want?

Will Your Dream Home Become a Nightmare?

Even if you decide to stay right where you are when you retire, that decision raises all the same questions that a new place would. You should still look at your location with fresh eyes and evaluate it from a new perspective. Will it support the kind of life you really want to live? Would a few changes make your current place into your dream place? How do you know what your dream place is, anyway? Your life changes so much from the Second Age to the Third Age to the Fourth Age that your dreams change, too. The place that was perfect for raising your kids and commuting to work may not be perfect anymore. Your dream home from the Second Age could even become a nightmare in the Fourth Age.

Not only is your choice of where to live a profound decision, it's also a high-stakes one. Making a move is such a major undertaking that you are unlikely to undo it, even if you get it wrong. If you discover you made the wrong choice, you may settle for just settling in because it's too difficult (and too expensive) to move again. Another move would likely be to another new place. You surely know the expression "You can't go home again." (That's because someone else is probably living there now.)

On the other hand, if you make plans for retirement based on not moving and then design a life around your existing place, it can be difficult to reconsider later. There are, in life, certain *windows of opportunity*.

Leaving your long-term career (and daily commute) is a major life transition that opens the window to living in a new place. If you don't make your move during that transition, the window may close. The window may be stuck—and you may be stuck, too.

The Geography of Freedom

The Four Ages depict the life stages, and life transitions, that are emerging in society. As you move from the First to the Third Age, your degree of freedom tends to increase, and that means more geographic freedom as well.

In the First Age, you lived wherever your family lived through high school, and perhaps college, too. You typically didn't have any choice about where you lived. It was just a given. Unless your family moved, you probably didn't think about moving. (There are those of us, though, who dreamt of faraway places from a very early age.) If you had a chance to go away to college that may well have been your first glimmer of geographic freedom. And for most of us, even that was quite limited freedom.

The Second Age opened up new horizons. You had the power to choose where to live. But the need to support yourself meant getting a job, which put limitations on your geographic freedom. You may have also been limited by a desire to be close to friends and family. Over the years, your work may have been a deciding factor, keeping you in place or moving you around. Having children may have kept you close to family for support. Getting your children into the schools you wanted for them may have shaped your geographic choices, too.

Yes, the Second Age is filled with responsibilities, and many of those have geographic requirements. But the Third Age offers the greatest freedom of place that you'll ever experience! Here are five reasons:

1. Your income may not be tied to living in a particular location. Unless you've been a telecommuter or a freelancer or you've done some other your-presence-is-optional type of work, your income and your geography have always been joined at the hip. But that loosens up

in retirement. Once you're receiving benefits, the Social Security Administration (and your pension plan, IRA account, bank, and so on) will send your monthly check wherever you tell them to.

2. If you want to work in retirement, you may be more geographically flexible in your search for work than you could be in the job that you retire from. Whether you work for the income, to use your strengths, or to be socially connected with other people, you can probably find work in a variety of places. There are even more options when you're open to—or even prefer—temporary or part-time work.

3. Your residence may appreciate in value by the time you retire, allowing you to sell it at a hefty profit. Or even if your residence doesn't appreciate, it may be much more expensive than a similar place in another location. In particular, if you live in a region or a metropolitan area with a thriving economy that has plenty of jobs and moneymaking opportunities, people still in the workforce will be eager to buy your residence. They need to live somewhere convenient for their work. But once you're retired, you may not need that same proximity. Many great places to live have poor job opportunities, which may not matter to you one bit!

4. Family responsibilities typically lessen in the Third Age, so geographical constraints loosen. As your brood left the nest (or flew the coop), they may have stayed nearby or moved across the country. But either way, you're not responsible for them. Staying connected with your family and being an important part of their life are affected by your geography, to be sure. But connection requires less proximity than responsibility did. In retirement, you may use your increased free time to visit them or stay in touch in other ways. If you live somewhere really cool, they may even be the ones who want to come visit *you*!

5. People you already know are blazing new trails for you. You have family, friends, and acquaintances who have moved to other places already, and they can provide you with opportunities to try out a different geography. It's an opportunity for you to sample places where

you may want to live. You may have had less communication with them since they moved, but planning your retirement is the perfect opportunity to reconnect with them, and possibly connect with the place that they've moved to. Getting inside information from the people who actually live somewhere is infinitely more informative than staying there on vacation.

It's great to have more geographic freedom, isn't it? Now what you need is a simple way to consider all the places you could live and compare them to where you live now. So on to this new perspective and new approach to analyzing your retirement geography.

The Four Layers of Retirement Geography

It's useful to think about any place in terms of *four layers*, the names of which form the acronym SALE. See the image that makes the acronym easy to remember.

S is for *sense of place*. The innermost layer, it's the meaning that you derive from a geographic location.

A is for *aging in place*. The micro layer, it's what most people hope to do in their retirement residence.

L is for *livable community*. The middle layer, it's a supportive environment for retirement and aging.

E is for *essential region*. The macro layer, it's the part of the country that you absolutely must live in.

THE FOUR LAYERS OF RETIREMENT GEOGRAPHY

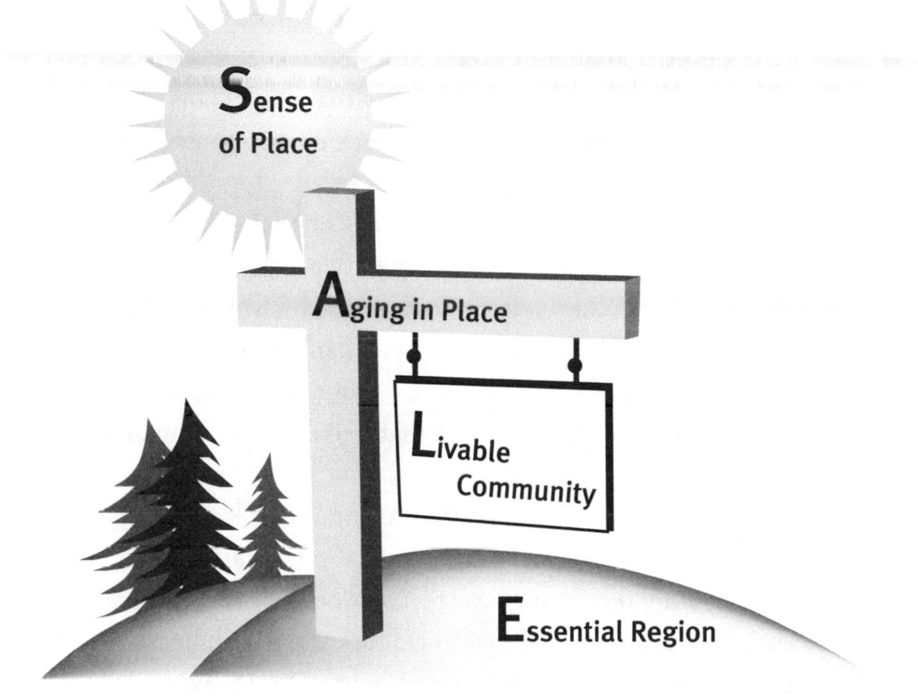

Does this acronym mean you should sell your place and move? Not at all. But you should at least evaluate your current place according to these four layers. That way, if you decide to stay there, it will be the result of a conscious decision. Consider the four layers in any order that makes sense for you. We'll explore them one at a time, starting with the big picture.

Your Essential Region: The Macro Layer of Geography

Assuming that you really could pick up and move to another part of the country (or another country altogether), where might that be? You may have visited other regions for business, while on vacation, or to visit friends or family. Certainly there are regions that you're curious about, or even attracted to deep down, but have never been to. Retirement may be just the opportunity you've needed to visit those places or hang out in them for a while—for weeks, months, or even years. But although retirement can have a vacation quality, it's important to make a distinction between the places you plan to sample and the one or two places that you may really want to call home. You know that expression "It's a nice place to visit, but I wouldn't want to live there"? It's not just a cliché; it holds a deeper wisdom than we give it credit for.

Whether a region is just nice to visit or is one where you'd happily live out your days depends, of course, on whether that region holds what you need to truly live. When you think about the life you want in retirement, there are probably certain things you can't imagine living without; you view those as essential. If some of your essentials are tied to a geographic region of the country, then that makes it an essential region for you.

Now, you may not have an essential region. Your essential requirements may be the kind that can be found in many geographic locations—say, a first-rate symphony, year-round golf, a professional sports team, or a huge outlet mall. But a good way to explore the possibility is to consider what you absolutely couldn't live without, then see whether those things are connected to a particular area.

To identify your essential region, ask yourself these questions:

1. Is there a region that supports you socially—that is, your most important relationships? Where are the people who are essential in your life (possibly children, grandchildren, lifelong friends, elderly parents)? You may not need to be right next door, but within easy traveling distance, perhaps? Consider, too, that these loved ones may relocate someday.

2. Is there a region that offers compelling opportunities to use your skills or strengths in a way that's psychologically engaging for you? This could be a particular retirement job, an unusual volunteer opportunity, a chance to go back to school, or a once-in-a-lifetime special project, such as working to help protect the flora or fauna of a threatened ecosystem.

3. Is there a region that would allow you to pursue your interests or passions in a way that you could nowhere else? This could be physical geography like mountains or water, or cultural offerings such as the arts or entertainment.

4. Is there a region that could be particularly supportive to your health, especially if that might become more of a challenge, as you get older? You may need a climate that's beneficial to a physical condition, or proximity to uncommon medical specialists or alternative practitioners. Even basic access to medical care, such as a Veteran's Administration hospital, HMO, or PPO, could be a factor.

5. Is there a region that would make it easier to make ends meet financially, if that's an issue for you? This could mean a lower cost of living or the chance to pool resources with family or others as a way to cut costs.

6. Is there a region that's somehow connected to your deepest values? It could be the center of your religious tradition, cultural heritage, or family roots.

7. Is there a region that would uniquely support your chosen ways to live? This means the area somehow pulls together the social, psychological, biological, medical, and financial elements to support the life you want to live.

As you answer these questions, keep in mind that retirement changes over time. What's important in early retirement is different than what will be important in later retirement. At the beginning, in the Third Age, you're young and healthy enough to be very active in the world, so amenities and opportunities are at the top of your checklist for evaluating regions. Toward the end, in the Fourth Age, you'll likely want and need more help and support from others, and you may need significant medical care. This evolution may necessitate two migrations during your retirement. A first migration could be made so you can do the things you want to do. Demographers call this an *amenity migration*. A later move to get some help from your supportive relationships is called an *assistance migration*. That could be to a new place altogether, wherever your family happens to live. Or it could be back to the region where you lived before—a *reverse migration.* It's not that you made a mistake and moved to the wrong place. You may have moved to the right place for the Third Age but know in advance that it won't be the right place for the Fourth Age.

Keep these migration types in mind as you think about what's important to you and where that's located. Your essential region for retirement may be a place that's very different from your essential region for your working years. And if your essential region has anything to do with people (and I hope it does!), your essential region could change if those people migrate. After all, you may be looking at thirty years of retirement.

Of all the changes in geography that you may consider, migrating to another region is the most expensive, labor-intensive, and logistically complex, and it has the greatest effect on your relationships. It's also the least common. You may already be living in your essential region and just haven't thought of it that way! All this adds up to the obvious conclusion that migrating to another part of the country is a level of geographic change that you need to research and consider most carefully. With a fresh perspective and a bit of ingenuity, you may be able to create your Ideal Retirement in the region where you already live. Perhaps you could instead make changes at another level, such as your community or residence. (In which case you might decide that another region that had beckoned you is a nice place to visit, but you wouldn't want to live there!)

Your Livable Community: The Middle Layer of Geography

What exactly is a community? For purposes of your retirement geography, think of a community in the broad and varied sense of the term. It's simply an area that you live in during your retirement, and it usually has little in common with that specialized planned development that's marketed as a "retirement community." Livable community, as the middle layer of your retirement geography, is the area around your home that you typically travel within to fulfill your daily needs and desires.

Think about your current community. How far do you need to travel to the coffee shop, the grocery store, your faith community, the pharmacy, the post office, the doctor, the library, or dinner and a movie? How much farther, if at all, do you travel to see friends and family? How much farther for something a bit out of the ordinary, such as an airport, a major sporting event, or a top-notch regional hospital? (Although in the later years of retirement, having a hospital close to home could well become more essential.) Whatever area you travel within to fulfill those daily needs is probably what you think of as your community. At some distance from home, you know the feeling that you have left your community behind.

If you think you might even consider looking around for a new community for retirement, it's worthwhile to think about all the different kinds that exist. In looking at types of communities, you might even redefine what you think of as the boundaries of your own community. **A community can be described in a number of ways:**

- It could be a political entity with easily identifiable borders, such as a city or county (for example, Santa Fe, New Mexico, or Door County, Wisconsin).
- It could be a political entity that is contiguous with others but still retains its own character (such as Sarasota, Florida).
- It could be an area bounded by certain landforms or by water (such as Cape Cod, Massachusetts, or Bainbridge Island, Washington).
- It could be a well-known urban area in a large city (such as Buckhead in Atlanta or Wrigleyville in Chicago).
- It could be an area shaped by the presence of a university or other institution (as Clayton, Missouri, is by Washington University).
- It could be a real estate development organized by a corporation (such as Sun City, Arizona).

It could even be what was once called a neighborhood, even if it doesn't have a specific name (but these are getting harder to find). Many large cities have these enclaves, but knowledge of what makes each neighborhood special may be jealously guarded by locals.

Communities are wonderful things; more wonderful still is a livable community. This concept is a fairly recent one, but it is developing rapidly. Livable communities are good for everyone, whether they're in the first, second, or third box of life. In fact, one of the features that can make a community particularly livable is that it integrates people from all three boxes. Rather than separating age groups—young singles, families with children, retirees—from each other, all are included. People have lived in these kinds of age-integrated communities for most of human history, and there is a deep wisdom in it. You may even have spent your childhood in an environment like this, and you probably benefited greatly from your interaction with retired folks. They probably benefited from their interaction with you, too!

At the same time, there certainly are livable communities composed mostly of retirement-age people. Where these arise organically through the maturing of a neighborhood, they're called naturally occurring retirement communities, or NORCs. On the other hand, where these are created synthetically through land development, we might call them developer-organized retirement communities, or DORCs. Not all DORCs are created equal, and a few are even shining examples of livable communities. But please recognize that although DORCs always look very nice, looks can be deceiving. They may be more "lookable" than livable.

You can start thinking now about your current community and how livable it may be through your retirement years. After you retire, your awareness of the community may be heightened. For example, you could become more aware of how rich and varied the available activities are. In looking for activities, memberships, and environments to invest yourself in, you'll be able to explore your community at a deeper level. One part of that exploration will be getting to know other people in your community to build fun, engaging, and meaningful relationships with (because you'll be seeing less of your old friends from work). The more interesting and vibrant the activities are in your community, the more rewarding your explorations can be. The good news is that those activities attract interesting and vibrant people (like you!).

Is your community up to the task of being a livable community for your retirement? Or is it a dud? And you may want to gaze into your crystal ball. Not only will your own life change over the coming years, but the life of your community will, too. Is it the kind of town that relies too heavily on just one or two industries, with a Main Street that's been abandoned as strip malls sprout just outside the municipal limits? Or is your town too appealing for its own good, attracting newcomers from pricier areas, so longtime residents' children can no longer afford a starter home (if they can find one)? As your community develops, do you see yourself wanting to live there more than you do now, or less? Is there another community, or are there several (right in your own backyard), that would be a better fit? Only by making a comparison will you know. You may discover that yours stacks up very well and you didn't even realize it. Lucky you!

The Self-Contained Community

Another facet of your community is more mundane: How self-contained is it? For many, retiring from work also means retiring from commuting. Commuting is an activity that automatically routes you near many services that you need. In fact, you've probably become a loyal customer of some retailers just because they're on your commute route. Or you may have gotten into the habit of shopping or running errands near your workplace. At lunch and along the way from home to work and back again, you may often fit in the side trips needed to keep the household functioning. They're just stops along the way. But once you don't need to commute, if those services aren't available in your community you'll need to make specific trips to obtain them.

You might think that's a good thing in retirement—it will get you out of the house and into the world. That may be true for some folks. But because you're reading this book, I suspect you're not looking for meaningless time fillers just to keep yourself busy in retirement. You'd prefer to take care of as many of your needs as easily and close to home as possible. Sure, you want to get out of the house, but for meaningful, engaging activities. If your retirement has the potential to be the high point of your life's journey, it would be a shame to spend it running errands, don't you think?

Some communities are called by a single name and thought of as a single entity, but they are actually composed of several self-contained neighborhoods. Their lucky residents can fulfill their daily needs within just a few blocks from where they live. If they walk those blocks (in decent weather) instead of driving a car or taking public transit, they tend to stay more physically fit. The more activities they can participate in within walking distance, the more likely they are to know their neighbors, shopkeepers, librarians, pharmacists, and other nice folks. As people make their way further and further into the third box of life, these relationships become more valuable.

These self-contained neighborhoods exist in every region, in most cities, and in both low-rent and high-rent districts. Many smaller towns still operate on this principle. If you've never lived this way before, you owe it to yourself to experience it. Go stay a while with a friend who's fortunate enough to live in one. For a vacation, sublet an apartment or a house in an area that appears to operate this way (even though you may not get to know many residents in that short a time). There are no advertisements or marketing brochures (let alone salespeople) for these neighborhoods. They aren't trying to entice anyone, so you need to seek them out. You need to be a sleuth!

Calling It a Community Doesn't Make It One

On the other hand, there are also places that are called "communities" but are communities in name only. You've seen the signs at the gates of developments: "A Community for Those 55 and Better," "A Community of 38 Distinctive Homes," "A Community for Active Living!" These places, whatever you call them, often put their residents at a disadvantage, because they don't offer what people actually need to live day to day. (Unless all you need to do is play golf or tennis or swim.) These "communities" are isolated enclaves that force residents to rely on a car or public transportation, which can be an inconvenience or a hardship, depending on the situation. (Strangely, both gated communities and ghettos can share this limitation.) Because residents don't walk to the services they need, exercise isn't as naturally integrated into their daily lives. Because they don't walk outside as much, they are less likely to know their neighbors and others outside the gates.

As you move from the Third Age into the Fourth Age, living in this kind of "community" can easily make you more socially isolated. Although the architecture and landscaping may be pleasing to the eye, the residents may or may not interact very much. This isn't something you can normally spot from photographs or even on a tour. But a little feet-on-the-ground research should reveal how residents get around and how well they know each other.

The social life of a community is often revealed in its physical configuration. There is a saying in the field of geography: "The spatial is social, and the social is spatial." The idea is that the configuration of a neighborhood affects the social relationships of the residents. The flip side is that the social relationships of the residents will in turn affect how they create and modify the spatial configuration of the neighborhood. **Every community offers social clues:**

- Are there sidewalks? Are there people walking on them?
- Are there courtyards or parks with benches? Are residents gathering and visiting there?
- Are there commercial establishments where people linger and socialize? Or do they just hurry in and out?

Such distinctions may not be a big deal for you in the early part of retirement, when you're healthy, active, out and about in the world, and reveling in your new free time. But much later, when you may not be as active and may prefer to spend more time closer to home, this distinction could mean the difference between inconvenience and hardship, between a community that is livable and one that is not.

Your Aging-in-Place Residence: The Micro Layer of Geography

When the time comes, as it may, that you need assistance with the activities of daily living, would you prefer to continue living in your own home or move to a nursing home? (Surveys, over and over, overwhelmingly report that people want to "age in place.")

Although this question deals with the Fourth Age, you should consider it as early as possible—right now, when you're thinking about the Third Age. The decisions you make at this point will determine, far down the road, how long you can live in your own home. Will the home in which you choose to spend your retirement be one that allows you to live out your days there? (Hand in hand with choosing that home, of course, goes making every effort to preserve your health and physical self-sufficiency, the focus of another chapter in this book.)

At the middle layer of retirement geography—your community—the key concept is livability. At the micro layer—your residence—livability is the key concept, too. Just as you'll spend more time in your community in retirement, you'll also spend a lot more time in your residence than you ever have before. The question is not simply "How livable is it?" but also "How long will it be livable?" Based on what happens to you as you age, how easy or difficult will it be to live there? As you're planning your retirement, you need to take the long view. The very long view.

Of course, even though many people claim that they want to age in place, not everyone wants to. Perhaps you imagine living in one residence for the Third Age when you're vigorous and active, then moving to another residence for the Fourth Age when you can't get around as well. That's a perfectly good plan, if you really do that kind of two-stage planning. Just don't ignore the Fourth Age because you find it unpleasant to think about. A little long-range planning now can save you (and your loved ones) a lot of frustration, work, money, and heartache down the road.

You may have been thinking of moving to a new home for your retirement, or not. Perhaps you're definitely moving, because you want to downsize and get equity out of your home for retirement income. Perhaps you're definitely not, because you have so many memories and friends (and so much stuff) associated with your home that you can't imagine moving. In that case, if you need to draw equity out of your home for retirement income, you'll look into a reverse mortgage or a home equity line of credit.

Perhaps you've hedged your bets by buying a vacation home that you plan to make into your retirement home. This will eventually lead to a sort of hybrid move, as you bring the remainder of your belongings to join those you've been keeping in the second home and adjust to living there as opposed to limited vacation visits. Perhaps you're open to moving but aren't sure yet what exactly you would be looking for, or whether a new home would be worth all the trouble. Whatever possibilities you're considering, remember this: think both near term and long term. When you evaluate a residence—existing or contemplated—ask yourself two questions:

1. How well would that residence support your active early retirement life?
2. How well would that residence support your aging in place, later in retirement?

Six Possible Ways to Use Your Home in Retirement

Let's look at some examples of the active early part of retirement, in the Third Age. Think of people you know who have recently retired; you've probably noticed that they use their homes in variations on the following six basic approaches. As you read each description, consider it in light of your own chosen Ways to Live. How have you been using your home during your working life? Is that how you'd really like to use it in retirement?

1. **Home as a Job.** These folks retire from their regular job and, in effect, take on a new job as the caretaker, handyperson, and housekeeper of their own residence. They take personal responsibility for just about every aspect of maintenance. These hardworking folks throw themselves into duties for which they might previously

have hired a professional (or a local teenager). Some retirees may find this truly rewarding; others may just be trying to keep busy, because they really don't know what else to do with their time. Either way, handling physical and technical responsibilities helps keep us sharp as we age, so some of it may be a good thing for everyone. How about you?

2. **Home as a Project.** These folks use their newfound freedom (and sometimes their retirement money) to finally get to the major home improvements they've contemplated for years. Whether they use the do-it-yourself or have-it-done approach, it's the focus of their interest and attention. If they're not careful, the remodeling ideas can be leftovers, fitting their old life more than their new one. But ideally the ideas are fresh and relevant to the way they want to live in retirement. The improvements really increase quality of life. At some point, though, the home improvement phase must come to an end. That's when these folks discover whether just living in their home is enough for their Retirement Well-Being. How about you?

3. **Home as a Museum.** These folks have accumulated a lot of physical possessions during their time in the second box, and their home is the place they display and store everything. Retirement is an opportunity to seek out and find even more of just the right stuff. Some people are true connoisseurs; others are true pack rats. For both, though, the thrill of acquiring more things or the sense of security in keeping them may be more important than the residence itself. Some may get involved as buyers or sellers at flea markets or in online auctions. The home may be just a warehouse or the ultimate display case, showing the entire collection. They may hope that their prized possessions will one day become family heirlooms. (If you're such a collector, one of the best ways to test that hope against reality is to talk with your family about it. Really, really talk with them. You may find that they treasure the time spent with you more than they would treasure having your treasure.) How about you?

4. **Home as a Community Center.** These folks turn their residence into a setting for finally spending more time with other people. In Western society, life in the second box is typically time deprived, and social relationships often suffer. Some people use their additional free time in retirement to entertain—seriously entertain. They get friends and family into their home for large and small gatherings, and they encourage overnight guests whenever possible. Unlike the first two uses of a residence, this approach is focused less on the physical structure itself and more on its usefulness as a venue. Of course, if these folks have let their relationships slip away during the second box, they may be beyond reviving in the third box, regardless of the venue. How about you?

5. **Home as a Base of Operations.** These folks may not really be interested in their residence at all. They yearn to be somewhere else, traveling hither and yon. Whatever form their travels take, their home becomes more or less the base camp. These folks feel that they've been tied down long enough in the Second Age, and as long as they've got health and money, they'll seek their happiness on the road. But consider this: Sooner or later we all must stop to rest, and rest becomes a bigger issue the further we progress toward the Fourth Age. At some point these folks will need to decide whether the residence they have is the one that they want to spend time in as their travels wind down. How about you?

6. **Home as a Retreat.** These folks may or may not be interested in their home per se, but they are interested in the privacy and serenity that it can provide. They may have found the requirements of the Second Age tiring, forcing them into more contact with the world than they really liked. Now they want to be left alone in peace and quiet and interact with the world on their own terms. Although home is a refuge even during the working years, it's usually only for a few hours each day. The long, unbroken time structure of retirement certainly allows home owners to retreat if that's what they want to do. However, as they move from the Third Age to the Fourth, a social support network will be an essential resource.

The danger of residence as retreat is that unless the residents also emerge to keep relationships alive, those may not be there when they need them. How about you?

It all comes back to the essential message of this book: making plans for the life you want to live in retirement, then considering how your residence can support that life. Life planning comes first; residence planning comes second. This is really the foundation of your micro layer geographical decision. Only after you're clear about your own Retirement Well-Being can you think clearly about whether you should stay put or go looking for your retirement dream home.

Thinking about what you'll need in your residence in the later, aging-in-place phase of retirement is more straightforward than planning for the active early retirement years, because your options are narrower. The natural process of aging, even healthy aging, means that sooner or later it can become a challenge for you to live independently. However, you probably can't foresee what your own specific challenges will be, when and if that time comes for you. There is a broad range of infirmities that become more common as you age, and you don't get to choose them; they choose you. It may be a loss of strength or balance, physical dexterity, eyesight or hearing, cardio or respiratory capacity. If you knew in advance which infirmities might eventually force you to leave your home for some type of assisted living, you could plan better. You could make sure that the home you settle on, early in the Third Age, would be hospitable to the infirmities you expect to have later on. Your family genetics, your health history, any existing conditions, and your health habits are all factors, but these are far outweighed by the unpredictable. Seeing as you can't accurately predict, it's a good idea to consider some general ideas from the new concept of universal design (see the sidebar on page 147).

PRINCIPLES FROM UNIVERSAL DESIGN

Universal design offers great guidance for planning the micro layer of your retirement geography. To look at your home with a universal design perspective means asking, "If someone with [fill in the limiting health condition] were going to live in this residence, what would allow them to be self-sufficient; what would make it a lifetime home?" *Lifetime home* is a new term to describe the residence that we hope will support us in both the early and the later parts of our retirement. It has a nice ring to it, don't you think?

So what makes a home a lifetime home? Mostly, that it can accommodate your changing needs. It can be as simple and easy as adding sturdy handrails in bathrooms, or more complex and expensive, such as installing lower counters and cabinets or a chair lift on a stairway. But some livability fixes can be almost impossible to implement in the layout of many homes. For example, if rooms are on multiple levels—even if they're separated by just one or two stairs—there may not be space for a wheelchair-accessible ramp.

Thinking about your physical needs as you age may be something you'd prefer to put off. And even when you do address the issue, you don't have a crystal ball. But evaluating your residence now with these ideas in mind could eventually make the difference between continuing to live there and being forced to leave.

A Sense of Place: The Inner Layer of Your Geography

Your inner experience of your retirement geography is as important as the outer layers that we've already explored. Sense of place is that connection you feel to a particular place, your emotional reaction to it, the symbolic meaning that it has for you. Sense of place is not easy to pin down, because it is something different for each of us. It has to do with how unique or generic a place is, how personal or impersonal.

This idea has arisen in the context of sweeping changes in the way we live in Western society. Many people are uncomfortably aware of the sameness, the lack of authenticity, the *placelessness* that has proliferated across the country. Subdivisions filled with look-alike houses, business parks filled with work-alike offices, interspersed with standard-issue strip malls. National chains driving out local retailers and franchises replacing family-owned restaurants. Places that once had a distinctive local character are being made over to fit into the same mold. There are parts of many cities that look just like parts of any other city. And they don't just look the same—they feel the same. It's difficult, if not impossible, to have a sense of place in such environments. Of course, many jobs are geographically connected to them, and in your working years you may need to live there. However, retirement offers your greatest geographic freedom. Are you curious where you might discover your own personal sense of place?

Universal or Personal?

Sense of place ranges from the universal to the personal. Certain landscapes evoke a strong sense of place for just about everyone. You have surely visited some unfamiliar places that you felt an immediate connection with—the mountains, the seashore, a deep forest, green rolling hills, the desert in bloom. You could say that those locations have a universal sense of place, and most humans would probably agree.

You have surely visited other places to which you felt a culturally based connection—for example, a classic Main Street in a small town, a setting that resonates with your childhood and the image presented in your schoolbooks and in magazines. Many people who share your upbringing would experience the same sense of place.

Finally, there are places that you connect with because of your own personal life experience; you would not expect others necessarily to experience the same sense of place that you do. You may have lived there in the past or dreamed about living there in the future. You may have gone to school there or vacationed or visited relatives there. Or you may have never set eyes on the place before, but once you do, you say, "This is the place." For your retirement geography, your own personal sense of place is the one that matters most.

You can't predict what will create that sense of place for you. You can't tell from pictures or descriptions alone. You can't tell from what other people say about it. You certainly can't tell from the statistics about it. No, sense of place comes from direct experience. It could be the evident features of a place: its climate, topography, vegetation, or architecture. It could be the people you interact with there. It could be what you know about its history or its importance in the larger scheme of things. It could be your own personal memories, distinct from your current experience of the place. You may even get the sense that a particular place will support your chosen Ways to Live.

The only way to really know whether a location has a sense of place for you is to become an explorer; you need to be there and experience it. You may need to move to a new place, or you may instead need to see the place you live now as if for the first time. Only you can explore the geography of your Ideal Retirement. But it's worth exploring, because your retirement will last a very long time, if all goes as you hope.

Two factors that are critical to just how long it will last are the biology and medicine elements that make up the health dimension of your Retirement Well-Being, which is the focus of another chapter. In this chapter, as we've explored where you might spend your retirement, we have frequently touched on the need to plan for both the natural aging process and the unpredictable infirmities that may arise. It's wise to choose a livable community and a home that incorporates universal design to support your aging in place. Having done that, you'll want to do all you can to preserve your physical vigor and independence for as long as possible.

But first, you get to brainstorm the geography of your Retirement Well-Being.

LIVING IN MY GEOGRAPHICAL PLACE

You've used the Four Layers of Retirement Geography to imagine the kinds of places that could best support all the other elements of your Retirement Well-Being. You should now have plenty of raw material for your final geography exercise: identifying the geographical element of your Ideal Retirement. That place could be the one you're living in now or someplace new.

You can approach the four layers in any order that makes sense for you. The acronym SALE doesn't mean you need to sell your home; it's just a way to help remember the layers.

If it's earlier in your career, you can note just the broad or general features of each layer. If it's later in your career, you should be more specific. If you're approaching retirement, you may have all the particulars completely worked out.

My Sense of Place: The Inner Layer

What places could create a particular feeling or a sense of connection for you in retirement? These might have a sense of place on a universal, cultural, or personal level, or be especially symbolic or meaningful for you. Think of places you've already experienced and ones you would like to explore. Write the names of several types of places, or specific places, for this layer, for example, "Ocean shore; Colorado Rockies; Taos, New Mexico."

____

____

____

My Aging-in-Place Residence: The Micro Layer

What role will your residence play in your retirement? Is it likely to become a job, a project, a museum, a community center, a base of operations, a retreat, or something else? To fill that role, what physical features would your home need? Financially, would your home be a significant expense, a low-cost place to live, or a source of income? Would your residence accommodate aging in place, or do you plan to move as you get older? If it's early in your career, identify a general type of residence (such as a city apartment, resort-style condo, or country house). If it's later in your career, try to identify a specific type of residence, or even a specific house (say, in your town, seen on vacation, or found on the Internet).

My Livable Community: The Middle Layer

Considering how far into retirement you plan to live there, how supportive does your community need to be at different stages? Which livability issues are most crucial to you? A walkable neighborhood? Access to medical care and other services? Transportation? Social interaction? Activities? A retirement-age population or one that's age-integrated? What other features or amenities are most important for you? Financially, will your community provide opportunities to upscale or to economize?

My Essential Region: The Macro Layer

Which part of the country offers what's most important to you? Could it involve the people you have relationships with? The opportunity to connect with your interests, strengths, or values? A supportive environment for your health or health care? A lower cost of living? Where are the things that you absolutely wouldn't want to live without? Is it likely your essential region will change during your retirement years?

LIFE CIRCLES EXERCISE

Now go back to your responses for all four layers and choose the most appealing or significant responses for each layer. (These aren't set in stone; you can revisit and revise your choices later as your planning evolves.) Enter these on the appropriate lines of your Life Circle to use for your One Piece of Paper in chapter eleven.

My Ideal Retirement
includes inhabiting this
geographical place:

S ______________________________

A ______________________________

L ______________________________

E ______________________________

"It's not a health care system at all;
it's a disease management system."

—Dr. Andrew Weil,
integrative medicine pioneer

Chapter SEVEN

Medicine—Who's in Charge?

How much retirement medicine are you planning to buy? A lot or a little? What kind?

During the Second Age, those questions might not have made sense. But for the Third Age, they make complete sense. That's because, when we were younger, most of us didn't have much interaction with the medical system. If we needed care, it was often the *urgent* kind. An infection that required antibiotics. An accident that caused cuts or broken bones. An acute condition like appendicitis that demanded surgery. We didn't expect to need treatment, but then we needed it in a hurry. For treatment, we *entered* the medical system, it *fixed* us, and we *exited*. We went back to our Second Age world, where medicine didn't play much of a role. The questions "How much care?" and "What kind?" wouldn't have been relevant then.

But, for the Third Age, those are very relevant questions. That's because we begin needing treatment not just for urgent conditions but also for *chronic* ones. The ones associated with aging. You know the list: high blood pressure, high cholesterol, high blood sugar, arthritis, depression, digestive problems, and so on. These chronic conditions are very different than the *enter-fix-exit* ones of the Second Age. When these develop, it's not usually urgent. Instead, it's usually *permanent*. Whatever it is, it's going to be with us, more or less, forever. So the question changes. Instead of "How quickly can I get this fixed?" it becomes "How will I manage this over the next couple of decades?" How you answer that question affects how you design the next stage of your life!

That's why this chapter is about *retirement medicine*, which addresses how to get the treatment you want for illness (if you need to). The next chapter is about *retirement biology*, which addresses the physical aging process and how to choose practices for building and maintaining your vitality. Here's one way to think about the distinction: We each have our own personal biology, the body we walk around in. We're responsible for taking care of it, and it's the aspect of our health that we have the most control over. In contrast, medicine isn't part of us. It's a system that's outside of us, out there in the world. We use a medical system, or systems, for treatment. The system doesn't act *upon* us—we choose to interact with the system, *consciously*. That's one difference between medicine and *veterinary* medicine—conscious choice on the part of the patient!

The Medical System Is in Turmoil

Making plans for how we want to access medicine in retirement would be a complicated subject under any circumstances. But with the Patient Protection and Affordable Care Act of 2010, our society has started down a long path of change. Economic constraints and an aging population mean there will be *short-term and long-term changes* to the system. How will we pay for it? Under what conditions can we access it? What's covered, and what's not? Those questions just scratch the surface of issues that our society will need to address over the next few decades.

You can't answer those questions now. You'll need to learn about new options as they emerge and make the best decisions you can as you go along. However, you can develop a long-term perspective for how you want to access medical care in your next stage of life. You can identify what your goals are and create a foundation for your future decision making that's unique to you and your life.

There Are Really Two Medical Systems

One of the core issues you need to address is what you consider the medical system to be. On the one hand, there's the *conventional* Western medical system composed of medical schools, MDs, hospitals, and drug companies, which is completely connected to and supported by state licensing laws, insurance plans, and federal tax laws. And there is also the enormous, expanding, unconventional *alternative* medical system that has not been connected or supported in the same way until fairly recently.

When you walk into a pharmacy to fill your prescription from the conventional medical system, you walk by an entire *aisle* of alternative treatments. It includes everything from herbs to vitamin and mineral supplements to homeopathic remedies. Huge quantities of these are sold at the pharmacy (and in natural foods stores), but because they don't require a prescription, few pharmacists have any in-depth knowledge of them.

Similarly, an entire section of the bookstore is devoted to alternative treatments, but because the topic is generally avoided in medical training, you won't find many medical doctors browsing there. And even though offices of alternative practitioners such as acupuncturists and chiropractors are often right next door to offices of MDs, there is generally little acknowledgment or interaction between these different practitioners. It's as though they're from different *planets*. More accurately, they're from different *paradigms*. Yet, research has shown that up to half of Americans have used alternative approaches not recognized by conventional medicine. And when they do use alternative approaches, they tend not to tell their medical doctor.

This topic of alternative medicine becomes particularly relevant for the Third Age. Urgent conditions of the Second Age are a perfect fit for conventional treatment. But for the *chronic* conditions of the Third Age, many people view complementary and alternative medicine (CAM) as an option. Rather than take a prescription drug for the *rest of their lives*, some wonder about "natural" alternatives. You probably don't know which chronic conditions you're likely to develop, or what CAM treatments for those might possibly be. So let's start with a baseline: your medical history. Or rather, your complementary medical history. See the exercise on page 158.

YOUR COMPLEMENTARY MEDICAL HISTORY

Have you used complementary or alternative medicine (CAM) at one time or another? A good way to anticipate whether you might use CAM therapies in the future is to consider which ones, if any, you've used in the past. You may have had direct experience with some of the approaches listed below, heard about others, and some may be new to you.

CAM Approaches	***Have you ever used this?***	***Would you consider using it?***
Ayurveda	No / Yes / Not Sure	No / Yes / Not Sure
Biofeedback	No / Yes / Not Sure	No / Yes / Not Sure
Botanical medicines or herbs	No / Yes / Not Sure	No / Yes / Not Sure
Chiropractic	No / Yes / Not Sure	No / Yes / Not Sure
Energy therapies such as Reiki or Healing Touch	No / Yes / Not Sure	No / Yes / Not Sure
Homeopathy	No / Yes / Not Sure	No / Yes / Not Sure
Mind-body approaches such as hypnosis or visualization	No / Yes / Not Sure	No / Yes / Not Sure
Movement practices such as yoga or tai chi	No / Yes / Not Sure	No / Yes / Not Sure
Prayer or meditation for healing	No / Yes / Not Sure	No / Yes / Not Sure
Nutritional supplements or vitamin therapy	No / Yes / Not Sure	No / Yes / Not Sure
Therapeutic massage	No / Yes / Not Sure	No / Yes / Not Sure
Traditional Chinese medicine or acupuncture/acupressure	No / Yes / Not Sure	No / Yes / Not Sure
Unconventional or unproven science	No / Yes / Not Sure	No / Yes / Not Sure
Other	No / Yes / Not Sure	No / Yes / Not Sure

Now read down the answer columns. Do you notice a pattern or theme in your use—or nonuse—of CAM? Even if you haven't discovered anything new, it is worthwhile to document your past and consider your future. How does this fit into your planning for the next stage of life?

For When You're Not Feeling Up to PAR: Your Retirement Medicine Cycle

What's your medical philosophy? Do you have a medical philosophy? You've probably never been asked! Instead of asking what your philosophy *is*, most books and practitioners tell you what it *should* be. If they're based in conventional medicine, they offer the truths from that paradigm as though they were the only truths. If they're from one of the alternative systems (such as the approaches in the history exercise), they offer the truths from that particular paradigm as though *they* were the only truths. All these sources of information seem to pretend that they exist in a vacuum, without considering the philosophies or principles of other systems. (Unless it's to attack them.)

There is one essential truth, though. The essential truth is that you're stuck in the middle and you need to make up your *own* mind. That's why you need to have your own philosophy of medicine. If you wait until you're sick to try to identify it, you won't be at your best. You'll be more likely to just accept a philosophy that's thrust on you by a medical practitioner or a well-meaning relative or friend. You may be so overwhelmed that you may not realize you have a choice. It's better to figure this out now, while you're of sound body and sound mind. Your medical philosophy is a little bit like having an advance directive or living will. Except instead of addressing end-of-life care, it addresses *all* of your medical care. Instead of being a guide for others, it's a guide for *yourself*.

The Retirement Medicine Cycle is a way to think about, and plan for, the kind of medicine you want. It has three components: your medical philosophy, your access to medicine, and your medical relationships. You can think of it as philosophy, access, and relationships, which creates an easy-to-remember acronym: PAR.

Regardless of the changes that happen to the medical system, you'll be able to make sense of your options by understanding how the Retirement Medicine Cycle operates.

- *Philosophy* includes your preference for conventional or alternative approaches, as well as your preference for greater or lesser medical intervention in general. Your philosophy determines what type of medical services you want access to. (Conventional or alternative? High-tech or low-tech?)

- *Access* includes your methods for getting treatment. (Insurance? Out-of-pocket cash? Government plans?) Your methods of access determine which practitioners you can use and thus limit the medical relationships you can create and develop.
- *Relationships* with practitioners are your sources of both treatment and information. The information you get from those practitioners will be limited by the paradigm they operate within—their own truths—which in turn influences your medical philosophy. That's what makes it a cycle rather than a linear process.

You can see that, if you're not careful, the Retirement Medicine Cycle can become a *closed loop* system. If your philosophy leads you to

THE RETIREMENT MEDICINE CYCLE

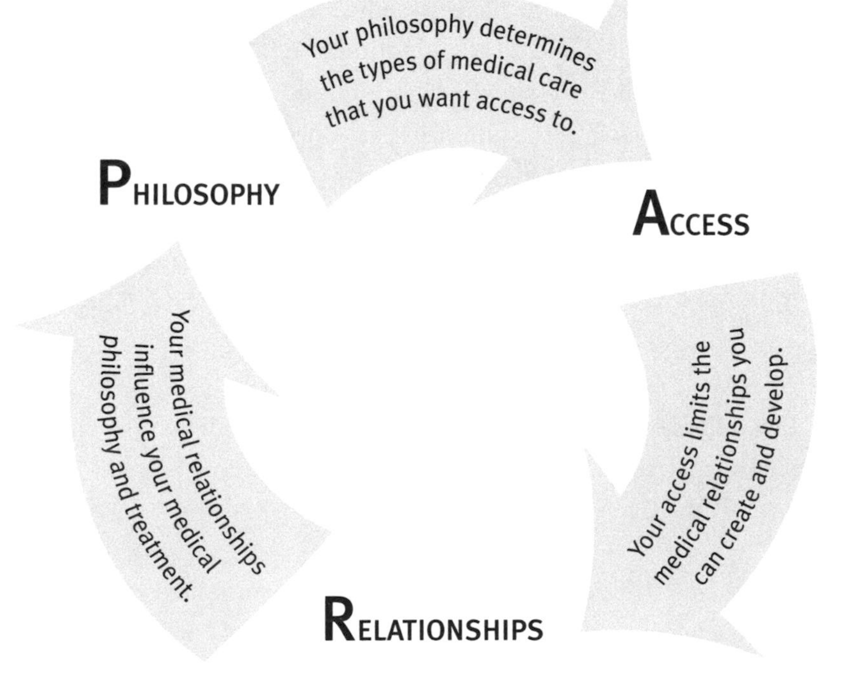

seek out access to one particular system and you develop relationships with only those practitioners, they will tend to give you only information from inside *their* system or paradigm. That's where they live and practice. However, that will only serve to further reinforce your original philosophy. You're not being presented with *other* perspectives or options, therefore you may have blind spots about your medical treatment, and you may not even realize it.

Let's take something common that most people simply *love* about aging—back pain—as a simple example. If you have a purely conventional philosophy, you may seek access only to medical doctors, who then offer treatment options only within conventional medicine (drugs, surgery, or maybe physical therapy). If you have a particular alternative philosophy—say, Chinese medicine or nutritional approaches—you may seek access only to *those* practitioners, who then offer treatment options only within *that* system. In both scenarios, you probably wouldn't be referred to a chiropractor, even if that might be a beneficial treatment in your particular case. (Although alternative practitioners may be more aware of and supportive of other alternative practices than conventional practitioners are.)

That's why it's so important to enter into your Retirement Medicine Cycle consciously, rather than getting swept along unconsciously. You need to be the one who's in charge! The following section will help you clarify your philosophy, identify your likely methods of access, and determine which medical relationships you'll need to support your health and well-being in the Third and Fourth Ages.

PAR: Philosophy of Medicine

Your medical philosophy combines two ingredients: your perspective on conventional versus alternative medicine and your tendency toward medical intervention in general.

First, where do you stand along the conventional versus alternative *continuum*? Do you see medicine from the narrower, more orthodox perspective or from the broader, more unorthodox perspective? Those are the two ends of the continuum, and your outlook may be somewhere in

YOUR MEDICAL PHILOSOPHY

To identify your personal philosophy of medicine, consider the sets of paired statements below. For each pair, decide where your perspective is on the continuum from conventional to alternative and mark one of the boxes accordingly. Marking the far right or left box means you strongly agree with that philosophy; marking the next box in means you agree somewhat more with that philosophy than with the other; marking the center box means you're neutral or unsure. This topic is enormous and very complex, so it can't be reduced to just this set of paired statements. But this exercise can be an important step toward clarifying your philosophy.

Conventional Philosophy				***Alternative Philosophy***
Medicine should be based on modern and rigorous research methods.				Medicine can be based on forms of knowledge other than modern science.
❑ *Strongly Agree*	❑	❑ *Neutral*	❑	❑ *Strongly Agree*
Treatments outside of conventional medicine should be avoided.				Conventional medicine treatments should be avoided.
❑ *Strongly Agree*	❑	❑ *Neutral*	❑	❑ *Strongly Agree*
All treatments must meet the same standards for safety and effectiveness.				Treatments that pose little risk and could be beneficial are worth trying.
❑ *Strongly Agree*	❑	❑ *Neutral*	❑	❑ *Strongly Agree*
High-tech is almost always more effective than low-tech.				High-tech or low-tech has little bearing on effectiveness.
❑ *Strongly Agree*	❑	❑ *Neutral*	❑	❑ *Strongly Agree*
Medicine is the weapon of choice in the fight against disease.				The body seeks to heal itself; medicine plays a supporting role.
❑ *Strongly Agree*	❑	❑ *Neutral*	❑	❑ *Strongly Agree*
As the expert, the doctor's role is to diagnose and prescribe; the patient's role is to comply with treatment.				The practitioner and patient both have knowledge and must actively share the role of promoting the patient's health.
❑ Strongly Agree	❑	❑ Neutral	❑	❑ Strongly Agree

Now consider your tendency to seek medical intervention *distinct* from how sick or healthy you are. This isn't about how sick you've been or how sick you're likely to be. This is about how likely you are to seek treatment for any given level of health. Your propensity to seek out medical care during your healthier Second Age may be an indicator of your propensity to seek it out in the Third Age. You can't know for sure whether your history of getting a little or a lot of help for small aches and pains is a predictor of how you'll react to the chronic issues of old age. (Unless you've already had major health issues.) To the extent you think about this consciously, though, you may become aware of a certain *consistency* in your tendency to seek intervention.

For each of the following pairs of statements decide where your perspective is on the continuum from high intervention to low intervention, and mark one of the boxes accordingly. Marking the far right or left box means you strongly agree with that philosophy; marking the next box in means you agree somewhat more with that philosophy than with the other; marking the center box means you're neutral or unsure.

High-Intervention Philosophy				***Low-Intervention Philosophy***
Too much treatment is usually better than too little.				Too little treatment is usually better than too much.
❑ *Strongly Agree*	❑	❑ *Neutral*	❑	❑ *Strongly Agree*
It's better to seek care sooner rather than later.				It's better to wait; conditions often resolve themselves.
❑ *Strongly Agree*	❑	❑ *Neutral*	❑	❑ *Strongly Agree*
Relying on a range of specialists provides better care.				Relying on a single trusted practitioner provides better care.
❑ *Strongly Agree*	❑	❑ *Neutral*	❑	❑ *Strongly Agree*
Using multiple treatments for multiple conditions all at the same time makes sense.				Receiving multiple treatments at the same time can cause problems in and of itself.
❑ *Strongly Agree*	❑	❑ *Neutral*	❑	❑ *Strongly Agree*
Medical treatment is the most important thing, even when it may be inconvenient.				Medical treatment that is difficult or disruptive must be considered within the context of day-to-day life.
❑ *Strongly Agree*	❑	❑ *Neutral*	❑	❑ *Strongly Agree*

between. You already have one good indicator in your history of using—or not using—CAM approaches. However, that's a measure of your past actions, not your current perspective. Second, where do you stand on the *level of intervention* continuum? The high extreme of that continuum is hypochondria, where people seek treatment for symptoms that aren't real. The low extreme is denial, where people ignore symptoms or don't take prescribed medicines. But well within those two unhealthy extremes, there is still a significant variation in the level of intervention that reasonable individuals consciously choose. To discover your preferred ways of using the medical system, complete the medical philosophy exercise in this chapter.

Now we'll put these two aspects together to illustrate an overall way of thinking about your medical philosophy. In the following figure, you'll see that *conventional* is on the left side and *alternative* on the right, *high intervention* on the top and *low intervention* on the bottom. For each of these two aspects, mark the point that indicates where your philosophy lies on the continuum (the line with two arrows).

To identify your philosophy, mark the point where a line drawn across from your spot on the High Intervention–Low Intervention (ver-

THE FIVE MEDICAL PHILOSOPHIES

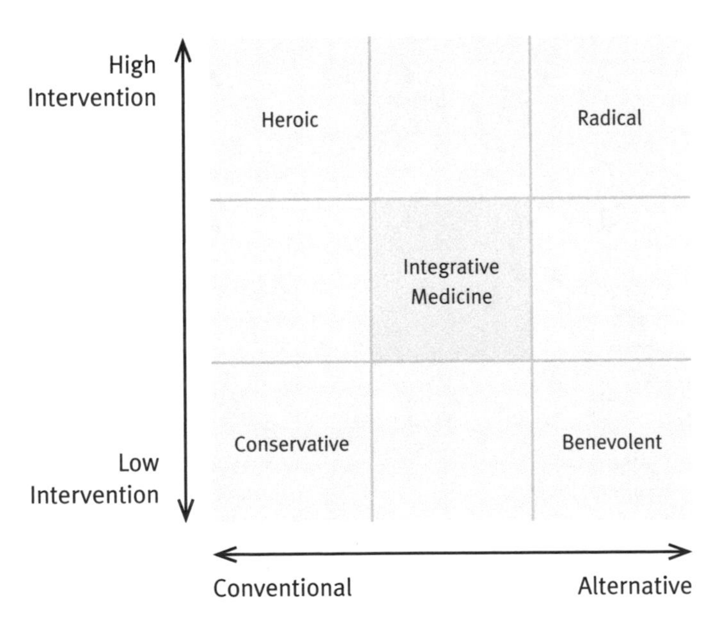

tical) continuum would intersect with a line drawn up from your spot on the Conventional–Alternative (horizontal) continuum.

The figure combines these two different aspects of your medical philosophy and provides a simplified way to think about them in the practical world. The four corners each crystallize a particular perspective. If you tend toward a high level of intervention using conventional treatments (upper left), that's a *heroic* philosophy. A low level of conventional intervention (lower left) is a *conservative* philosophy. That same tendency for low intervention, but using alternative treatments (lower right), is a *benevolent* philosophy. And if you use alternative treatments and also tend toward a high level of intervention (upper right), that's *radical*, dude.

An Integrative Approach

What if you're somewhere in the middle? You should be delighted to learn that there is actually a fifth perspective, and you can see it right in the middle of the shaded area. *Integrative* medicine is a fast-growing movement that integrates these different perspectives.

Integrative medicine is midway between conventional and alternative, and high and low intervention. Of course, even without integrative medicine, it's possible to use both conventional and alternative treatments in an eclectic way. You know, some of this and some of that. However, that's definitely not what integrative medicine does. At its core, it's based on adherence to the same *scientific method* that is the foundation of conventional medicine. However, for treatment options, it accesses both conventional *and* alternative approaches. It uses a rigorous approach to explore alternative treatments that are less dangerous and disruptive to the body than many conventional treatments but are often just as effective. It looks for the best of both worlds.

The scientific approach that integrative medicine takes is somewhat different from that of conventional medicine, however. Conventional medical science is sometimes *skeptical* toward phenomena that it should be *curious* about. Or dogmatic about assumptions that it should be questioning. In terms of the Retirement Medicine Cycle, conventional medicine can act like a closed loop system that isn't open to some types of new information.

In contrast, integrative medicine is open to information from *more sources.* Specifically, it studies treatments from alternative medicine that may be beneficial, yet because it does adhere to the scientific method, it's rigorous about which alternative medicine treatments to use. However, there may be different standards for evaluating the safety of traditionally used natural substances that are less likely to cause harm versus newly developed powerful pharmaceuticals that may have strong side effects.

As for a low or high level of intervention, integrative medicine assumes that the lowest level that supports the body's own healing is the place to start. (Often the best intervention is a healthier lifestyle!) If a condition doesn't respond to the lower-level intervention, then it's time to move up the ladder. For example, instead of prescribing the standard dose of a drug, integrative medicine may start with the *minimum* dose, to see whether that's effective. If so, there are few side effects. But if a higher level really is necessary, so be it.

Specific to the Third and Fourth Ages, integrative medicine suggests that biological aging is a natural part of life. Technically speaking, there is no such thing as an "antiaging" treatment. No one has figured out yet how to reverse the natural aging process that inevitably ends in death. But it's possible to optimize your health at any age. And it's definitely possible to optimize how healthy you feel and act in your daily life. Often, ironically, when you focus on the symptoms and diseases that you *don't want*, they expand to assume a bigger role in your life. When you instead focus on how to support your body's own *self-healing* process, that's what expands. Which would you prefer?

Integrative medicine helps you (1) build habits that support your biology and (2) use any natural treatments that are effective for your condition (with fewer adverse side effects). This helps you focus on (and expand) your awareness of health and healing, rather than focus on diseases or treatments. This issue becomes more and more important as you age. In the First and Second Ages of life, because health conditions are the *enter-fix-exit* type, they go away and may be quickly forgotten. But in the Third Age, many conditions related to aging can't be cured. Even if you need to gracefully accept those conditions, do you want *disease* to be the focus of your life? Or would you prefer to focus on the *health and healing* that are operating in your life?

The goal of integrative medicine is healthy aging, even though you may also have chronic health conditions.

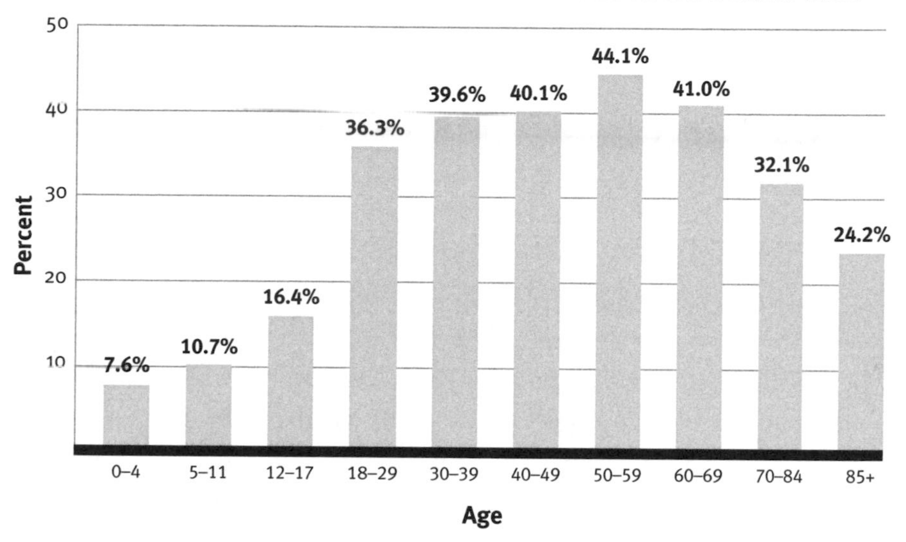

Barnes, P.M., B. Bloom, and R. Nahin. *CDC National Health Statistics Report #12.* Complementary and Alternative Medicine Use Among Adults and Children: United States, 2007. December 2008.

Now that you've had a chance to identify the fundamentals of these five medical perspectives, you'll have an easy way to identify them in the real world. If you read a book or magazine, talk to a practitioner, or get a recommendation for treatment, you'll have an idea which perspective it's coming from. Before you consider the specific information, you can consider your *compatibility* with the source. How does that perspective relate to your medical philosophy?

You need to ask, "How valid is that perspective, approach, or paradigm in general?" And if it's valid, you can ask, "How knowledgeable is that practitioner within the scope of that perspective or approach?" Even after you determine that your perspective and the practitioner's perspective are compatible, there's always the question of whether the individual practitioner is experienced or inexperienced, competent or incompetent.

So, for the first stage of the Retirement Medicine Cycle, would you describe your medical philosophy as heroic, conservative, benevolent, radical, or integrative? Is there yet another term that better describes you? The answer is an important part of planning your Ideal Retirement.

PAR: Access to the Care You Want

Now that you know your medical philosophy, you can plan how to gain *access* to the types of medical care that you want.

First, will conventional treatments be enough for you? If not, which alternative approaches do you plan to use? How will you gain access financially? One of the first observations we made about these two systems is that conventional medicine is supported by insurance companies, the Medicare system, and the tax laws. Much alternative medicine is not supported (although that's been changing), which leads to higher out-of-pocket costs. However, who knows what will be covered, and not covered, under future health care system reforms? If you didn't have access to an expensive conventional treatment, would you then consider an inexpensive alternative treatment? Another part of your access can be geographical—if the provider for that type of treatment is far away, it may not be feasible. If you live in a remote area, most treatments may be out of reach. If you want a particular specialist, or a particular CAM practitioner, can you travel to see them? What will it cost to live near the treatments you want or to travel to gain access to them? Geographical access becomes a bigger issue in the Third Age and especially in the Fourth Age.

Second, what level of intervention do you expect? Do you tend toward more intervention rather than less? Are you more likely to pay a visit to your practitioner? More likely to pursue advanced treatments? This isn't about how sick or healthy you'll be (although that is another important question). Rather, the question is, for a given level of sickness or health, do you tend to *seek out* a lot of care or just a little? Do you tend to be lured by those prescription-drug commercials that coax you to "Ask your doctor if this New Miracle Drug is right for you"? Even when you have insurance, if you tend toward high intervention, you'll have higher out-of-pocket costs.

Let's review our medical philosophy table from the perspective of cost. In the figure, total cost means the actual true cost, *ignoring* subsidies such as insurance plans or tax breaks. Out-of-pocket cost means what you might typically pay, taking into account subsidies such as insurance plans or tax breaks. Again, who knows how the health care reforms will affect what treatment is covered under your plan at that time? However, the general principles underlying this table should operate for the foreseeable future. If you favor an "expensive" approach, you need to think about how to pay for it!

RELATIVE COSTS OF EACH MEDICAL PHILOSOPHY

	Conventional		Alternative
High Intervention	High Total Cost / Medium Out-of-Pocket		Medium Total Cost / High Out-of-Pocket
		Medium Total Cost / Medium Out-of-Pocket	
Low Intervention	Medium Total Cost / Low Out-of-Pocket		Low Total Cost / Medium Out-of-Pocket

Now consider common methods for accessing medicine in retirement, recognizing that all of these may well be *changing* over the course of your retirement:

- Social programs, such as Medicare A and B, the Prescription Drug Plan (Medicare D), or your state's "Senior Care" type plan
- Insurance plans, such as a working spouse's group insurance, your own retiree medical coverage, a former employer plan through COBRA, or an individual medical policy

- Membership rights, such as access to the Veteran's Administration for those who served in the armed forces, or facilities that serve members of religious or fraternal organizations
- Out-of-pocket expenditure, such as earmarked funds like health savings accounts, or general funds—any of your PERKS (see chapter five) that you would draw on to pay for out-of-pocket medical costs

Based on your philosophy, which one of these is likely to provide your primary method of access? Which one will take some advance planning to make it available? Where should your focus be?

PAR: Relationships with Practitioners

Now that you know your medical philosophy, you can identify the practitioners to help you implement it. Although you'll probably be looking for good practitioners as long as you live and breathe, this is about identifying *types* of practitioners. Is your family practice MD's expertise enough? Do you already have a condition that will make a medical specialist important? If you want to use alternative medicine, which approaches will you use the most? Which types of practitioners will provide the most treatment and be your sources of information and advice? To stay healthy, this is an important part of your Ideal Retirement.

It's time for a reality check. Look back over your Retirement Medicine Cycle. Does it fit together as a whole? Does your philosophy fit your method of access? Will your access pay for the types of treatments and relationships that you want? Will your relationships provide treatment and advice that fit your philosophy?

In addition to your relationships with medical practitioners, there's an even more important relationship for you to develop. That's your relationship with your *own body*. If you're like most people, the relatively good health of the Second Age allowed you to pay less attention to your biology than you probably should have. The next chapter will give you a chance to start making amends. As you think about your next stage of life, remember to think about how you'll take care of your body. It's the only one you've got!

LIFE CIRCLES EXERCISE

Looking back over the Retirement Medicine Cycle sections, consider the three components: philosophy, access, and relationships. In your Life Circle, write the name of your medical philosophy next to the "P." Next to the "A," write your primary method of access, or the method that you most need to focus on in your planning. Next to the "R," write the medical relationships that will be most important for you to develop. All together, these help you create a vision of how medicine will support your Ideal Retirement, and you will use this when you fill in your One Piece of Paper in chapter eleven.

My Ideal Retirement

includes accessing this medicine:

P ______________________________

A ______________________________

R ______________________________

"For an individual, the pattern of growth, plateau, and decline is mandated by personal biology."

—James Fries, MD,
renowned longevity researcher

Chapter EIGHT

Health from the Inside Out

For retirement, are you more concerned about staying alive—or staying healthy?

As average human longevity has increased and more people are living into their eighties and nineties, the issue is becoming less and less whether we'll live long enough. We may know people who've lived longer than they expected to, or even wanted to. No, for most of us it's about staying healthy as we spend decades in old age. What we really want is a health span that matches our life span. However long our journey lasts, we want to be healthy along the way. But how do we make that happen?

The Equation Is Biology + Medicine = Health

In the Retirement Well-Being Model, health is called the Bio-Medical dimension. No one ever forgets about the medical part, but the biological part is easily overlooked. The term *biology* reminds us that, before we even consider medical care, we're first and foremost biological organisms. We're in charge of our own bodies, and the way we live affects our health—our *physical vitality*. Everything we do either supports or depletes that vitality. Once we become conscious of our vitality, we may decide to build it up the way we build our personal savings or build our social networks. We can even think of all of these things as unique forms of *capital* that we draw on in different ways, for different purposes, during retirement.

Even though our personal biology is unique, it's also governed by universal principles. The biological trajectory is the same for everyone: growth, plateau, and decline. We need to factor that trajectory into every other aspect of planning our life. But we can influence our trajectory in two ways. One way is through accessing the medical system out there in the world. The other is to act in ways that support our own biology directly. So, how's that been going for you?

We each have our own measures of how it's been going for us, of course. The most basic one is purely subjective: It's simply how good we feel. (Which is actually a good measuring instrument, when we take the time to calibrate and use it.) We may have other, more objective measures, too: our clothing size or weight measured on a scale; how many days of work we've missed; whether we're meeting the goals of our exercise program. These are probably all good measures, but on occasion we realize we need something more objective, more official. We go for a physical.

Measuring Your Biological Health

In the early days of the old retirement, a checkup with a medical doctor involved a lot more poking and prodding than it usually does now. For example, to assess a patient's health, physicians would listen as they palpated and gently thumped on different points of the patient's abdomen, sort of like testing a watermelon or cantaloupe for ripeness. A healthy organ has a certain *sound*. If it doesn't sound right, that's a reason to investigate.

These days, doctors don't spend as much time *listening* to their patients. They gather data using much more high-tech methods. They take biological samples from us and run laboratory tests. Our body chemistry supplies the raw data, which is then analyzed using sophisticated statistical methods. How do we measure up compared to thousands of other people? For most tests, the goal is simply to be in the normal range. But for others (such as cholesterol) the goal is actually to be better than normal. Gathering raw data and doing a statistical analysis is much less personalized than thumping on our organs, it's true. But it does provide a different, and extremely helpful, kind of analysis. Biotechnologies made the new kind of checkup possible.

Now, there's another technology that's making another kind of new checkup possible. It's called a *health risk assessment* (often available through your medical insurance plan or hospital). But instead of collecting your bodily fluids, it collects your biological data. Then it does what you'd expect: It statistically analyzes your data against that of thousands of other people. But a health risk assessment is completely different from a lab report. Instead of telling you that you may have a particular health condition in the *present*, it tells you whether you're likely to have a particular health condition in the *future*. A health risk assessment is like a crystal ball, but it's powered by statistics.

You may wonder why people would want to know what diseases they're more likely to get. You may even feel that you wouldn't *want* to know. Wouldn't it just be better to live a healthy lifestyle and forget the crystal ball? After all, many of your health risks are inherited from your parents, and it's too late to choose different ones now.

Some people find health risk assessments useful, because they put the information to good use. Let's take an example: Say that a person—based on her heredity, her health history, her current data, and her general lifestyle—discovers that the area she should be most concerned about is heart disease. One possibility is that she *wasn't* aware of her elevated risk for heart disease. But now that she has this new information, she'll adjust her behavior accordingly, make lifestyle changes, and reduce her risk.

However, another possibility is that she already *suspected* she had an elevated risk of heart disease. She knows her family history. She knows she's overweight and that her cholesterol is too high. She just hasn't been motivated to exercise more control over her biology. But seeing the health risk assessment changes how she *feels*. It's right there in black and white. It motivates her to finally make the changes that she already knew she should make.

In our society, the problem isn't a lack of information about healthy lifestyles. We live in a sea of information. Haven't you already been told a million times to exercise and eat healthier? How many more times do you want to be given the same suggestions? No, information isn't the problem—*motivation* is the problem. And not just motivation to make healthy lifestyle changes. Motivation to really stick with them over the long term and make them a part of our lives.

How Old Are You Really?

So, back to our biological question: How are you doing? Well, there's a new way for you to answer that question. It's an entirely *new form* of measurement. This form of measurement is beyond your subjective feelings, beyond being thumped like a melon, beyond giving up bodily fluids, and even beyond a health risk assessment. From a technical standpoint, in relation to a health risk assessment, it's just a small step forward. But from a conceptual standpoint, it's a giant leap. It's a form of measurement that uses statistics to tell you how old you are. Not your chronological age, but your *biological age*.

Let's review this whole *concept* of age. For most of human history, people didn't have a record of when they were born. The concept of how old they were didn't require mathematical computation; it was *functional*, not chronological. Age was how a person looked, sounded, moved, and thought. Age was a function of appearance, strength, flexibility, and mental sharpness. But then we started to keep written birth records, and by the industrial era, chronological age had become the standard. Industrialists standardized everything, including people. So of course retirement was based on chronological age rather than functional age. That kind of thinking still drives the timing of retirement all these years later. Don't people plan when to retire based on their date of birth rather than their appearance, strength, flexibility, and mental sharpness?

Now imagine for a moment that you're fifty-seven years old. That's what it says on your driver's license. However, your "age" of fifty-seven is only a tally of how many times the earth has orbited the sun since you've been in residence. That's an astronomical description, not a biological one! But that tally of orbits determined when your school allowed you to attend first grade and also when the state allowed you to take a driver's test. It will determine when the Social Security Administration allows you to apply for retirement benefits. Other than satisfying legal red tape, your chronological age has never done that much for you. (Although the birthday parties were nice.) But what if you also could measure your *biological age*? How would that affect your life stage planning?

Biological Age

Imagine again that you're looking at your driver's license and it says you're fifty-seven years old. You plan to retire in five years, when you turn sixty-two and first become eligible for Social Security. By then, you'll have enough PERKS (see pages 103–106) to afford the retirement that you want. Now, imagine that you take this assessment that measures your biological age. Much to your horror, you discover that your body's age is *already* sixty-two. According to the government you're only fifty-seven, but according to your body, you're five years older than that.

You do the math in your head and realize that in five years, when your driver's license says you're sixty-two, your biological age by *then* could possibly be . . . (gulp) . . . sixty-seven! You need to stop and reconsider the retirement life you had imagined. You realize that it may not be as physically *active* as you had hoped. You realize that it may not last as *long* as you had hoped. According to your financial plan, you thought you were retiring on the early side (going by your driver's license). But for your biology, you may actually be retiring a bit on the late side. Multiple-choice question: What should you do?

A. Focus on your driver's license age, ignore your biological age, and retire in five years as planned. If your retirement is short and sedentary, so be it. At least you probably won't run out of money. And maybe you'll beat the statistics and have a long and healthy retirement anyway.

B. Focus on your biological age and retire as soon as you can possibly afford to. If you need to reduce your cost of living to make ends meet, so be it. You want to make sure you have as healthy and active a retirement as possible. If it turns out you beat the statistics, then that will be a bonus.

C. First, find out what health changes you can make to reduce your biological age. Make those changes and monitor your biological age. Second, reduce your cost of living and save money like crazy. Third, create a new plan for when to retire.

There is, of course, no right answer. But look at how powerful the concept of biological age is. Now, change the scenario so that your biological age is five years *younger* than your driver's license, and the entire story changes dramatically.

AGING: A REALITY CHECK

- Remember that aging is a basic biological process for humans.
- There is currently no science or technology that can stop or reverse aging.
- The most useful way to think about biological aging is to focus on healthy aging.
- The measurement of biological age is an incredibly powerful tool for education, motivation, and planning.
- If you were to make lifestyle changes that reduced your statistically calculated biological age, you wouldn't really reverse the aging process—you would just get healthier. Sound good?

We don't know what the correct answer to the problem is. But there's no question that biological age should be factored into retirement planning *somehow*! And although the stakes are much higher in the years close to retirement, knowing your biological age at every stage of your career is useful information. Like any health risk assessment, it can provide you with information on the changes you should make to become healthier. And probably *more* than any other type of health risk assessment, it can motivate you to make those changes. Any way you look at it, knowing your biological age is a good thing.

Other than a health risk assessment through your medical plan, how can you gain access to this new form of electronic data *checkup*? The original method for calculating your biological age is www.RealAge.com. A different approach to this concept can be found at www.BlueZones.com. Or, if you're looking for a good life expectancy calculator, use www.LivingTo100.com. Although you'll need to register to take these, the assessments are free. You'll find related books in the Resources section.

Why has staying healthy and "young" become the hot topic for retirement biology? Because longevity has already been steadily increasing, for generations. However, understanding how long you're likely to live isn't easy. Even when people calculate their life expectancy, it doesn't show them how it changes over time. To see another perspective on how life expectancy works, take a look at the Longevity Class Reunion in this chapter.

THE LONGEVITY CLASS REUNION

To see how long you're likely to live, consult one of the online calculators in the Resources section. But to really understand your life expectancy, you need to see how it changes over time. So let's pretend you're part of an imaginary group, during the heyday of the old retirement. Even though your group is imaginary, the mortality and life expectancy data is real, compiled by the Center for Disease Control over the last hundred years.

You're one of a thousand babies born in Longevity, USA, in the year 1900. The infant mortality rate is high, so the life expectancy for your group is only forty-nine years. That doesn't mean you'll all die at age forty-nine, of course. Half of you are expected to die before age forty-nine and half of you after.

Due to sickness and accident, some of you don't live to graduate from Longevity High. Of the original thousand babies, 781 are still alive. The unhealthy and unlucky have died off. But the healthier and luckier teenagers who remain have a longer life expectancy. You now have a remaining life expectancy of forty-five years—which means the ripe old age of sixty-three! Isn't that better?

You all begin your careers and families. In the year you turn thirty-five, the Social Security Act is passed. Your class is so excited that you hold a reunion at the Longevity Hotel. Everyone attends, except that "everyone" means 691 of you. However, because you're the healthy and lucky ones, your life expectancy has now increased to age sixty-seven. So on average, each of you can expect to enjoy a Social Security retirement that will last for two years. Yahoo!

You all return to managing careers, raising children, and saving money. Thirty years pass, and now you're sixty-five. You hold a class retirement party. The room at the Longevity Hotel isn't as full as last time—there are 409 of you left. However, you had all anticipated living for just two years in retirement. But now you have a remaining life expectancy of twelve years! That will take you to age seventy-seven. You all agree to return in ten years for a Diamond Gala.

You all go off into lives of leisure. At first it's wonderful to simply not work. But boredom sets in, and you wonder if you could have done something more engaging and meaningful in your retirement. Finally, you turn seventy-five, and attend the Diamond Gala. You're surprised to see only 230 are left. But you have good reason to party, because your life expectancy is now age eighty-two. Everyone has so much fun that you promise to meet in ten years.

You all go off to lives of friends and family. Ten years later invitations go out, but the post office returns most of them—unopened. When you arrive at the Longevity Hotel, you're one of only sixty-one classmates. At the age of eighty-five, some still enjoy dancing, while others are in wheelchairs. The hardy group that remains has only a four year life expectancy—to age eighty-nine. Instead of ten years, it seems wiser to meet again in five years.

You all go off to quiet lives of deep reflection. As you open the next invitation at the age of 90, you feel a sense of accomplishment. This time the reunion is held at the Longevity Nursing Home. The 19 who are left, amazingly, still have a three year life expectancy.

As the reunion is winding down, a classmate raises her glass to toast the paradox of life expectancy:

"When I was born, I was only supposed to live to forty-nine.

But I graduated from high school, and so was supposed to live to sixty-three.

Then when the Social Security Act passed, I was going to make it to sixty-seven.

But attending our retirement party meant I'd live to seventy-seven.

At our Diamond Gala, I was expected to live until eighty-two.

But then I made it to the next reunion, so I was supposed to live to eighty-nine.

Here I am at 90, and now my life expectancy is ninety-three.

It's strange that the longer I live, the older I'm supposed to get. It feels like I might live forever!"

But she didn't.

However, if you were born in 1950, you'll get significantly closer. At birth, your life expectancy wasn't forty-nine—it was over sixty-eight. Instead of nineteen classmates at your age ninety reunion, you'll have more than sixty. Of course, that doesn't mean you'll be in attendence!

REM: Your Dream Body for Retirement

When you decide to exercise more control over your biology, perhaps you'll go to your doctor for a checkup, take a health risk assessment, or calculate your biological age. Or perhaps you won't. Maybe you feel that you don't need additional information from experts suggesting changes you should make in your lifestyle. You may feel that you already know what you should do to become healthier. If you've had an epiphany and are now *motivated* to get started, that's wonderful—get going. Then go see your doctor too, for heaven's sake!

You support your biology by making healthy lifestyle decisions. You've certainly tried out various healthy changes in the past; some were likely short-lived, while others became a part of your life. Obviously, the ones that become a part of your life are the ones that help the most.

This section will help you identify three biological *practices* that you'd like to include in the picture of your Ideal Retirement to support your health in the next stage. These are three practices to do on an ongoing basis to increase your vitality from the inside out. There are three categories of practices that you'll want to include: relaxation, eating, and movement. By making sure you address all three, you're taking a comprehensive approach to supporting your vitality. You can remember them by the acronym REM (for your *dream* body).

THE THREE TYPES OF BIOLOGICAL PRACTICES

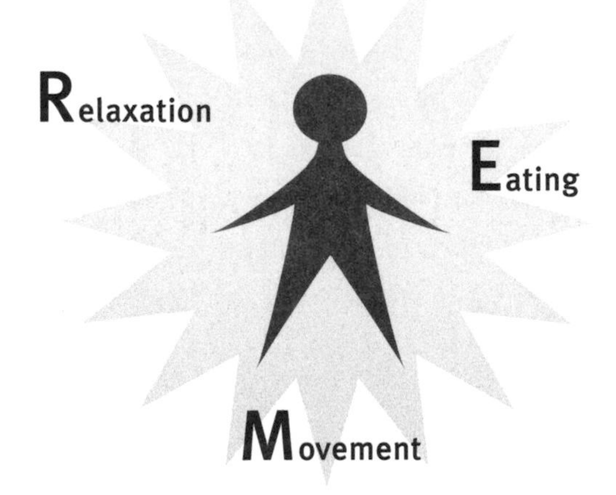

How Do You Get to Carnegie Hall? (Practice.)

The word *practice* in this case has a fairly specific meaning. To qualify as a practice, it has to pass a few tests. First, it's something that is *challenging* enough that you can't just learn it quickly. Or if you can learn it quickly, you may never fully master it. Or if you were to become a master, it's so engaging that it would draw you again and again. (You get the idea.) Second, it's something that offers a *body of knowledge* that will help you learn and grow in the practice. Others have explored it before you and have left accounts of their own practice that can inspire you. Third, it's something that has *other practitioners* for you to connect with, other people who are also learning and practicing it, so that you can either exchange information with them or do the practice together with them. When you complete the exercise below, you'll see why choosing something that meets these high standards is more likely to create *long-term* results for you.

Here's an example from the third category, movement. Martial arts could easily fit the definition of a practice; jumping jacks could not. A martial art (there are many types) is challenging enough that you might never master it. You could access a large body of knowledge about it. And you could exchange information with other devotees or practice it with them. A martial art might keep someone involved for many years, or even a lifetime. But how long could anyone keep up a practice of jumping jacks? For each of these three categories, you want to choose something that you can get really excited about, too!

These practices may be things that you currently do and want to make absolutely sure that you keep doing. Or they may be things that you tried in the past and they worked for you, but for one reason or another you stopped; now you'd like to incorporate them into your life again. Or they may even be things that you've never done but for some mysterious reason, you really want to give them a try.

Relaxation Does Not Involve TV or the Internet

Relaxation is the first category. Some people may think of it as stress reduction. We're not talking about sitting in front of the television or having a few cocktails. Far from it. A relaxation practice is a specific activity that elicits what Herbert Benson identified as the *relaxation response* in the famous book of the same name.

The relaxation response is the biological opposite of the much more famous fight-or-flight response. The fight-or-flight response triggers the release of chemicals that put us on edge to better deal with danger. In our society, that response is triggered many times every day, from obvious stressors like driving in traffic or dealing with work deadlines to seemingly passive and innocuous activities like watching TV or listening to the radio. We can expect to keep experiencing this response even in retirement. Being subjected to the fight-or-flight response so frequently has a strong negative effect on our biology. The best antidote is to *intentionally* evoke its opposite: the relaxation response.

A relaxation practice is a specific activity that you engage in to elicit the relaxation response. Benson originally focused on meditation but later identified many additional ways to do it. Prayer, especially repetitive prayer—such as with a rosary—is another way. So is visualization or self-hypnosis. There are also physical ways to elicit the relaxation response, including tai chi, yoga, and some types of walking. You can even make up your own relaxation practice, or perhaps you already have. You will find that your relaxation practice probably has a very small positive effect on you initially. Don't look for thunder and lighting. However, the nature of a practice is that it deepens over time—that's what makes it a practice! So be patient, and try a different practice if you need to, but keep going on this path. It will pay off. What relaxation practice are you going to start with as part of your Ideal Retirement?

You Are What You Eat and Eat and Eat

Eating is the second category. Of course, we all have to eat. And to a greater or lesser degree, at different times, we all try to eat "healthier," whatever that means for us. There is no shortage of official recommendations for healthy eating, no shortage of diet books, and no shortage of miracle diet supplements. (No shortage of fast-food commercials, either!) But the idea of an eating practice has nothing to do with following a diet or trying to eat more healthfully for a particular time period. An eating practice, like the other practices, is an approach that could be permanent, for you.

To follow an eating practice means adopting a way of thinking about the foods that you imagine *wanting* to eat. About what foods you imagine shopping for and buying. About how you would prepare the foods, and how you would actually consume them. How all that would affect your choices when you dine out. An eating practice is an approach that you've seen real people adopt in their lives, consciously or unconsciously, and then stick with for years. Some easy-to-identify examples of eating practices are low-fat, Mediterranean, vegetarian, and organic. But you could also create your own healthy eating practice. What about "home cooking" the way your grandmother thought of it? You resolve to simply never buy, prepare, or eat anything that comes in a box.

Think about people you've known who seem to have some internal guidance system for healthy eating habits. Can you identify what their internal standards might be? For example, you may know someone who simply doesn't eat any kind of fast food, ever. Or you may know someone who has an internal standard for eating at least one salad every day. Others may have a standard for what size portions they eat, regardless of what they're eating.

The casual observer wouldn't even be aware that each of these people has particular standards, and you probably couldn't fit their standards into any official approach. These people, intentionally or intuitively, came up with healthy practices for eating. You yourself may already be doing exactly that—if so, congratulations. If not, consider what your most *natural* inclinations would be for establishing your own internal standards. Rather than trying to adopt some system created by others, is there some healthy homegrown system already inside you, just waiting for you to give it a try? If so, how would you describe this eating practice?

Poetry in Motion

Movement is the third category. This means some type of *full-body* movement, although it doesn't have to be what you normally think of as exercising. What's more important than meeting specific guidelines for aerobic activities, or for strength and flexibility activities, is meeting your own internal standards for sustainability. It's about finding something that can become nearly automatic and a lifelong practice. For most people, this will be a specific activity, such as swimming, bicycling, or golfing (without a golf cart, please).

The lifelong part is what can make finding a movement practice trickier than finding a relaxation or eating practice. Most of those other practices are not affected by aging. But your ability to continue a particular form of movement is. There are some practices that you might not be able to keep up, such as running. What do you do then? Try to find a different practice, just when it becomes even more important to keep moving? So explore and experiment with practices that can be done at a higher intensity while you're younger and a lower intensity when you're older. Part of the equation is the expectation that you bring to the movement practice. If you anticipate that your running will someday scale back to jogging, and then someday scale back to walking, you'll find it easier to keep it up. On the other hand, if your movement practice is the pole vault, it's not so easy to scale back.

One opportunity you may want to consider is combining or pairing your relaxation and movement practices in some way. Again, the point is not to identify the "best" type, according to the experts. It's to identify—based on your own body and your own experience—what's likely to work for you over the long term. What would you call this practice that you want to put in your Life Circle?

LIFE CIRCLES EXERCISE

Looking back at the section on biological practices, consider the three categories: relaxation, eating, and movement. In the Life Circle, next to the "R," write the name of the relaxation practice that you can imagine engaging in. Next to the "E," write the name of the eating practice that you can most easily imagine following. Next to the "M," write the name of the form of movement that you could practice at a higher intensity first and then at a lower intensity as you get older. Together, your REM practices support your biological vitality and help you create your Ideal Retirement. Use these responses in your One Piece of Paper in chapter eleven.

My Ideal Retirement
includes deepening these
biological practices:

R ______________________________

E ______________________________

M ______________________________

"Your vision will become clear only when you can look into your own heart. Who looks outside, dreams; who looks inside, awakens."

—Carl Jung, pioneering Swiss psychiatrist

Chapter NINE

A New Chapter in Psychology

Without the well-being model, many people are a bit lost in their thinking about happiness. Some think that if they have prosperity, then *that* will bring them happiness. Others think that if they have health, then *that* will bring them happiness. But you, dear reader, know how well-being works. You know that being poor or sick can prevent a person from being happy, but no amount of prosperity or health can *make* them happy.

But who can blame them? They know they can focus their attention and energy on building prosperity or health in life, and they're likely to get results. They can use knowledge and specific approaches to improve their finances, their environment, their biological health, and how they access medicine. They can create results in those areas, directly.

This chapter reveals a similar way of thinking about creating our happiness. That's because recent breakthroughs within the research field of psychology offer knowledge and specific approaches for *learning how to become happy*. These are ways of focusing our attention and energy on building happiness directly, similar to the ways we can build prosperity or health, directly.

There's a special challenge, though, for the topic of retirement happiness. When people dream about creating a happy retirement, it's usually based on a version from the old retirement. Society still puts some pressure on us to simply go after carefree fun and enjoyment. But that's an outdated idea for worn-out old people. This new chapter in psychology tells us that lasting happiness is linked to a critical factor that the fun-and-enjoyment approach overlooks: *engagement*. The old retirement was sometimes even described as a process of *dis*engagement. That's definitely not what we want for the new retirement!

Engagement is the missing ingredient in lasting retirement happiness. And the key to engagement is identifying our *strengths*—those talents and abilities that we receive great satisfaction in using.

We can certainly get lucky and be happy without knowing how we did it. (If you win the lottery you can be prosperous without knowing anything about money.) But because the new retirement offers the greatest opportunity for our fulfillment in life, we shouldn't count on luck. Science is a better bet.

Moving Beyond a Problem-Focused Approach

As it turns out, psychology is finally learning as much about happiness as unhappiness. Instead of studying happiness, most psychological research studies over the past five decades looked at its opposite: depression, addiction, neurosis, and so on. Some very smart and well-intentioned people have spent billions of dollars to create a mountain of detailed knowledge about the *thousand and one* ways that people can be unhappy. This is important information, to be sure. It's also why, when we think of psychology, it's usually in the context of fixing people's problems, to help them lead normal lives. If you're *already* normal (or at least somewhat normal), then psychology hasn't had much to offer you. Psychology couldn't help you learn how to create happiness in your life. Trying to prevent or avoid unhappiness isn't *at all* the same as creating happiness.

To balance out all this knowledge about unhappiness, a new discipline called positive psychology emerged around the turn of the new millennium. This is *not* just a variation on "positive thinking." The inquiry into positive psychology was championed by the renowned research psychologist Martin Seligman and others. They take a clear-thinking, hard-nosed, let's-measure-it-and-see-if-it-stands-up approach to the study of human strengths, positive emotions, and other aspects of optimal human experience. Positive psychology has really caught on, and these days there are many more researchers who are studying how humans thrive.

Thanks to systematic research in other fields, we know about approaches for increasing our "economic well-being" as well as our "health and well-being." Finally, there is systematic research into our "psychological well-being," too.

Seligman suggests that there are, essentially, three approaches to happiness; that is, three basic *ways* to be happy. Although there are, thank goodness, an unlimited number of specific ways in which you can be happy, each comes under one of these three basic approaches.

Three Ways That You Can Be Happy in Retirement

What, you ask, are these three approaches to happiness?

- Pleasure
- Engagement
- Meaning

Let's explore them one by one.

Pleasure or Enjoyment

This one sounds obvious, doesn't it? When you first think of happiness, it's usually pleasure and enjoyment that come to mind, right off the bat. An afternoon at the ball game. Eating a delicious meal. Watching an entertaining movie. Buying something that you want. These involve being comfortable and *having fun* in an easy or relaxed way. Pleasure like this brings a burst of positive emotions that come and go quickly, though, usually not lasting much longer than the event itself. When you use this approach (and I sincerely hope that you do), you need to keep going back and doing enjoyable activities, over and over again, to get more of that happiness.

Engagement or Involvement

This one isn't very obvious. Another word for engagement is involvement. Positive psychology researcher Mihaly Csikszentmihalyi uses still another word for this experience that you can almost feel: He calls it *flow*. (His name, by the way, is actually easier to say than it looks; it sounds like "Me high. Chicks sent me high.") Flow happens when your abilities are well matched to some challenging task. You get so deep into the activity, whatever it is, that you lose all track of time. You may feel like it's been only a few minutes, but it's been much longer. Or a few seconds may feel like an eternity. Either way, when you're that engaged, you lose yourself in what you're doing. You may not even be aware that it makes you happy *while* you're doing it, but *afterward* you say, "That was great!"

Engagement involves challenge, and it demands something from you, so it's not as simple as pleasure. It can't be purchased or consumed in the way that pleasure can be. When you use this approach (and you may be using it more than you realize), it can stick with you *longer* than pleasure does. Over time, it can build up into a lasting satisfaction with life.

Meaning or Purpose

This approach to happiness is somewhat more obvious than engagement, but it's not so easy to pin down. Of course having meaning in your life would make you happy! But how do you get it? The way you get it, my friend, is to use your abilities in the service of something larger than yourself. This approach requires something from you, too. Note that meaning doesn't come from just *believing* in something larger than yourself; it comes from being in service to that something. This is part of living your life in alignment with your core values.

What's *larger* than yourself? Take your pick, depending on your belief system: God, your family, the environment, your political party, your ethnic culture, the free enterprise system, your community. It may not be service to something larger than yourself but to something *beyond*

WHAT ABOUT FIXING YOUR WEAKNESSES?

Look carefully at the three approaches to happiness. You'll notice that "fixing your weaknesses" appears nowhere on the list. Rooting out and eliminating your imperfections is not an approach to happiness. With the best of intentions, your loving parents, your well-meaning teachers, and every straight-shooting boss you've had since high school have attempted to correct your deficiencies. It's finally OK to place a bit less emphasis on that. In retirement, you won't need to focus on fixing your weaknesses. So take a lesson from positive psychology—develop and expand what's right with you. Focus on what you like about yourself, rather than what you don't like. Concentrate on what you do want, instead of what you don't want. Those are the scientific recommendations, anyway.

yourself: a neighbor who needs help with chores, a child who needs help with school, a litter-free walking path, a safer neighborhood, the sick, the needy. You can't buy or consume meaning, just as you can't buy or consume engagement. And contributing your *money* to something you believe in doesn't provide the same sense of meaning or happiness that working for it provides (although giving money is still a good thing). You can be aware of this happiness before, during, and after a meaningful experience. When you use this approach (and I highly recommend it), the sense of satisfaction can last a lifetime.

By the way, Seligman suggests there's a fourth way to be happy, which he calls *victory*. He's right. If this book were focused on the First Age or Second Age, victory would be a whole section. On the other hand, for a book that's about designing the Third and Fourth Ages of life, we'll focus on the other three paths to happiness.

Societal Expectations Make Them into Three Levels of Happiness

If you'd like to increase your happiness in retirement (or even right now!), you can use the three approaches to design your life. All three are equally valid—one of them is not better or more important than the others. But there is a connection between them, and what society tries to tell you *retirement* happiness should be about. Society may still be thinking in terms of the old retirement. For people who didn't have all that many years to live and weren't in the best of health, just retiring from work was a blessing.

So society has created expectations about what kind of happiness is appropriate for worn-out old people in retirement: the easy, relaxing, leisure-oriented kind of happiness. The message from society has been that happiness in retirement should be based on pleasure.

That message may have made sense years ago (and still may for those who earn their living with hard physical labor), but for the legions of modern workers whose sedentary lives require the intervention of gym workouts, a good long rest is *not* what they need. At retirement age now, most of us are burned-out but definitely not worn-out.

So even though there is no hierarchy among the three approaches to happiness, society has created a hierarchy for retirement happiness. Society's expectations are that enjoyment and pleasure should be enough. If your expectations are *higher* than that and you want engagement and meaning in retirement, you have some work to do.

If a pleasant retirement is all that you want, that's perfectly OK. But if you decide that you'd like to set your sights higher and plan for a retirement that's engaging, or possibly even meaningful, that's OK, too. You should realize that if you haven't worn yourself out on the job, those two approaches give you a better chance at achieving a more lasting kind of happiness—the true well-being that this book is all about.

You can see that the Three Levels of Retirement Happiness look like a mountain.

THREE LEVELS OF RETIREMENT HAPPINESS

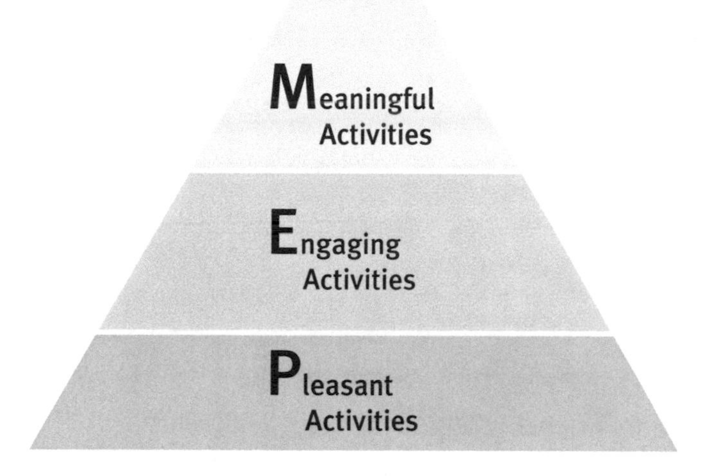

Mountain Climbing in Retirement?

Does all this sound like you're hoping for too much happiness from retirement? After all, many of your friends and coworkers will be relieved to simply not have to drag their sorry rear end back and forth to work every day. They will be content just resting their duffs, like on that old three-legged stool. They will wonder why you're putting so much thought and energy into planning for your happiness in retirement. Isn't discovering your strengths a lot of *work*? And just who do you think you are, climbing *mountains* of happiness? Who are you to climb beyond pleasure to engagement, and beyond engagement to meaning? Why do you deserve to have all three levels of retirement happiness? You will get push back, and resistance, and pressure from many of your friends and coworkers for even trying to design the new retirement.

The answer, of course, is that we all deserve all the approaches to happiness. But you may not be able to talk with some of your friends about it. They'll notice later, when you're out having the time of your life, and they're just "relaxing." That will be the time to invite them along!

Pleasure: Your First Level of Retirement Happiness

When you initially imagine the retirement you want, it's probably a *pleasant* retirement. You want to be secure and comfortable and simply enjoy yourself. You want to spend time with friends and family. You want to play. A pleasant retirement is based on leisure, relaxation, and finally getting a chance for some fun in life. Like a vacation.

This is the original idea of retirement, as people have imagined it, for generations. You probably already know a lot about what it would take to create this level of retirement happiness. It's usually based on your *interests* in the world outside of work. It's the same kind of stuff that you pursue whenever you have enough free time: hobbies, entertainment, spectator events, travel, socializing. It's the WHAT, from chapter three. These things are enjoyable partly just because they're not work. And they're enjoyable partly because there's something about the subject or pastime that you find interesting.

Some of these interests may keep you tuned in for years or for a whole lifetime. Others you may casually pick up, explore, and let go again, moving on to new explorations and new interests, as those interests aren't necessarily a very fundamental, or lasting, aspect of yourself. (Think how much your interests have already changed over the years.)

During your working life, these low-involvement activities bring a welcome *counterbalance* to your work. In retirement, though, these activities are no longer counterbalancing work (unless you are still doing some work to pay the bills), and they may not have enough weight to stand on their own. They may not be rich enough to bring the amount of happiness that you expect from them. They were up to the task of filling your all-too-short weekends and a week or two of vacation. And it helps if you can choose from a wide range of pleasurable activities that you've already lined up and experienced. But they may not be up to the task of filling weeks and months and years and decades of retirement.

Memory versus Imagination

How do you go about actually *planning* for the first level of happiness—pleasure and enjoyment? You'd think it would be as easy as falling off a log! After all, you're naturally drawn toward what's fun and enjoyable, and no doubt you've found ways to fit it in during your free time. You've done it during the Second Age, so you should be an old pro at planning for it in your Third Age, yes? (If you're one of those who has taken little or no time out for fun and enjoyment during the Second Age—and sadly, there are more than a few—it will take some effort to reconnect with your natural inclinations and rekindle your interests.) So for your retirement, can't you simply *imagine* how to do more of it—a lot more of it?

The answer is yes, you can and should use your imagination. And that's the tricky part. It's easy to imagine all sorts of new activities for the first level that seem like they would be fun, but you've never tried them before. They're unrelated to your actual experience. It's great to try new things and discover new ways to have fun. However, the bad news from the research front is that we humans are spectacularly inaccurate at predicting what will make us truly happy. It's not often that we appreciate something *completely* new. When we like something that seems new, it usually has elements from our past experience that we enjoyed. There's just enough new to make it feel novel and exciting.

Low-stakes experiments into new ways to have fun are ideal. Think of them as experiments into what you find to be fun. No big risk. (For example, trying a new sport or a membership organization.) On the other hand, high-stakes experiments that aren't based on some elements of your past experience can be *disastrous*. (Such as buying a boat, an RV, or a vacation home. We've all heard horror stories, haven't we?)

So when you're planning for the first level of retirement happiness, don't rely solely on your imagination! **Use this three-step process:**

1. Remember previous fun experiences. After all, when you plan how to create a pleasurable retirement, you have lots and lots of information to go on. You've been accumulating data on yourself whenever

you pursued your favorite leisure activities outside of work. So the first step is to search your memory bank. Cruise back in time for some of the most fun experiences you can remember having.

2. Identify, specifically, what it was about these experiences that brought you the most enjoyment. Use the basic questions you learned in high school: Who? What? Where? When? How? These are hints, or clues, based on your real experiences for how to create more enjoyment like this.

3. Now imagine new ways to have fun in retirement. You're not trying to re-create the old experiences, of course. But by using the hints and clues from your real life, you're pointing yourself in the right direction. Find opportunities to test out, in a low-stakes way, your ideas for new types of retirement fun.

Engagement: Your Second Level of Retirement Happiness

In addition to the first level of happiness that comes from pleasure, people are beginning to imagine something more: a second level that comes from engagement. This level introduces a new element: *challenge*. This is definitely part of the idea for the Third Age of Life. So it's an essential part of the design for the new retirement!

Here's what Csikszentmihalyi's research discovered. When the challenges in your life are too far above your level of skill, they create *anxiety*. You've probably had a job like that at one time or another. But when the challenges in your life are too far below your level of skill, they create *boredom*. You probably wouldn't want a retirement like that. (Remember, the old retirement is dying.) Perhaps you'd like more of a middle ground? That's what an engaged retirement is about. The secret is regularly finding interesting challenges that are a good match for your favorite skills and strengths. When you find these interesting challenges and become actively involved in them, you get a sense of accomplishment from doing them well.

CONSUMING HAPPINESS VERSUS CREATING IT YOURSELF

Because pleasure can easily be packaged and sold to you as a product or service, the first level of retirement happiness is a very big business (as we explored in chapter three). Magazine advertisements and television commercials are filled with entertainment, travel, and luxury goods that were developed and marketed based on the narrow view that retirement happiness is based only on pleasure. It's a big business because the marketing works—we consume pleasure, and it generates a healthy profit.

Marketers know that we want other forms of happiness, too, like engagement or meaning, but those are difficult to package and sell because they require more involvement from us than just buying something. However, let the buyer beware: the marketing messages for products that can really provide only pleasure often imply that you'll get engagement or meaning if you buy the product. That's just hogwash.

It's not easy to buy engagement or meaning—they're more self-created. You need to build these kinds of happiness yourself, even if you do use a product—tools, books, sporting goods, learning opportunities—in conjunction with the activity. Even the simplest approach to retirement happiness—pleasure—has been a do-it-yourself project for most of human history. Not until the twentieth century did packaging and selling it become such a gigantic business.

When you plan for your retirement happiness, you can make a choice about how much to consume and how much to create yourself. It's a little bit like making food choices. The Second Age of life is so hectic that many of us end up eating a lot of fast food along the way. But the Third Age opens up new possibilities, so with planning (and a bit of luck) we'll all have the time for more of those good home-cooked meals.

"Go with the Flow" Doesn't Mean What You Think, Dude

But what about actually *planning* for the second level of retirement happiness, engagement? What about designing it into your life? Remember, flow is about enjoyable effort; it isn't even remotely like the laid-back, whatever attitude of "go with the flow." No, the second level is more like "make the flow."

Here's how you can begin to make plans for going beyond the first level to the second level. Pure enjoyment is most closely linked with your interests. And your level of involvement with an interest can be *passive* or *active*. Let's say you're interested in baseball. You could choose to be a spectator at a baseball game, or you could choose to be a player on a team. The low level of skill needed to be a spectator would produce a pleasant experience. But the higher level of skill needed to be a player would produce an engaging experience (not to mention the boost to your health from being physically active).

So when you're planning for the first level, you need to know what your *interests* are. But when you're planning for the second level, you need to know what your *skills* and *strengths* are. When you get an opportunity to use those parts of yourself, you tend to experience engagement—you go into the flow state. The surest way to successfully plan for the second level of happiness is to set up ways to use your strengths. It does take more research and planning. You need to discover your strengths so that you can begin to investigate opportunities to use them in your retirement. The Ideal Retirement exercise in this chapter will help you identify your top five strengths so you can be on the lookout for where to use them in the world.

Strengths Are Deeper Than Skills

What's the difference between skills and strengths? Since you have more experience with skills, let's start there. Skills are the abilities or talents that you use to accomplish tasks with people, data, or things. In the world of work, skills are king. A key aspect of the job hunter's *What Color Is Your Parachute?* is helping you identify your skills (especially the ones that you love to use). Knowing your skills and being able to effectively communicate them is the basis for showing a potential employer what you can do. How valuable you are as an employee depends, to a large degree, on your skills. In the workplace, skills have a paycheck attached to them. As you may already know, it's possible to have skills that you absolutely *hate* to use. Perhaps you became an expert at something, somehow, but you don't like to do it. Or you may have loved that task at one time and developed the skills to do it, but now you don't like it anymore. Or you may never have liked it. Competent, conscientious person that you are, though, you retained the skills.

However, for the most part, you probably like using your skills. If you found a job made up *entirely* of tasks that used your skills, and those tasks had just the right level of challenge (this is obviously a fantasy), you'd be in job heaven. You wouldn't be spending (wasting?) your time on tasks that didn't make use of your skills. Because the challenge wouldn't be too high for your skill level, you wouldn't feel anxious. And because it wouldn't be too low, you wouldn't feel bored. In fact, you'd be feeling engaged all the time. You'd probably be in a perpetual flow state (if that's humanly possible). You'd be a model employee. Employee of the Month, over and over and over. (Could your job in the new retirement be like this?)

Of course, for regular jobs, it doesn't work that way. And yet, people are more likely to experience flow *at* work than *outside* of work! How can this be? Because they typically get to use their skills more at work than they do anywhere else. If you experience much flow in your work, you'll undoubtedly *miss* it when you retire. The first level of a leisure-based retirement just ain't the same thing.

Now let's make some distinctions between skills and strengths, as we did in chapter three. Your skills are mostly useful within some context—usually work. Your strengths are useful across *all* contexts—your whole life. Skills are narrow and specific enough that they often can have a paycheck, or some type of responsibility, attached to them. Strengths are broad and general enough that they may not. (Yet your strengths are the parts of yourself that you're happy to use, whether you're supposed to or not.) Skills are usually related to being a worker, while strengths are related to being a human. Strengths are more fundamental.

Strengths Are Like Positive Personality Traits

Strengths may sound a bit like something else that humans have: personality traits. These are intrinsic and enduring behaviors, such as introversion and extroversion. Personality traits are partially inherited, like the color of your eyes. Strengths are a little like that, because you also have *tendencies* toward certain strengths, developed through both nature and nurture. But here's a big difference between traits and strengths: expressing your personality traits is more automatic, and you just do it. But using your strengths is more of a *choice*, and you can choose to develop them or not. (Skills are that way, too.)

Here's another distinguishing characteristic of strengths: They are always *positive*. In contrast, personality traits and skills can be either positive or negative. For example, the most widely validated personality test measures the level of neuroticism as a trait that's present in each person. Neuroticism is useful in the world of personality traits, but it would never be classified as a strength. In the same way, there are workplace skills that would be valued only by unethical employers. For example, cooking the books and roughing up adversaries are certainly skills but not positive ones. In contrast, strengths are abilities that are *recognized and esteemed* by the individual and by society at large.

Become an Expert on Your Own Strengths

Deep down inside, you know what your greatest strengths are. You are, without a doubt, the world's leading expert on yourself.

But you are also so accustomed to some of your strengths, so familiar with them, so at ease in using them, that you may have kind of *forgotten* about them. Perhaps you noticed when you were young that you could do something in life easily and effortlessly while others struggled trying to do the same thing. Then, because doing that thing or acting in that way was effortless, you didn't need to focus on it. It *receded* into the background of your awareness as you focused on the things that didn't come easily and effortlessly. You needed to really apply effort and attention to the areas that were *not* your strengths (we won't call them weaknesses), and so those other things may have stayed in the foreground of your awareness.

You probably have other strengths that you've never been aware of, even when you were young. They're so much a part of you, so automatic, that they've been in the background *all along*, quietly helping you to effortlessly excel in that particular area. What's more, they haven't stayed the same over time. As you've used them—whether you were aware of them or not—you've continued to develop them. You've probably gotten better at using them over time. In fact, the Third Age may offer life's greatest opportunity for you to develop them to their fullest potential.

You can think of your strengths as being like *the paint colors on an artist's palette* (or in a kindergartner's watercolors box). If you were to look back at the scenes of your life, you'd notice that over the course of time you've been painting with mostly the *same colors*. You may have used red or blue over and over again. That's the way you use your strengths—they're your favorite colors in the pictures of your life. In the scenes of your life, sometimes your favorite colors, or strengths, were in the foreground. In other scenes they were in the background—less obvious, but there just the same. You may find it helpful to line up a bunch of your scenes alongside each other to notice which colors are the most recurring. Once you do, they just jump out at you: Those same colors, those same strengths, are in so many of your life's pictures and in your best work—your greatest achievements.

THE SIX STRENGTH THEMES

The three different methods in this chapter's exercise are designed to help jog your awareness of your own strengths so you can plan how to incorporate them into your next stage of life (or right now). The picture of your Ideal Retirement needs to include those best parts of yourself, so it's well worth a bit of reflection to identify them. Although, again, deep down you know what they are, these exercises are about *naming* them and more clearly articulating them, so they'll be easier for you to plan with.

The naming system we'll use is the VIA (Values in Action) Classification of Strengths. This classification was developed through the collaboration of dozens of experts, all focusing on the best of human nature. It's the most thoughtfully conceived, broadly researched, thoroughly articulated, and painstakingly validated system of character strengths that's ever been created. As an online survey, it has now been taken by more than a million people! This classification is a very powerful tool for identifying what's best about you so you can design your next stage of life.

This system consists of twenty-four individual Signature Strengths, which are organized into six groups. The system's developers, Chris Peterson and Martin Seligman, call these six groups Virtues; for our purpose here, you might also think of them as Strengths Themes. Each of these six broader Strengths Themes contains three to five of the more specific twenty-four Signature Strengths. You could spend years learning about the relationship of all these (and some people have), but you'll get the general picture just by looking over the Strengths list on the following pages. Which sounds most like you?

THE STRENGTHS THEMES AND SIGNATURE STRENGTHS[1]

Transcendence

Strengths that forge connections to the larger universe and provide meaning

Appreciation of beauty and excellence (awe, wonder, elevation) / Noticing and appreciating beauty, excellence, and/or skilled performance in all domains of life, from nature to art to mathematics to science to everyday experience

Gratitude / Being aware of and thankful for the good things that happen; taking time to express thanks

Hope (optimism, future-mindedness, future orientation) / Expecting the best in the future and working to achieve it; believing that a good future is something that can be brought about

Humor (playfulness) / Liking to laugh and tease; bringing smiles to other people; seeing the light side; making (not necessarily telling) jokes

Spirituality (religiousness, faith, purpose) / Having coherent beliefs about the higher purpose and meaning of the universe; knowing where one fits within the larger scheme; having beliefs about the meaning of life that shape conduct and provide comfort

Wisdom and Knowledge

Cognitive strengths that entail the acquisition and use of knowledge

Creativity (originality, ingenuity) / Thinking of novel and productive ways to do things; includes artistic achievement but is not limited to it

Curiosity (interest, novelty seeking, openness to experience) / Taking an interest in all of ongoing experience for its own sake; finding subjects and topics fascinating; exploring and discovering

Open-mindedness (judgment, critical thinking) / Thinking things through and examining them from all sides; not jumping to conclusions; being able to change one's mind in light of evidence; weighing all evidence fairly

Love of learning / Mastering new skills, topics, and bodies of knowledge, whether on one's own or formally; obviously related to the

1. The VIA Classification of Strengths is adapted with permission of the VIA Institute.

strength of curiosity but goes beyond it to describe the tendency to add systematically to what one knows

Perspective (wisdom) / Being able to provide wise counsel to others; having ways of looking at the world that make sense to oneself and to other people

Humanity

Interpersonal strengths that involve tending and befriending others

Love / Valuing close relations with others, in particular those in which sharing and caring are reciprocated; being close to people

Kindness (generosity, nurturance, care, compassion, altruistic love, niceness) / Doing favors and good deeds for others; helping them; taking care of them

Social intelligence (emotional intelligence, personal intelligence) / Being aware of the motives and feelings of other people and oneself; knowing what to do to fit in to different social situations; knowing what makes other people tick

Justice

Civic strengths that underlie healthy community life

Citizenship (social responsibility, loyalty, teamwork) / Working well as a member of a group or team; being loyal to the group; doing one's share

Fairness / Treating all people the same according to notions of fairness and justice; not letting personal feelings bias decisions about others; giving everyone a fair chance

Leadership / Encouraging a group of which one is a member to get things done and at the same time maintain good relations within the group; organizing group activities and seeing that they happen

Courage

Emotional strengths that involve the exercise of will to accomplish goals in the face of opposition, external or internal

Bravery (valor) / Not shrinking from threat, challenge, difficulty, or pain; speaking up for what is right even if there is opposition; acting on convictions even if unpopular; includes physical bravery but is not limited to it

Persistence (perseverance, industriousness) / Finishing what one starts; persisting in a course of action in spite of obstacles; "getting it out the door"; taking pleasure in completing tasks

Integrity (authenticity, honesty) / Speaking the truth and, more broadly, presenting oneself in a genuine way; being without pretense; taking responsibility for one's feelings and actions

Vitality (zest, enthusiasm, vigor, energy) / Approaching life with excitement and energy; not doing things halfway or halfheartedly; living life as an adventure; feeling alive and activated

Temperance

Strengths that protect against excess

Forgiveness and mercy / Forgiving those who have done wrong; giving people a second chance; not being vengeful

Humility and modesty / Letting one's accomplishments speak for themselves; not seeking the spotlight; not regarding one's self as more special than one is

Prudence / Being careful about one's choices; not taking undue risks; not saying or doing things that might later be regretted

Self-regulation (self-control) / Regulating what one feels and does; being disciplined; controlling one's appetites and emotions

EXERCISE: DISCOVER YOUR STRENGTHS

Your choice of method for discovering your strengths depends on how much time and effort you can spare for it. However, there's something you should know. The process of reflecting upon your character strengths is actually a way of developing them! Think of it as strengths training—but not for your muscles—for your character. Naturally, the more of yourself you invest, the greater your likely return, and the more personalized, relevant, and meaningful the outcome will be. Taking more time will begin to develop your strengths more. The good news is that the following three methods are not mutually exclusive. You could end up using all three methods over time. Speaking of time, they're listed in order from the smallest to largest investment of time and effort.

The Fastest Method for Discovering Your Strengths

Choose them from a list. (Requires about ten minutes.)

You can use this method right now, with just this book. You'll jot down your answers, notes, observations, and so on, in the margins and spaces around the strengths listed on pages 205 through 207. Or if you prefer, make photocopies.

First browse the six Strengths Themes to get the big picture. The themes are a bit more abstract than the strengths, so you're starting at the broader level, then narrowing things down. Even the strengths may seem a little abstract to you, because they're more general than the kinds of narrow skills that relate to the context of work.

Next, browse through the twenty-four strengths, studying the synonyms and descriptions. As you consider each of the strengths, ask yourself, "Is this strength not like me? Is it somewhat like me? Is it very much like me?" Remember, you're looking for the parts of you that have shown up, over and over, across many different life situations. Make note of the strengths that seem very much like you. There should be no more than ten of these.

Now your goal is to identify the five strengths that are most like you. Go back through your list of "very much like me" strengths to narrow it down to five. One way is to ask yourself two questions:

1. Which strengths, when I'm using them, make me feel most engaged?
2. Which strengths, when I'm not using them, make me feel most frustrated?

The five that you ultimately select are your Signature Strengths, which you will fill in on the Life Circles exercise on page 215.

The Second-Fastest Method for Discovering Your Strengths

Take the VIA online survey at www.viacharacter.org. (This requires free registration and takes about thirty minutes to answer the questions.)

This method is the most high-tech; to use it you'll need to set aside this book and go on the Internet. When you're done, return to the book and fill in your Signature Strengths in the Life Circles exercise on page 215.

The VIA survey was designed to be used online. It's the primary method for figuring out which of the twenty-four strengths are most characteristic of you. I strongly recommend that you take the free online survey, if you can. It provides a much more accurate way of discovering your top five strengths than browsing the names and descriptions. An in-depth optional report showing your Signature Strengths is available for a fee. A different online strengths assessment is available from the Gallup organization for a fee at www.strengthsfinder.com.

The Third-Fastest Method for Discovering Your Strengths

Find them in stories from your life. (This takes the longest—several hours.)

This method is the most thorough, because it requires you to write down stories about your strengths or tell them to another person who will take notes for you. The danger of this method is that, with the best of intentions, you may set aside reading this book to pursue writing your stories. Then you may not get around to finishing the stories right away, so time passes, and before you know it, the whole process of creating a picture of your Ideal Retirement has come to a halt. I strongly recommend that you first complete one of the two quicker methods. If you can't resist the prospect of writing some stories, allow yourself a rough first draft, review it for your five Signature Strengths, then keep moving forward to finish this exercise, followed by the remaining chapters and your other Life Circles. You can always come back later for a deeper exploration.

Using this method, you'll identify at least three stories from your life. The stories that you choose are ones that fit a very specific description, first articulated by Bernard Haldane, which forms the core of what he called the Dependable Strengths process. Each must be a true story from your own life in which you actively participated in something. (Remember the baseball game distinction between being a spectator and playing on the team?) Also, it must be a specific event, not simply a type of event or one of a series of events. (Not just "playing on a baseball team"; something more like "playing in that game on the Saturday before my birthday, two summers ago, when I hit a home run.")

Now that you know what can qualify as a story, here are the criteria for the stories that you want to pick out. They are all experiences of something that you:

- Enjoyed doing while you were doing it
- Feel that you did well
- Are proud of

Notice that the story criteria get you to identify experiences that cover all three types of happiness. If you enjoyed it while you were doing it, that obviously relates to pleasure. If the story was about something you did well, it was possible to not do it well, meaning that there was a challenge. You met that challenge successfully, which relates to engagement. Finally, if you're proud of what you did, it meant something to you—the definition of meaning. Essentially, a *trifecta*. At the same time, your stories don't have to be big life-changing events. (That baseball game probably didn't change your life, and you're probably the only one who knows how important it was to you.) Are you getting a good idea of the kind of stories that you're looking for? Remember the artist's palette? This exercise lines up the best scenes from your life so you can identify which colors you used to paint them. These three stories are some of your greatest artistic achievements. Aren't you curious which colors (strengths) you used? Think of these stories as though a gallery were showing a retrospective of your best paintings—your life's work. If possible, the gallery would want something from your early period, as well as your middle and later periods. It would also want your works of art from different contexts. Not just from your job or hobbies or social life but ideally all three. So the stories you choose will be most helpful to you if they're from different times, and different contexts, of your life.

You may be thinking that finding such particular types of stories will be a difficult search. But trust me, you have tons of these stories in your memory bank. An entire collection. True, these positive experiences are sometimes pushed farther back in the memory warehouse, whereas experiences of disappointment and defeat are much more readily at hand. So as you start your internal inventory system running and let these stories come to your mind over the next twenty minutes or twenty hours, realize that it's perfectly normal to bring up all kinds of stories, not just those that meet the three criteria. Then you get to choose.

Now let's begin with one of your stories. What do you do with it for this exercise? You can write it longhand or type it into your word processor and print it out to work with. If you love to write, you may tell it with perfect spelling, grammar, and syntax, but you can also just note phrases, fragments, and key words, as long as you use plenty of them. Remember, you'll be trolling your stories for your strengths.

If you're telling the story to someone else who is kind enough to take notes, there is one rule that they absolutely, positively must follow. They don't have to write down every word that comes out of your mouth, but every word they do write down must be one that did come out of your mouth. The words that end up on the paper need to be your actual, exact words, from your own vocabulary. Your friend must not translate your words into other words or try to summarize your story. This is your story in your words. Ask your friend to take down as many of your important words as possible. You need enough material to comb through to look for your strengths.

Whether writing it yourself or telling the story to a "reporter," what matters is that you record the parts of your story that answer the following questions:

1. What, specifically, were you doing?
2. What was fun about it? (Remember, you enjoyed it at the time.)
3. More important, what was the challenge, and how did you meet that challenge? (Remember, this is something you did well.)
4. What is meaningful to you about this, now, as you look back on it? (Remember, you're proud of it.)

And one more question:

5. What did you bring to that experience that was unique? (That is, no one else would have brought quite the same thing that you did.) After you have your story down on paper, you can look for your strengths—the colors that you've used over and over—through two basic methods: color-by-numbers and freehand.

Color-by-numbers. Start with a small box of markers, colored pencils, or crayons. Assign the six basic colors (red, orange, yellow, green, blue, violet) to the six Strengths Themes. Make enough photocopies of the twenty-four strengths list to take notes on one for each story.

First, go back through your first story and underline the words that describe, or closely relate to, a Strength Theme. Don't expect to find many examples of each; you may have just one or two of the Strengths Themes showing up.

Second, go back to the underlined words and think about what you were really doing in the context of the story. Which of the Signature Strengths within that Strength Theme is the best descriptor of what you were doing? Make relevant notes on one copy of the strengths list.

Do the same for each of your other stories. By the time you get to the second and third stories, you'll be much better at spotting the Strengths Themes and the Signature Strengths within them. Whichever colors seem to you to be the ones you've colored with the most in the scenes of your life, those are the clues. Write them down in the Life Circles exercise on page 215.

Freehand. This method starts with the same markers, colored pencils, or crayons, but doesn't use the Strengths Themes. Instead, you simply comb through your stories for your own words that describe your strengths. After reading this chapter and familiarizing yourself with the concept of strengths from the lists on pages 205 through 207, you're completely qualified to select your own labels for these inner qualities that we've been calling strengths. Choose the words that you used frequently and that describe the best parts of you, then assign and mark each with its own color (your choice). Whatever language you use to capture those parts of you—your ways of thinking, feeling, or acting that make you feel engaged when you use them—is fine. When you think you've found the five colors from your palette that are most common in the masterpieces of your life's experiences, those are your Signature Strengths. Write them in the Life Circle on page 215.

By the way, regardless of the quality of these scenes from your life, keep in mind that some of your best artistic achievements are still ahead of you.

Meaning: Your Third Level of Retirement Happiness

In addition to a pleasant and engaged life, some people imagine having a *meaningful* life, too. Of course, they still want to be secure and comfortable and enjoy themselves. And they want to be actively involved in life, using their strengths in a personally rewarding way. But they also want a sense of meaning and purpose. This usually comes from feeling that you are part of something larger than yourself, something that makes you *proud of the personal contribution you're making*. Which brings us to the third level of retirement happiness.

If pleasure is most closely related to your interests, and engagement is most closely related to your strengths, then meaning is most closely related to your values. You may well find that the third level of retirement happiness has a connection to your core values from chapter three.

If you *already* knew, in the Second Age of life, what gives you a sense of meaning—perhaps from a fulfilling career—congratulations! If your sense of meaning comes from something outside of your work, that's even better, because you won't leave it behind when you retire from your career or move from the Second to the Third Age. On the other hand, if you're not sure whether you really have a sense of meaning in your life, the Third Age just might be your *best chance* to look for it. It could be your golden opportunity! In fact, discovering your purpose in life could be one of the most important parts of the new retirement. (More on this in chapter eleven.)

Of course, you don't need to decide in advance how far up the levels of retirement happiness you want to go. But the clearer your vision of life and, especially, the clearer your vision of yourself in retirement, the more likely you will be to get there. And frankly, when it comes to developing a vision, sooner is better than later. You may even start to have a new vision of your life before you've finished reading this book.

So keep your mind wide open. In the picture of your Ideal Retirement, see yourself using your strengths in the service of something you believe in and really enjoying doing it. And if you see yourself not alone in these scenes but *connecting with others*, sharing the experience with people you hold dear, so much the better! You're envisioning both elements of the happiness dimension: the psychological, which you've learned about in this chapter, and the social, the subject of the next chapter. The three levels apply to relationships, too—and in retirement, we generally need to make a more active effort to build relationships that bring us happiness and fulfillment on all three levels. That's what we'll be delving into in chapter ten.

LIFE CIRCLES EXERCISE

Using one of the three methods to discover your retirement strengths, you should now have a list of five strengths. Enter these in the Life Circle to use for your One Piece of Paper in chapter eleven.

My Ideal Retirement
includes developing these
psychological strengths:

"Call it a clan, call it a network, call it a tribe, call it a family: Whatever you call it, whoever you are, you need one."

—Jane Howard, American journalist

Chapter TEN

Happiness Is Only Real When Shared[1]

It's the rare person who wants to be alone. For most of us, inner psychological happiness is enhanced when we're socially connected with others. And it's a two-way street. Social connection with others is one of the surest paths to our own psychological happiness.

That's why it's amazing to realize that most of our social connections are based on *convenience*! How can something so important to our happiness be seemingly left to chance? Certainly, we maintain some very close relationships even when they're decidedly *inconvenient*. But much of our interaction with others is based on where we happen to work or live.

In the First, Second, and Fourth Ages, convenience may well rule the day. However, the Third Age is the greatest opportunity we'll ever have to build social connections and relationships, *consciously*. A deeper, more mature understanding of ourselves means that we seek activities in life that align with our interests, strengths, and values. In consciously seeking out those activities, we're more likely to connect with others who are also doing the same thing. That's a different dynamic than mere convenience.

Like many people, you may not realize that when you retire, most of your social connections and friendships from work will wither and die.

1. Christopher McCandless, quoted by Jon Krakauer in *Into the Wild* (1996).

You can end up socially isolated. Or you can develop new connections, based on new conveniences. Even better, you can choose to make your Third Age the happiest time of your life because of the *conscious connections* that you create in that stage of life.

A note about terminology: If you don't spend much time reading or thinking about "relationships," feel free to substitute any of the following:

- Contacts
- Connections
- Friends and family
- Kith and kin
- People you know
- Social circle

The Automatic Relationship Generator

During the First Age of life, the world of education was often an awkward place. Acceptance by our peers was the most important thing in the world to us, and yet we were just beginning to figure ourselves out. We felt socially insecure. Some of us were in the popular crowd (probably you) and some in the geeky crowd (that was me), but we all had relationships with other students. That's because, day in and day out, we were thrown together into similar circumstances and activities. It was natural to get to know other people because we interacted with them every day. Something called the Automatic Relationship Generator went to work on our behalf, and it created a social network for us.

Then we changed to another school or left the world of education altogether, and what happened? How many of those school relationships kept going, and how many withered and died? Dig out your school yearbooks and leaf through them. How many of the friends who wrote those long, heartfelt notes are you still in touch with? A few of those relationships may have survived, or even grown and developed. But chances are, most of them are only a distant memory. (Perhaps they weren't dead, but merely dormant—look at Facebook!)

From the First Age, we moved on to the Second Age, and the world of work. Luckily, there was *another* Automatic Relationship Generator whirring away in that world, too. We were thrown into frequent contact with another group of people, again sharing similar circumstances and activities. The Automatic Relationship Generator took over and built another social network for us.

In the Second Age, we had other responsibilities, outside of work, that operated in a similar way. Children (if we had them) tend to pull us into environments with their own Automatic Relationship Generators: the neighborhood, sports teams, school events, a religious community, and so on. These generators kept creating social networks for us. How convenient.

Often, as we progress through the Second Age, we move around. New jobs, new neighborhoods, new towns, new states. Kids get older, change schools, find new interests; they drop old friends (and their parents, who may be our friends) and take up with new ones. How many of those relationships kept going? How many withered and died? Again, we're fortunate (or dedicated and loyal) if more than a few of those friendships stay active. Can you see a *pattern* emerging here?

There Is No Automatic Relationship Generator in Retirement!

When you think about retirement, you may not give much thought to your social connections. After all, you've made life transitions before. And even though you've left friends behind before, you've always made new ones, haven't you? We don't stop to realize that school, work, parenting, and other responsibilities have been our Automatic Relationship Generators. But when we enter a life stage that doesn't have those responsibilities—and those natural social connections—what will happen *then*?

You have, of course, been building deep, long-term relationships with friends and family members that will continue with you into your next stage of life. And, depending on how your life is structured, you may have some of those shared similar circumstances and daily activities that will get the Automatic Relationship Generator up and running again. Or you may not. (For some retirees, television or the Internet becomes an Automatic Relationship Generator. They build relationships with people who aren't real or who aren't real enough to have true relationships with.) Because most of us consider our personal relationships to be the most rewarding part of our lives, it's worth a little *planning* to have plenty of good ones in it, wouldn't you say?

What Is a Relationship, Anyway?

To design a new retirement that features social engagement instead of disengagement, we need to look at the structure of relationships, not so much from an emotional perspective as from a social science perspective. (Emotions are in there, though, whether we acknowledge them or not!) First of all, the potential variety of relationships is endless. It could take *lifetimes* to truly experience them all: parent, child, sibling, friend, lover, confidante, mentor, cheerleader, partner, caregiver—you could go on and on. You could compile another list of less personal, more instrumental relationships, too: colleague, teammate, coworker, client, vendor, supervisor, collaborator, neighbor, and so on. You could even compile a list of contentious relationships that are mostly based on friction, but let's focus instead on supportive ones.

Trust and Reciprocity

Robert Putnam, a sociologist at Harvard, has an idea about what all strong and healthy relationships share. Even though they're endlessly different, they're all the same in one basic respect: They're based on trust and reciprocity. Those two factors, together, are the basis for the kinds of relationships that most of us want to create in the Third Age.

The first factor, trust, is a familiar concept. It's almost impossible to have a positive relationship with someone you don't trust. The word *trust* is frequently used in an adjective form to describe a relationship; that is, a trusted friend, a trusted source, a trusted teacher or counselor.

You want relationships with people you feel are trustworthy. But you have different levels of trust for different relationships. You may trust the paperboy to have your paper on the doorstep at 7:00 A.M.; you may also trust your adult child to make medical decisions for you if you're in a coma and on life support. Those are two very different *levels* of trust. Also, trust can have different qualities, even at the same level. Trusting your lover with your heart and trusting your cardiac surgeon with your heart are both very high levels of trust. But each has a different quality. What about the second factor, reciprocity? That's not as familiar a word. But we all know what it means when it comes to relationships. If you do something for someone and they don't reciprocate, you may not do something for them again. You don't build a relationship, in that case. Or perhaps you've had a relationship that was reciprocal and then one of you stopped reciprocating and the relationship changed. Reciprocation could be emotional support, money, information, food, communication, back rubs, understanding, or whatever. (Remember the reciprocal exchange within family members in retirement economics?) And it doesn't have to be like for like; it can be mix and match. The bottom line is this: You know it when you're getting it, and you know it when you ain't getting it. That's reciprocity.

Bonding and Bridging

There's another important thing to know about relationships, and it relates even more particularly to Third Age planning. Putnam also suggests that there are two broad types: bonding relationships and bridging relationships. This is a bit of a simplification, because relationships can exist somewhere along a continuum between them rather than at just one end or the other. But it's a good way to start thinking about your relationships for the next stage of life (and right now, too).

Bonding relationships are the ones you have with people who are *like you*. You can make anything you want of "people who are like you." You're the only judge of which people in your social network are "like you." However you identify this, you feel that these people are more like you, and you bond with them. Bonding means that they are a source of support for you. (There are lots of different kinds of support: emotional, financial, logistical, informational—think of all the kinds you've given and received.) These people also provide what is sometimes called your *strong ties*.

What about the people in your social network who are not like you? Those are the people with whom you're more likely to have a bridging relationship—that is, you are, in effect, crossing over your *differences* to have the relationship. You rely on these people for information rather than support. The very fact that they're not like you means that they probably have different sources of information than you have. People who are more like you are more likely to have the same sources of information that you do, which isn't that helpful! By bridging out, you tap into additional sources of information. These people provide what are sometimes called your *weak ties*.

A strong social network for making life transitions, including the Third Age and your retirement, has both types: bonding relationships for support, and bridging relationships for information. Without your social network, you'd be all alone and in the dark. You can easily think of times when you've drawn on your social network for *support*, be it emotional, financial, or logistical. And you can easily think of times when you've drawn on your social network for *information* about getting a job, deciding where to live, or choosing which products or services to buy. You'll need to do this for the new retirement, too. This is especially true if you may be looking for a job; one of your pillars of retirement income, remember, is Keep Working. The best jobs usually come from social networking, *not* from job listings! So totally aside from preventing loneliness, having a strong social network—relationships—helps you get along in the world. That's why you need to do some planning, well in advance, to ensure that you'll have a network you can continue to count on as you transition through life.

Build Third Age Relationships in the Second Age

At the beginning of the Second Age, we start to build relationships related to our work. The more of these relationships we develop, the more *successful* we're likely to be in our career. In fact, a good predictor of our productivity on the job is whether we have a best friend at work for support or information or both. And by the same token, the more successful we are in our career, the more our relationships can end up being concentrated among people we know through work, if not exclusively at work. That's the way it is for most of the years we spend in the Second Age, and it's a *good* thing.

But when we approach the end of our career, if a big part of our social network is *still* concentrated among people we know through work (rather than outside of work), we may be headed for trouble. Most of those work-related relationships will fade away. So as you get closer to the end of your career, it makes sense to do two things:

1. Consciously build social networks that are not related to your job. Those relationships won't be affected when you retire the way that work relationships will be. If anything, they may be affected in a positive way, because you'll have more time and energy to devote to them after you retire.

2. Consciously build deeper relationships with some of the people in your job-related social network. Some of these folks have the potential for being your lifelong friends. But if you wait until after you leave that job, you may have lost your chance. It's easier to build lasting relationships with these potential lifelong friends while you're still working with them, particularly if you make the effort to share time outside of work. By putting in the time and energy to establish relationships that extend beyond the work environment, you increase the likelihood that the relationships will survive when you leave the workplace.

THREE LEVELS OF RETIREMENT RELATIONSHIPS

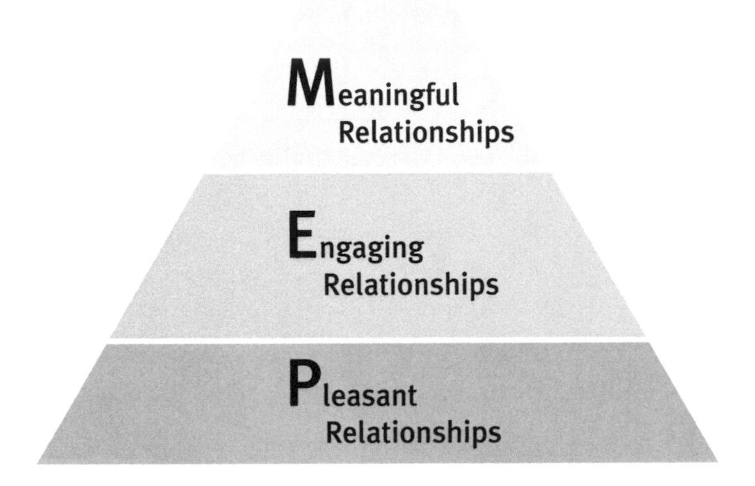

Three Levels of Social Connections

Now that you know about the Three Levels of Retirement Happiness, introduced in the last chapter, you can apply the same thinking to the happiness that you get from your social connections and relationships. When you think back on the ones in your life that have brought you the most happiness, you can even see which type. Some were mostly *fun*, some were mostly *engaging*, and some were mostly *meaningful*. And it stands to reason that some of your best relationships embraced all three approaches to happiness. A trifecta!

Even though these relationships may have originated through the Automatic Relationship Generators in the worlds of education or work, they went on to become rewarding and valued because they incorporated your approaches to happiness. Because this process has been operating in your life already, imagine how it might operate in the new retirement, too. Remember, there is no Automatic Relationship Generator in retirement.

If you can, you'd probably like to preserve your relationships from your career and also build new relationships for the next stage of life, whatever it ends up being. How might that happen? Let's apply the Three Levels of Retirement Happiness:

- **First Level.** This level is about pleasant, lighthearted fun, and some of your work relationships are built on just having a good time. These are people that you like hanging out with, and you may have common interests outside of work. Work relationships based on pleasure may be more likely to survive if they expand to the second level (engagement) or the third level (meaning); for example, you both take up a challenging hobby together (for shared engagement) or join a community project or political organization (for a shared sense of meaning).
- **Second Level.** This level is about engagement, or using your skills and strengths for a well-matched challenge. These relationships are based on shared flow experiences, which can definitely happen in some jobs. When you're really in sync with coworkers on a project, you can develop this kind of strong relationship. But when you leave that work, that shared flow generally disappears along with the shared challenge.
- **Third Level.** This level is about meaning, or feeling that you're in the service of something larger than yourself. If you and your coworkers really care about the greater purpose of your work, that creates a bond. This could be especially true if you consider your work to be a type of calling. Of course, retirement changes that; it takes you out of the context in which you're sharing that sense of meaning. What might these relationships be based on after you no longer work together? The following exercise will help you identify three examples of involvement for building relationships based on the three levels of happiness.

BUILDING MY SOCIAL RELATIONSHIPS

The worlds of education and work usually function as Automatic Relationship Generators, creating social relationships through shared daily activities with other people. These relationships bring happiness in the form of pleasure, engagement, meaning, or some combination of these.

Because the world of retirement doesn't have an Automatic Relationship Generator, to have the social relationships that you want in retirement you need to identify your own relationship generators: life activities, memberships, or environments that perform a social function similar to that of education or work. Getting involved in these creates the shared activities from which relationships grow.

For each of the Three Levels of Retirement Happiness, you can identify examples that would be likely to create and build social relationships. When you think about building these relationships from the perspective of the three levels, you're thinking about involvement in activities, memberships, and environments based on your values, strengths, and interests.

Involvement in activities, memberships, or environments based on your values is more likely to create meaningful relationships. Involvement that's based on using or developing your strengths is more likely to create engaged relationships. Involvement based on pursuing your interests is more likely to create pleasant relationships. Of course, all forms of involvement, and all social relationships, can develop on all three levels.

Beginning with the general list that follows, think of specific examples that could provide opportunities for social involvement during your next stage of life. Try to think of three or four opportunities for each of the levels. You will then choose one from each level as an example of the kind of involvement you'd like to explore and write them in the Life Circles exercise on page 228.

Examples of Relationship-Building Opportunities

Alumni organizations
Athletic teams
Charitable organizations
Educational opportunities
Employment
Environmental groups
Extended family
Faith communities
Performing arts organizations
Political organizations
Service clubs

Meaningful Relationships

What types of involvement would I like to explore, based on my values? These are social activities, memberships, or environments that would offer an opportunity to serve something larger than myself and could create a shared sense of purpose with other people.

______________________ ______________________

______________________ ______________________

______________________ ______________________

Engaging Relationships

What types of involvement would I like to explore, based on using or developing my strengths? These are social activities, memberships, or environments that would present a challenge and could create a shared sense of flow with other people.

______________________ ______________________

______________________ ______________________

______________________ ______________________

Pleasant Relationships

What types of involvement would I like to explore, based on just having fun? These are social activities, memberships, or environments that allow me to pursue my interests and could create a shared sense of enjoyment with other people.

______________________ ______________________

______________________ ______________________

______________________ ______________________

LIFE CIRCLES EXERCISE

Now choose one specific example from each of the levels—meaningful (M), engaging (E), and pleasant (P)—and write it on your Life Circle to use for your One Piece of Paper in chapter eleven.

My Ideal Retirement includes building these social relationships:

You Can Choose Your Friends, but You Can't Choose Your Family

For some, it may feel weird to contemplate where and how social connections and relationships might be built in retirement. They may wonder whether deliberately taking this action means they're being insincere or manipulative. Is it like being a social climber or using other people? The answer is ABSOLUTELY NOT. On the contrary! Building genuine relationships based on shared pleasures, shared engagement, or shared meaning is a very sincere and respectful way to connect with fellow human beings. It's at least as honest and respectful as convenience, wouldn't you say?

As is the case with any friendship, the underlying requirement for building and maintaining relationships this way is genuine connection. Aside from the shared experience of happiness, if the genuine connection is there, then it's there. If it's not, it's not. By using the three levels as a starting point, at least we know where to look.

What about people who just happen to have DNA that's very similar to our own? The old saying "You can choose your friends, but you can't choose your family" implies that we like our friends better. After all, we build those relationships from scratch. If our friendships don't operate on at least one of the levels of happiness, they don't endure.

But that may be true of our families as well. We all know that family relationships can become estranged—between parents and children, or among siblings. Perhaps the family relationships that endure are operating on the three levels, too. Many people use the greater time and freedom of the Third Age to reconnect with family. The three levels can even be a guide for connecting with family, and with old friends, too. In particular, this is a time of life to pay attention to what's most *meaningful* to you!

Retirement with That Special Someone

In retirement, there's one family relationship that's in a category all its own. It sometimes even seems to transcend the requirements of trust and reciprocity. Ideally, it anchors the bonding end of the bonding and bridging continuum. And it has probably operated, at various times, on each of the three levels. This is, of course, your relationship with your significant other. There are many variations on this type of relationship, but for simplicity we'll use the terms *marriage* and *spouse*, because they are the most common. (Even if you don't have a significant other at the moment, keep reading. Who knows what the future may bring?)

One way to describe what happens to our relationship with our significant other in retirement is *marriage on steroids*. It becomes a bigger version of itself. Whatever a marriage is like before retirement, left to its own devices, tends to become *more* that way in retirement. A marriage that's harmonious and loving can tend to become more harmonious and loving. A marriage that's discordant and intolerant can tend to become more discordant and intolerant.

Why? It's a simple matter of space and time. It's the laws of physics, applied to marriage. Let's assume that at least one marriage partner works outside the home—and these days, often both do. When the partners are still in full-productivity mode, they each have their own space at work and a space at home. On a daily basis, the two partners occupy two or three distinct locations in space. Also, because of the time allocated to work, the time that they spend interacting with each other is limited.

How are space and time altered in retirement? First, space is compressed. Instead of having two or three spaces to occupy, both partners occupy the *same* space—home. Second, time is expanded. Instead of time being allocated to work, it's mostly spent *interacting* with each other. So what happens when these two highly energized particles come together in retirement? They're either attracted to one another or repelled by one another. Marriage is like physics—or maybe more like rocket science. (To the moon, Alice!) Anticipating both partners' *shifts* in space and time is an element of good life transition planning. Sometimes, what people think is an insoluble problem in physics is just a minor glitch in physical surroundings.

You've probably heard of at least one couple who were together for many years until one or both partners retired, then not long afterward, to everyone's surprise, they filed for divorce. In some cases this isn't due to the simple physics of space and time. It runs deeper. Once the two got to know each other again, they may have discovered that their interests or values had evolved in such diverging directions that they were no longer in sync. They decided that life was too short—or the retirement stage of life was too long—to put up with each other.

From a life stage planning perspective, what should you do about this possibility? If you're in a bad marriage in the Second Age, should you accept the inevitable and jettison your partner to finally have the life you want in the freedom of the Third Age? Or should you try to repair that troubled relationship in advance, so it has a better chance of surviving the concentrated conditions of retirement? Each marriage is unique, and you could be happily surprised. There are marriages that limp along during the couple's work life, languishing from inattention, and then become revitalized through conscious application of the more abundant time and energy of the Third Age. A new stage of life was *exactly* what the marriage needed!

When it comes to building a strong partner relationship, the stakes are high. No matter how socially engaged we are in the Third Age, as we approach the Fourth Age, our social circles inevitably become smaller. Our worlds shrink, our activity levels decline, we spend more and more time at home and in the company of our spouse. This tends to happen even for those of us who are relatively healthy and active. Our relationship with our spouse becomes a larger and larger part of our lives.

With age comes infirmity. In the Fourth Age, frequently one partner needs some type of care and the other partner provides it. The burden on the caregiver is great (and we can be thankful for the many books, groups, and other supportive resources now being devoted to the special needs of caregivers). Across the life course, many relationships are based on convenience. Becoming a caregiver is just the opposite. Nothing is more inconvenient than *caring* for another person. At the same time, *needing care* from another is very inconvenient, too. Our society values and promotes independence, and the loss of independence isn't an easy adjustment. It's not easy for either partner.

For a moment, think about your relationships—especially your marriage—in the Fourth Age. Imagine the inconvenience (and burden) of being the caregiver and also the inconvenience (and loss) of being the one who needs care.

Now stop for a moment to recognize your spouse as the person *most willing* to care for you, should that need arise. (This could apply to a caregiver who is not a spouse, too.) Pause to consider what that means, and to reflect on your relationship with that person in the following way:

1. Reconnect with what made the two of you fall in love with each other in the first place. What special chemistry brought you together so strongly? That's what grew into this willingness to care for you.
2. Think of all of the times that your spouse has supported you, comforted you, and seen the best in you over the years. Remember that your spouse has *already* been your caregiver, in many other ways.
3. Imagine how grateful you would feel in the future, knowing that your spouse has truly come to your aid. Of course, you don't need to wait to feel this gratitude. You can begin feeling it today and every day that the two of you are together. Ideally, you have a spouse who is your truest and closest companion on your journey.

Although your social connections and relationships are absolutely essential to your well-being, they are still only one part. The real power of designing your next stage of life is in bringing all the parts together. The final chapter of this book is where you'll be able to collect the best of all these parts to create a unifying vision for the retirement you want to have.

"What a long time it can take to become the person one has always been."

—Parker Palmer, American author, educator, and activist

Chapter ELEVEN

The New Retirement—an Undivided Life

The modern world has encouraged us to live *divided lives*. One division is the *time* of our lives, segmented into efficient industrial boxes called education, work, and retirement. Another division is the *why* of our lives, split between our own core values and the larger forces at work in society. Another is the *what* of our lives, represented in the division of well-being into prosperity, health, and happiness. It's true that these divisions help us understand what's going on and make our way in the world. But it's also true that we yearn for wholeness. We yearn for completeness. We yearn for integrity.

The new retirement is our opportunity to have what we yearn for. It's our opportunity to live an *undivided life*. That's why this chapter is about integrating all the parts of life.

As you've worked on the chapter exercises, you've been filling in the circles that represent parts of the life you want to live. Now you'll bring all the circles together to create a larger overall picture of your Ideal Retirement. At this point, I hope you have done the exercises and aren't merely *reading* this book! If you haven't done them yet, go back now and fill them in quickly, as a first draft. You can always get more detailed later.

Let's review the elements: The outer circles represent six fields of knowledge that relate to six parts of your life (and also six chapters of this book). These are paired up to create the three dimensions of well-being: prosperity, health, and happiness. The icon in each outer circle represents a key idea related to that element and chapter. Each chapter offered an exercise that allowed you to fill in a Life Circle at the end. The exercise provided a process, but you provided the content. So the circles are really more about you than they are about those fields of retirement knowledge. The picture of the Ideal Retirement that you're creating is really a picture of *you*!

THE ELEMENTS OF YOUR IDEAL RETIREMENT

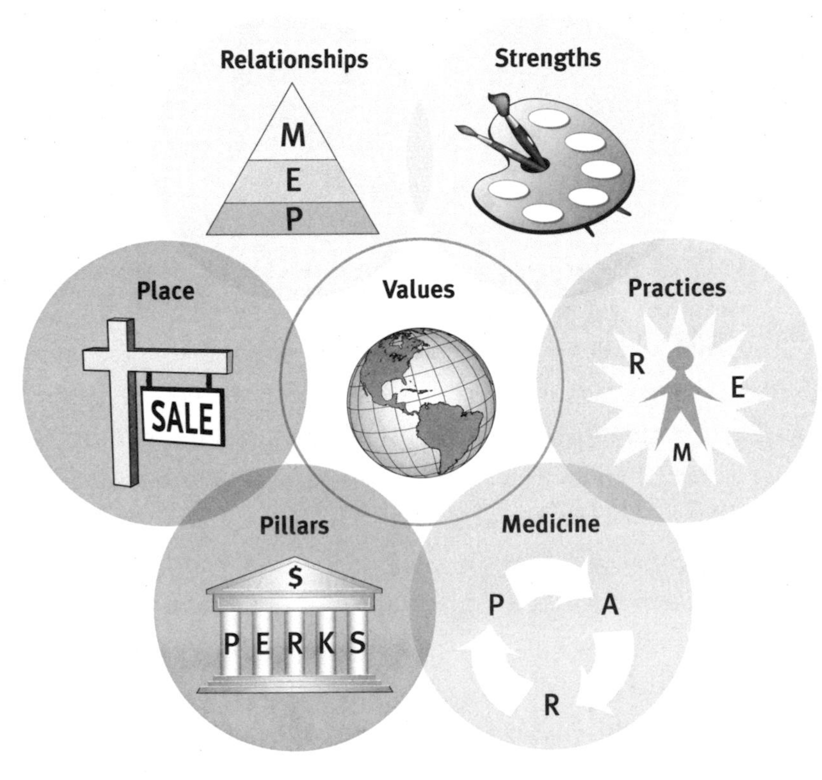

The icon for the central circle is a picture of the world, to remind you to *activate* your values in your everyday world. Your values are at the center, because hopefully they're at the center of your life. The exercises in chapter three gave you a taste of them. The more deeply you get to know them, though, the more you can bring your other circles into alignment with them. You can consciously use your values to help you make decisions in all the other circles—to create your own unique version of well-being.

This values-based guidance is crucial, because there aren't obvious, objective answers to all your retirement planning questions in the six outer circles. Based on the knowledge in each field, some decisions are obviously the right ones. But for other decisions, there is no objective standard, no right or wrong, no shining truth. Your answers will be subjective and personal. You really need to design your next stage of life from the inside out.

Putting Your Life Circles Together

You can choose from a variety of methods to assemble the picture of your Ideal Retirement. If you wrote your answers in the pages in this book, just flip back to each of those exercises to get your answers for the fill-in-the-blanks exercise that follows. If you wrote your answers on photocopies of the exercises, you can assemble those Life Circle sheets onto a larger sheet of paper or poster board. Just paste or tape them on the appropriate spots. Being the resourceful and adaptable person that you are, you may think of even more interesting ways to assemble your complete picture.

Whichever methods you use, the point is to create that One Piece of Paper that allows you to see the *whole picture at once*. Seeing a visual representation of these connected elements helps create a compelling vision of the retirement life that you really want.

Retirement planning has traditionally focused on just one dimension—financial. When it has included others, it's been arbitrary—there hasn't been a natural way to select, and then connect, the dimensions. They've typically been isolated from one another. And when we plan for each part of life in isolation, it's easier for them to be out of sync with each other. When that happens, we may not be able to really see it, but at some level we'll probably feel it. Because we're wired to want all three dimensions of well-being, being able to finally see it all *connected* on our One Piece of Paper can be a real breakthrough. It's a way to get our lives in sync!

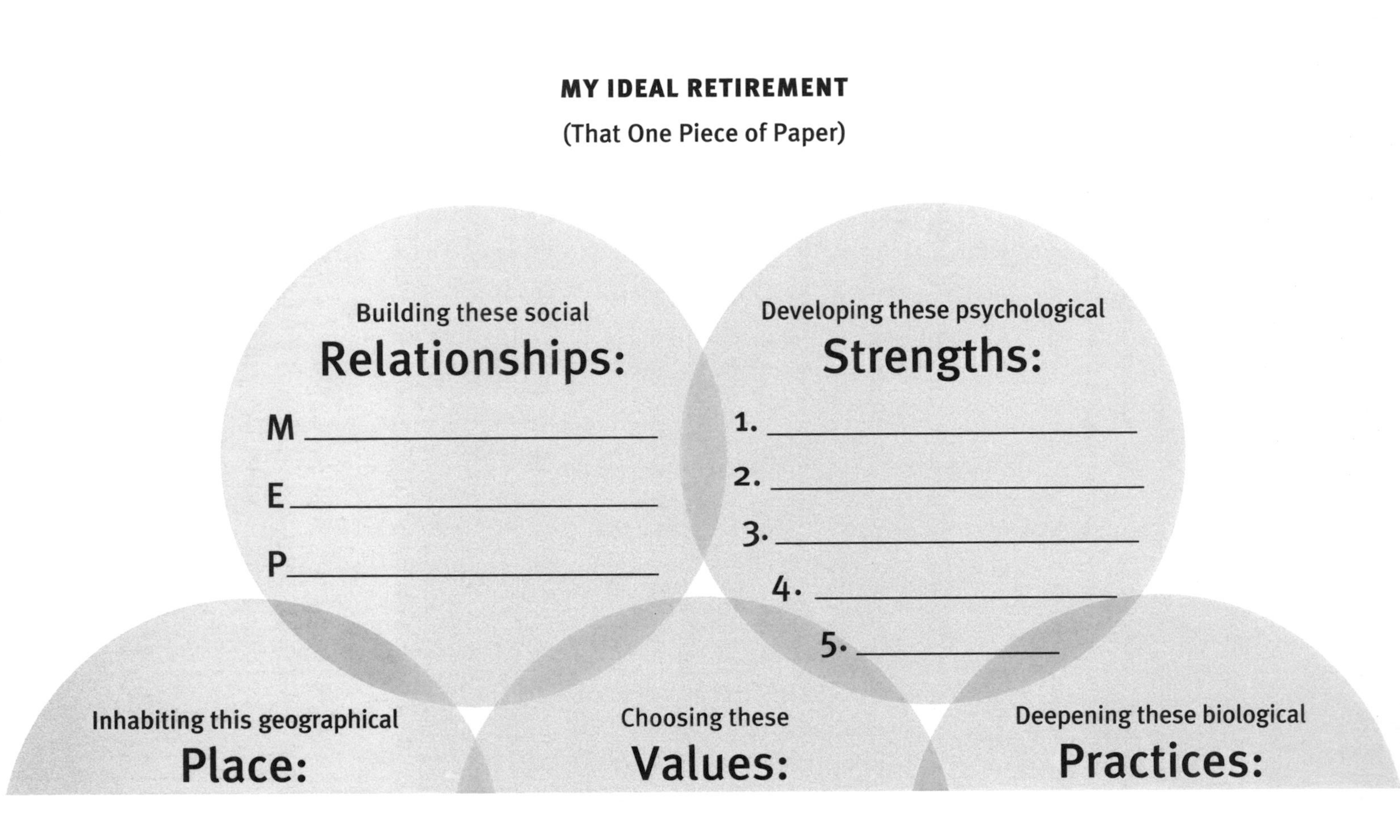
MY IDEAL RETIREMENT
(That One Piece of Paper)
Building these social
Relationships:
M
E
P
Developing these psychological
Strengths:
1.
2.
3.
4.
5.
Inhabiting this geographical
Place:
Choosing these
Values:
Deepening these biological
Practices:

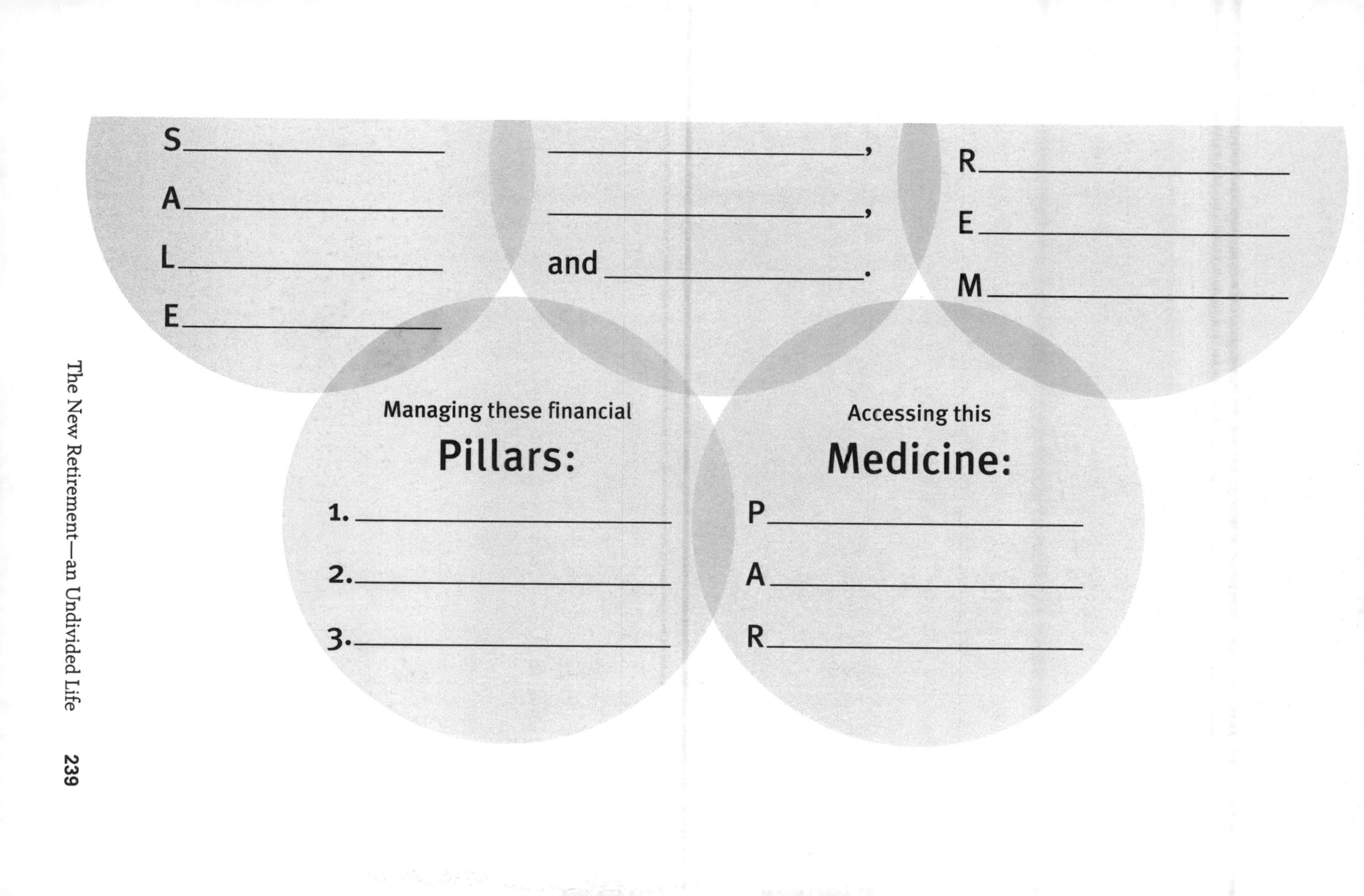

S______
A______
L______
E______
______,
______,
and ______.
R______
E______
M______
Managing these financial
Pillars:
1. ______
2. ______
3. ______
Accessing this
Medicine:
P______
A______
R______

For our life design, some of the easiest connections to spot are between adjacent circles. We've already seen the close connections between the two elements that make up each dimension of well-being: biological and medical, psychological and social, geographical and financial. But there are also many close connections between the other *adjacent* elements.

For example, geographical and social are next to each other because they have a strong connection. Remember "social is spatial, and spatial is social"? Also, financial and medical are next to each other, and it's obvious why—access to medical care is usually based on finance. Finally, psychology and biology are next to each other because psychology has a strong biological aspect. And on a practical level, we know that psychology has an effect on biology, too: Research is starting to show that happier people tend to be healthier. So these connections between the six circles are easy to see, even when they're from different dimensions of well-being. But *all* the circles are connected in our lives, even if they're on opposite sides of the Well-Being Model.

The assembled picture of your Ideal Retirement as seven circles is a unique and powerful planning tool. However, you can go beyond seeing it as seven circles to seeing it as an integrated whole. The purpose of the seven circles isn't to *break down* your planning into smaller parts—modern life does that already. No, the purpose is to help you *put it all back together.* As an integrated whole, you might think of your picture as:

- a retirement dream.
- a strategic plan.
- a treasure map.
- a life plan.
- a vision.

Or use any other term that comes to mind and makes sense for you.

Your Retirement Calling

Could this picture of your Ideal Retirement offer something more? Might it offer a clue to your *calling* in retirement? If you think that you may have had a calling, you should know that it's not always easy to find it again in later life. Even though the Third Age can offer the greatest freedom, we may have trouble knowing what that freedom is for. Sometimes it's actually easier to hear our calling earlier in life. Life is generally simpler then. Things get much more complex as the responsibilities pile up on us in the Second Age. We can become so strongly conditioned by what *society* wants that we sometimes mistake it for what *we* want. Then when we get to the Third Age, the marketing messages go into overdrive, selling us prefabricated lifestyles based on products and services. It's not easy to hearken back to the small voice of calling that we may have first heard in the First Age. But we probably did hear a call, and on some level still yearn to fulfill it. It may be why we're still here.

So—why *are* you still here?

Is it because there's still something important left for you to do? As you get closer to retirement and realize the freedom that it brings, it may become easier to get a sense of your calling.

When you look at the picture of your Ideal Retirement, does it give you a hint about some contribution that you still want to make? That contribution could be connected to one of your circles. Or it might be inspired by your *total* picture rather than being just one part of your picture. Either way, something calls to you, beckons you, draws you toward it. You're willing to do whatever is necessary to get there. In fact, you'd like to start tomorrow!

On the other hand, when you look at your Ideal Retirement, it might look wonderful but doesn't feel like a calling. That's OK. Maybe your next stage of life is still too far away for you, and this exercise is more like planning than it is like living. Or maybe your circles are about important things but not necessarily connected to your core values at the center. Values are usually where motivation comes from. To get closer, try *activating* your values more in your daily life now and see how it feels!

Remember that your picture is a work in progress; it is always open to revision as you reflect more on what you truly want.

That means that finding your retirement calling isn't a onetime, now-or-never deal. The ability to look for your heart's desire and hear a call improves with practice. In doing these exercises, you may be tapping into parts of yourself you haven't been in touch with for a while. Maybe not since your First Age. As you continue to visualize your Third Age, you'll get better and better at it, and you may discover that the picture of your Ideal Retirement contains a calling.

Whether you've identified a calling or not, there may be some changes you should make to your picture right now. Would you like to change or add something in any of your circles? Is there a name, a title, or a label that you'd like to give this picture? A phrase, a sentence, or even a paragraph that you could add that would be meaningful to you? You can do any of these things anytime you want. It's your picture!

Share Your Picture with Your Dream Team

Who's coming with you to the next stage of life? Some companions? Some helpers? Should you let them in on part of your picture? Let's see who those folks might be.

Your companions are the people with whom you have personal relationships. If you have a spouse or significant other, that loved one should know about your picture. It will help immensely if your partner is also creating a picture of his or her Ideal Retirement. Initially, it's better to do these exercises separately and create your own individual pictures. When some couples work together, one partner can end up driving the process, and the other doesn't get enough of a voice. It's important for each of you to have your own authentic vision that comes from your own heart, then put your hearts (and minds) together. You'll want to get on the same page—or at least adjoining pages. Two compatible pictures can be even more powerful than one!

Beyond your spouse or significant other, who else might be your companions? Your children? Your parents, if they're alive? Your best friends? Who are the people you most want to spend time with in your retirement?

You might do some of them a great service by inspiring them to create their own picture. But at the very least, they'll gain a deeper understanding of you, what's most important to you, and where you're headed on your journey. When you become really clear about what you want and other people can see it too, they may even want to help you. (Although you may have some companions who tend to be jealous, or naysayers. You're the best judge of who will help and who might hinder you.) Who knows what wonderful things might happen when you share your picture?

You may have some helpers and advisors, too. They provide assistance along the way, especially at key points. Do you have, or can you imagine having, any of these helpers?

- Accountant
- Alternative medical practitioner
- Attorney
- Benefits counselor
- Career counselor
- Financial planner
- Human resource professional
- Life coach
- Medical doctor
- Personal trainer
- Realtor
- Religious or spiritual guide
- Therapist, counselor, or psychologist

You may choose to share the full picture with them, but more likely you'll just share the part that's relevant to them. Some of these will be true helpers who genuinely want to assist you. Of these well-meaning helpers, some are competent, others less so, but at least they have your best interests at heart. However, along the way you may discover others who appear in the *guise* of a helper but seek only to serve themselves. You may need to be careful sharing much of your vision with them until you know whether you can trust them.

Returning to the Everyday World

How do you bring this vision back with you into the everyday world? Even when you gain clarity and can see what you really want, it's not always so easy to keep it alive. But it is essential for designing your next stage of life, because the everyday world is where you actually *prepare* for retirement. That's where you gain the knowledge and make the changes in your life that will put you on the path to your Ideal Retirement. The more clearly you hold on to that vision, the more your day-to-day planning and preparations will come into alignment with it.

There are three effective approaches to bringing the vision of your Ideal Retirement into your everyday life: the no-brainer approach, the left-brain approach, and the right-brain approach. Although quite different from one another, they share a common perspective that *retirement is not a problem to be solved, but an opportunity to be created.* (A problem-solving and fixing perspective works well for things like machines. When a machine is working and then malfunctions, troubleshooting is the way to get it back up and running. But a life stage isn't like that at all. You're not troubleshooting it; you're creating it.)

Brief descriptions of the three approaches follow, and you'll find instructions and worksheets for using each at the end of this chapter.

1. The No-Brainer Approach

Is your brain tired after your long journey through this book? Rest assured, this approach doesn't take a lot of hard thinking. (Although it's actually very smart!) It's a no-brainer only because it's such an obviously good idea. This approach comes from the psychology of human performance, and it has been used by athletes for many years. It's based on the idea that we don't always need to think consciously about something we want to achieve—we can turn it over to our automatic, unconscious mind. This approach brings your vision into everyday life in three distinct ways: as pictures, words, and feelings. If you want to try just one approach right now, this is the one for you.

On the other hand, if you're up for a bit more thinking, try one of the other two approaches. They come from a very different source—organization management. Management is a discipline that coordinates a wide variety of disparate elements to reach a goal. That sounds a bit like retirement planning, doesn't it?

2. The Right-Brain Approach

Do you see yourself as a right-brain person? Are you intuitive, creative, and focused on the big picture? If so, this may be the approach for you. It's loosely based on appreciative inquiry, a revolutionary field of organizational development. Appreciative inquiry looks for the best in people, searches for their highest values and abilities, and helps them expand. Using this approach, you discover positive experiences grounded in the past, dream of an even better future, design conditions that make that future possible, and then deliver it through inspired action. If you want an approach that increases your energy and helps you see new options, try this one!

3. The Left-Brain Approach

Do you think of yourself as a left-brain person? Are you logical, linear, and focused on the details? This could be your ideal approach. It's loosely based on an approach for strategic planning and execution called the Balanced Scorecard. This system creates performance standards not only for financial assets but also for nonfinancial ones. By establishing objectives, measures, targets, and initiatives across multiple domains, it offers quantitative feedback from a balanced perspective.

You're the sole judge of which of these three approaches is best for you. At different times you may even use all of them. But please try at least one as soon as you finish this chapter, before you get caught up in those day-to-day realities again. You wouldn't want all of your hard work to be lost!

Don't Wait Until Retirement to Live Your Ideal Life

Here's one final thought for you, dear reader: You can begin bringing your life into more alignment with your core values right away! You can begin doing all the things you imagined in all of your circles, to greater and lesser degrees. Instead of living a divided life, you begin living an undivided life—you don't need to wait until retirement.

Wouldn't that be *grand*?

In the words of American mythologist Joseph Campbell: "If you follow your bliss, you put yourself on a kind of track that has been there all the while, waiting for you, and the life that you ought to be living is the one you are living."

BRINGING THE VISION OF YOUR IDEAL RETIREMENT INTO THE EVERYDAY WORLD

The No-Brainer Approach: Visualization and Affirmations

This approach brings the vision of your Ideal Retirement alive in three distinct ways: as pictures, words, and feelings. Follow these three simple steps. You may want to use a blank sheet of paper to record your answers and ideas.

Pictures. Expand or embellish the picture of your Ideal Retirement just as you please, with clippings from magazines, fine-art reproductions, or your own drawings. Then keep it where you can see it easily and refer back to it often. Where might that be? Your office wall? Your refrigerator? In front of your exercise equipment? Where you sit to pay the bills? Over time, you'll notice that the words and images have seeped into your subconscious, forming an internal image of your Ideal Retirement that is more portable—and powerful—than That One Piece of Paper. The goal is to keep visualizing it in as much detail as possible.

Words. Are you familiar with affirmations? These are statements in the present tense about conditions and accomplishments you would like to realize in your life. You can use the terms, phrases, and statements from all of your Life Circles to create your own affirmations—a set of statements about your retirement. Be as specific and clear as possible, and state them in the present tense. Although there are all kinds of affirmations out there, in self-help books, magazine articles, websites, greeting cards, and so on, those that come from you will be a perfect fit. They will feel natural, will be easy for you to memorize and repeat to yourself every day, and they can have a significant positive effect. Internalizing those words makes them even more powerful than just displaying them on your picture. Repeat some of your affirmations several times every day—indeed, anytime you think of them—until they become automatic.

Feelings. Positive feelings in your body about your Ideal Retirement are usually triggered by your pictures or words (whether external or internal). With a little practice, you can learn to cultivate those positive feelings and connect them strongly to your pictures and to your affirmations. The stronger your positive feelings, the more effective this approach will be. So when you use your visualizations and affirmations, remember to recognize and welcome these positive feelings. Your goal is to feel confident and excited when you think about your retirement. Practicing the no-brainer approach all by itself will bring you closer to your vision, and it will also bring your vision closer to you. You'll find yourself acquiring knowledge and accumulating resources without consciously planning to do so. Before you know it, you'll catch yourself taking actions that move you in the direction of your Ideal Retirement.

The Right-Brain Approach: Appreciative Inquiry

Appreciative inquiry helps you discover positive experiences grounded in the past, dream of an even better future, design conditions that make that future possible, and then deliver it through inspired action. You'll complete this process separately for each element of your Life Circles, beginning with the ones that give you the most pride in your accomplishments. Use a blank sheet of paper to record your answers and ideas.

Choose the first circle that you'd like to learn about and explore. Regardless of how well you think the planning and preparations have been going for this circle, you will focus on what has worked, not what hasn't. And no matter how much success you feel there has been already, you'll focus specifically and completely on what you want more of.

Discover. Think back to a specific time when things were going well in this element. Remember one of your high points or a peak experience. What were you grateful for or excited about? What did you do that was so successful? How did that make you feel? What made that success possible? What was the root cause of your success?

Dream. Now, based on your Life Circles exercise, consider the role this element plays in your Retirement Well-Being. What is the best possible future for this element? What would that future feel like?

Design. Now, keep in mind what has really worked in the past for this element when things have gone well. To bring about that best possible future, what values or principles would you need to act from? What conditions would you need to create?

Deliver. Brainstorm a wide variety of actions that you could possibly take. Generate options that are exciting but also tangible. Which actions would be a stretch for you but that you would feel confident about taking? Which actions would be the most inspiring to take and follow through on? What structure could you put in place to support those actions? What could you celebrate as a result of taking those actions successfully?

You can expect the actions you take as a result of this exercise to lead to more experiences of success. You can make them part of another discover, dream, design, and deliver exercise. You can consciously create a virtuous cycle that repeats itself.

The Left-Brain Approach: The Balanced Scorecard

The balanced scorecard is an approach for strategic planning that creates performance measures not only for financial assets but also for nonfinancial ones. By establishing objectives, measures, and initiatives across multiple elements, it offers feedback on your progress from a balanced perspective.

For designing your retirement, your strategy is built upon your core values. This worksheet will help you implement your strategy across the six elements of your Life Circles.

First, as a reminder, list your three core values:

____,

____,

and ____.

Second, consider (1) the objectives you can identify that will bring you closer to your Ideal Retirement, (2) how you might measure your progress toward the objectives, and (3) what initiatives you can take to get there.

Objectives. When you filled in each of your Life Circles, you identified a state that you want to achieve for your Ideal Retirement. You can probably identify many other intermediate objectives that could lead up to it. Some of your objectives will be about accomplishing something specific, but many could be about learning, investigating, or making future plans.

And for all six elements, a worthy interim objective is simply sharing your goals and plans with someone!

Here are examples for each Life Circle.

Geographic: Researching potential retirement places; evaluating your existing place; taking a vacation or visiting people you know; making lifetime home improvements; interviewing a realtor about trends and opportunities.

Financial: Checking your Social Security projections; calculating how much income you'll need; retaining a financial planner; setting up an autopilot for saving or investing; reaching an account balance goal.

Biological: Calculating your biological age; establishing a practice through a club or class, or tracking your frequency of participation; replacing an unhealthy habit with a healthy one; reaching a target weight, fitness measure, or lab result.

Medical: Researching the terms of your retirement medical plan; comparing Medicare Part D or other prescription plans; investigating your Veteran's Administration benefits; getting age-appropriate medical screenings or tests; completing a medical power of attorney; interviewing a new potential doctor or practitioner.

Psychological: Taking the VIA survey online; shifting job responsibilities to better use your skills; exploring opportunities to use strengths outside of work; trying a new hobby for enjoyment; exploring a potentially meaningful responsibility or opportunity; testing the waters for engaging retirement work.

Social: Meeting with coworkers outside of work; looking up old friends; investigating a club or other membership; volunteering for an organization to meet new people; joining an athletic team; making specific arrangements to help family or friends.

Measures. How can you measure your progress toward each objective? It could have a numerical measure, as for a financial account or a biological test. If it's a goal for participation in appealing groups or activities, it could be a simple count of memberships or dates. You can't measure your progress toward some objectives numerically, but you should be able to identify milestones that show you're getting closer to your objective. It's good to set target dates for reaching numerical goals or milestones, then celebrate or treat yourself when you get there.

Initiatives. What specific actions can you take toward your objectives that fit your numerical or milestone measures? Better yet, what systems can you put in place to automatically reach your objectives? What can you put on autopilot?

Now use the following table to record your important objectives, measures, and initiatives for each element that will bring you closer to your Ideal Retirement. You may have one or many objectives for each element.

Element	Objective	Measure	Initiative

Appendix

THE RETIREMENT WELL-BEING PROFILE

Are you on track for your best life? To find out, first rate all your areas subjectively, from your own point of view. Then go back and rate them all objectively, from an outside point of view. Consider your early years and also your later years.

		Subjective: ***How you rate your well-being in this area.***	***Objective:*** ***How an expert advisor or trusted friend would rate your well-being in this area.***	***Totals***	
Overall	Your overall level of satisfaction with your life as a whole these days.	1 2 3 4 5		____/5	
	Your level of confidence that you'll have overall well-being in retirement.	1 2 3 4 5		____/5	
		____/10			Overall ____/10
Prosperity	FINANCIAL: Income vs. expenses. Assets vs. liabilities. Adequate liquidity and insurance. Suitable investment risk. Job security. Sufficient retirement income.	1 2 3 4 5	1 2 3 4 5 6 7 8 9 10	____/15	
	GEOGRAPHICAL: Personal safety. Sense of place. Aging-in-place residence. Livable community with key services. Regional amenities and assistance.	1 2 3 4 5	1 2 3 4 5 6 7 8 9 10	____/15	
		____/10	____/20		Prosperity ____/30

Health	MEDICAL: Access to desired types of information, practitioners, institutions, treatments. Quality of care. Freedom of choice. Total out-of-pocket cost.	1 2 3 4 5	1 2 3 4 5 6 7 8 9 10	____/15	
	BIOLOGICAL: Risk assessment by personal history, family history, bio-metrics. Fitness. Life expectancy. Healthy practices for relaxation, eating, movement.	1 2 3 4 5	1 2 3 4 5 6 7 8 9 10	____/15	
		____/10	____/20		Health ____/30
Happiness	PSYCHOLOGICAL: Regularly seek experiences of fun and enjoyment, engagement and challenge, meaning and purpose. Maintain mental sharpness.	1 2 3 4 5	1 2 3 4 5 6 7 8 9 10	____/15	
	SOCIAL: Partner relationship. Strong ties with family and friends for support. Weaker ties with broad networks for information and opportunities.	1 2 3 4 5	1 2 3 4 5 6 7 8 9 10	____/15	
		____/10	____/20		Happiness ____/30
		Subjective ____/40	Objective ____/60	**Retirement Well-Being** ____/100	

Add your responses left to right and top to bottom. Both should total the same Retirement Well-Being. Rather than comparing you to others, your scores compare your areas to each other. Which are your highest and lowest? How different are your Subjective and Objective? How different are your Overall and RWB? Why? Where do you want to improve?

Resources

Well-Being Resources

Few resources exist for comprehensive, individual well-being. That's because most *comprehensive* approaches aren't individual—they're for nations or communities. Conversely, most *individual* approaches aren't comprehensive—they emphasize one dimension, like prosperity.

The first national assessment to address all three dimensions of well-being was the United Nations' Human Development Index, at www.hdr.undp.org. It uses an *objective* perspective, from economics. But a seminal individual assessment is Michael Frisch's QOLI(r), at www.QualityofLifeInventory.com. It uses a *subjective* perspective, from psychology. Most recently, the Gallup Organization developed a national assessment that uses a subjective perspective. It's now available for individuals at www.wbfinder.com. The companion book by Tom Rath and James Harter is *Wellbeing: The Five Essential Elements* (Gallup Press, 2010).

The Retirement Well-Being Profile in this book is an educational model, based on ontology and lexicology. *Ontology* relates to the essential nature of "being," while *lexicology* refers to our common understanding of the word "well-being." So the profile doesn't emphasize just one field or dimension, and also allows for both subjective and objective perspectives. If you haven't completed it yet, stop reading and go to the appendix. It only takes a few minutes!

Values Resources

For a deeply researched theory about why consumer values have been taking market share away from other values in modern society, read Juliet Schor's *The Overspent American* (HarperCollins, 1999). It's a follow-up to her earlier book, *The Overworked American* (Basic Books, 1993). To see how consumer values are penetrating the next generation, check out Schor's *Born to Buy: The Commercialized Child and the New Consumer Culture* (Scribner, 2005).

Jim Wallis' book, *Rediscovering Values: On Wall Street, Main Street, and Your Street* (Howard Books, 2010) is a call to redemption. But rather than being a perspective on "Christian values," it offers a perspective on values, from a Christian perspective.

If you think of retirement as an opportunity to gain perspective on life's biggest questions, you may want to explore Ronald Manheimer's *A Map to the End of Time: Wayfarings with Friends and Philosophers* (Norton, 1999). It introduces classical philosophy through group discussions with retirees from all walks of life.

For an erudite examination of personal values formation, see Hunter Lewis' classically inspired tome, *A Question of Values: Six Ways We Make the Personal Choices That Shape Our Lives* (Axios Press, 2000). A similarly philosophical, but more narrowly defined approach is *Money and the Meaning of Life*, by Jacob Needleman (Currency Doubleday, 1994). It delves deeply into timeless wisdom regarding money and materialism—while also offering a personal account.

If all this philosophy about consumption and values seems a bit ponderous, and you yearn for something fresh yet insightful, pick up Lee Eisenberg's *Shoptimism: Why the American Consumer Will Keep on Buying No Matter What* (Free Press, 2009). Combine it with his previous book, *The Number: What Do You Need for the Rest of Your Life, and What Will It Cost?* (Free Press, 2006), and you'll realize that first and foremost, life needs to be an interesting story!

Life Stage Resources

The deep structure that life stages are built upon is time. Philip Zimbardo and John Boyd make our implicit perceptions of time more explicit in *The Time Paradox: The New Psychology of Time That Will Change Your Life* (Free Press, 2009). It provides experimental evidence for how we perceive time, along with personal assessments and recommendations.

The most influential model of how the human life cycle plays out across time is from Erik Erikson. Although stages of child development had been studied, Erikson's eight-stage model was the first to take us all the way from birth to old age. For this very deep psychosocial model, see *Vital Involvement in Old Age* (W.W. Norton, 1994).

At the same time that Erikson was theorizing about the life cycle, Richard N. Bolles was offering practical advice for navigating it. He created the field of life planning with his lighthearted guide, *The Three Boxes of Life and How to Get Out of Them: An Introduction to Life-Work Planning* (Ten Speed Press, 1978).

As an historian looking to the future, Peter Laslett predicted that the three boxes would evolve into four ages. His landmark *A Fresh Map of Life: The Emergence of the Third Age* (Harvard University Press, 1991) is scholarly, but not intimidating.

William Sadler picked up the trail with qualitative research about people entering into this newly created life stage. His two books are a travelogue: *The Third Age: Six Principles for Personal Growth and Rejuvenation after Forty* (Da Capo Press, 2001), and *Changing Course: Navigating Life after Fifty* (The Center for Third Age Leadership Press, 2008). For more richly detailed portraits of adventurers traversing Peter Laslett's landscape, take a tour with Sara Lawrence-Lightfoot's *The Third Chapter: Passion, Risk, and Adventure in the 25 Years After 50* (Farrar, Straus and Giroux, 2009).

Like Laslett, Richard Leider and David Shapiro were intrigued by the past. But they explored the traditional wisdom of indigenous cultures for *Claiming Your Place at the Fire: Living the Second Half of Your Life on Purpose* (Berrett-Koehler, 2004), and *Something to Live For: Finding Your Way in the Second Half of Life* (Berrett-Koehler, 2008). They suggest you keep your inner fire alive by becoming a New Elder.

Also tapping into timeless human experience, Jungian analyst James Hollis accesses the depths of our collective psyche for *Finding Meaning in the Second Half of Life: How to Finally, Really Grow Up* (Gotham, 2006).

Harry R. Moody and David Carroll suggest that stages are spiritual, as much as social and psychological. In *The Five Stages of the Soul: Charting the Spiritual Passages That Shape Our Lives* (Anchor, 1998), they distill thousands of years of wisdom—from many faiths—into this very readable book. Real-life stories illustrate the stages you may find yourself traveling on life's journey.

Parker Palmer knows that the stages of the inner journey are aided by entering into a community of trust with other seekers. Especially if you sense that the demands of earlier life stages have forced you to lead a divided life, you'll want to read his book, *A Hidden Wholeness: The Journey Toward an Undivided Life* (Jossey-Bass, 2004).

In *Callings: Finding and Following an Authentic Life* (Three Rivers Press, 1998), Gregg Levoy reminds us that we can be called to journey outward, as well as inward. This wonderful book offers a broad exploration of callings in history, myth, and religion, combined with intimate accounts from Levoy and others. In this down-to-earth book you'll discover the endlessly varied and fascinating ways that people hear and heed a calling. What's your calling?

Prosperity Resources: Financial

If your budget only allows one book on finance, start with Mark Miller's *The Hard Times Guide to Retirement Security: Practical Strategies for Money, Work, and Living* (Bloomberg Press, 2010). Then log on to his website (www.RetirementRevised.com), which *Money* magazine called the best retirement planning site on the web!

If you want something so comprehensive you may never need the web, try *The AARP Retirement Survival Guide: How to Make Smart Financial Decisions in Good Times and Bad* (Sterling, 2009), by Julie Jason. It's like a reference for your bookshelf. A truly unique book for your bookshelf would be *Live Long and Prosper! Invest in Your Happiness, Health, and Wealth for Retirement and Beyond* (Wiley, 2004). As an actuary, Steve

Vernon can address not only finances, but health and longevity, too. Get a glimpse into the strange mind of an actuary on Steve's blog, Money for Life, at www.MoneyWatch.com.

When it comes to money, though, we all have strange minds! Gary Belsky and Thomas Gilovich explain in *Why Smart People Make Big Money Mistakes and How to Correct Them: Lessons from the Science of Behavioral Economics* (Simon & Schuster, 2010 edition). Even if you're a rational agent, you might learn a thing or two. Instead of people who do the wrong things, Thomas Stanley studies those who do the right things—millionaires. See *The Millionaire Mind* (Andrews McMeel, 2001) and with William Danko, *The Millionaire Next Door* (Pocket Books, 1998).

At the other extreme, we can learn from those who choose to live on less. Buy (or borrow) *Your Money or Your Life: 9 Steps to Transforming Your Relationship with Money and Achieving Financial Independence: Revised and Updated for the 21st Century* (Penguin, 2008). You probably won't adopt the lifestyle described by Dominguez, Robin, and Tilford, but just reading this book will put you in an altered state of money consciousness—in a good way.

Prosperity Resources: Geographical

The micro layer of retirement geography is your residence. Adelaide Altman looks at that issue in *ElderHouse: Staying Safe and Independent in Your Own Home As You Age* (Chelsea Green Publishing, 2008). For a home that's friendly to your current and future selves, consult Wendy Jordan's *Universal Design for the Home: Great Looking, Great Living Design for All Ages, Abilities, and Circumstances* (Quarry Books, 2008).

Then step up a layer, and evaluate how friendly your community will be to your future self, too. A good guide is "Beyond 50.05," from AARP. It's called *A Report to the Nation on Livable Communities: Creating Environments for Successful Aging* (2005). Search for it on www.aarp.org, or request a free copy by email from fulfillment@aarp.org. Publication ID is 18316. If you decide your community is a "fixer-upper," see Jay Walljasper's *The Great Neighborhood Book: A Do-it-Yourself Guide to Placemaking* (New Society Publishers, 2007).

At the next layer, evaluating cities and regions has moved online as the number of geographical "calculators" has mushroomed. But it's still worth getting inside the heads of the experts who've assembled the classic books on where to live. Three examples are David Savageau's *Retirement Places Rated: What You Need to Know to Plan the Retirement You Deserve* (Frommer's, 2007); Bert Sperling and Peter Sander's *Cities Ranked & Rated: More than 400 Metropolitan Areas Evaluated in the U.S. and Canada* (Wiley, 2007); and Warren Bland's *Retire in Style: 60 Outstanding Places Across the USA and Canada* (Next Decade, 2005).

What's most important about a city or region sometimes can't be found in guidebooks or online resources. They can have a personality all their own, which brings us to the inner layer of geography—a sense of place. Richard Florida has touched upon this phenomenon in *Who's Your City?: How the Creative Economy Is Making Where to Live the Most Important Decision of Your Life* (Basic Books, 2009).

Health Resources: Biological

For a book that asserts biological aging is both natural and inevitable—but that you can still optimize your health—get Andrew Weil's *Healthy Aging: A Lifelong Guide to Your Well-Being* (Anchor, 2007). On the other hand, if your biological ideal includes *not* aging, that's the theme of *Younger Next Year: Live Strong, Fit, and Sexy—Until You're 80 and Beyond* (Workman, 2007). Authors Chris Crowley and Herbert Lodge also offer a separate version for women.

Looking farther afield, Dan Buettner traveled the world to find factors shared by the world's oldest people. The result is *The Blue Zones: Lessons for Living Longer From the People Who've Lived the Longest* (National Geographic, 2009). Take a personal assessment and also learn how to make your community healthier at www.BlueZones.com. John Robbins looked for the world's oldest people, too. His take on biological vitality is *Healthy at 100: The Scientifically Proven Secrets of the World's Healthiest and Longest-Lived Peoples* (Ballantine Books, 2007). However, for Robbins, sustainably healthy people and a sustainably healthy planet go hand-in-hand.

Instead of field research, some look to the laboratory for clues to extend healthy life. The only empirical evidence so far is for permanently reducing calorie intake. Take a nibble on *The Anti-Aging Plan: The Nutrient-Rich, Low-Calorie Way of Eating for a Longer Life—The Only Diet Scientifically Proven to Extend Your Healthy Years* (Da Capo Press; 2005), by Roy and Lisa Walford. It provides a small taste of Roy Walford's extensive research into calorie reduction.

Instead of a body-based approach, Ellen Langer has researched a mind-body approach. She placed older people in an environment filled with cues from their younger days, and discovered they effectively became biologically younger! It's not as simple as it sounds, so don't try it at home without the instructions: *Counterclockwise: Mindful Health and the Power of Possibility* (Ballantine Books, 2009).

Health Resources: Medical

The surest way to receive high quality medical care is to develop partnering relationships with your medical practitioners. But before you're qualified to partner with your doctor, you need some medical training!

For a fair and balanced account of how we ended up with the mainstream medical system that we have—and what your alternatives are—see *Health and Healing: The Philosophy of Integrative Medicine and Optimum Health* (Mariner Books, 2004). As a Harvard-trained physician, Andrew Weil dissects the conventional medical paradigm from both an insider's and outsider's perspective.

As you progress through the Third Age and into the Fourth, you'll have more and more interaction with doctors, whether you like it or not. Truth be told, most doctors are a boon to their patients and to society—but they're trained to see the world differently than we do. To get the inside perspective, read *How Doctors Think* (Mariner Books, 2008) by Jerome Groopman.

Another insider is Nortin Hadler. Unlike Andrew Weil, he doesn't focus on the difference between conventional and alternative treatments, but on the total amount of treatment that we consume. His concern is that too many of us end up on the high end of the intervention continuum. See *Worried Sick: A Prescription for Health in an Overtreated America* (University of North Carolina Press, 2008).

Regardless of your philosophy on conventional versus alternative treatment, and high versus low intervention, sooner or later you or someone you love will end up in the hospital. Before you check in, be sure to check out *YOU: The Smart Patient: An Insider's Handbook for Getting the Best Treatment* (Free Press, 2006), by Michael Roizen and Mehmet Oz. Or, for a non-insider's advice from an experienced patient, look into Jari Holland Buck's *Hospital Stay Handbook: A Guide to Becoming a Patient Advocate for Your Loved Ones* (Llewellyn Publications, 2007).

Happiness Resources: Psychological

The field of psychology recently turned over a new leaf. It didn't abandon the study of psychological ill-being, but added a serious commitment to also studying well-being. Martin Seligman planted the seed of what is now flowering as "Positive Psychology." To learn how it happened—and get plenty of practical advice—pick up his book, *Authentic Happiness: Using the New Positive Psychology to Realize Your Potential for Lasting Fulfillment* (Free Press, 2004). It's like a good textbook, interwoven with adventure travel.

This next resource actually is a text book! But *A Primer in Positive Psychology* (Oxford University Press, 2006) is nothing like what you were forced to read in school. Christopher Peterson makes you wish you were in his class at the University of Michigan. He also did the heavy lifting on the free VIA Strengths assessment at www.ViaCharacter.org.

Donald Clifton left academia to start what we know today as the Gallup Organization. His seminal work on strengths is *Now, Discover Your Strengths* (Free Press, 2001), with Marcus Buckingham. Tom Rath, Clifton's grandson, has carried on the family legacy with *Strengthsfinder 2.0* (Gallup Press, 2007). The profile at www.StrengthsFinder.com is oriented toward workplace outcomes.

If outcomes are what matter to you, you'll like Sonja Lyubomirsky's *The How of Happiness: A New Approach to Getting the Life You Want* (Penguin, 2008). Among the flood of happiness books, this is a practical, step-by-step guide. For a more philosophical approach, explore *The Happiness*

Hypothesis: Finding Modern Truth in Ancient Wisdom (Basic Books, 2006), by Jonathan Haidt. It integrates empirical research with the age-old questions of life.

Rather than age-old questions, Gene Cohen asks old-age questions. Prepare to be surprised by *The Mature Mind: The Positive Power of the Aging Brain* (Basic Books, 2006), and his earlier book, *The Creative Age: Awakening Human Potential in the Second Half of Life* (Harper, 2001).

Happiness Resources: Social

Our top priorities for retirement include spending more time with friends. But when we leave our jobs, we leave much of our social network behind! It doesn't help that the trend in society has actually been away from building and maintaining social relationships. Connect with Robert Putnam's *Bowling Alone: The Collapse and Revival of American Community* (Simon & Schuster, 2001). He documents the decline of "social capital," which can be just as important as financial capital to our retirement well-being. His follow-up is *Better Together: Restoring the American Community* (Simon & Schuster, 2003), which showcases programs that promote social engagement.

Promoting social engagement for the Third Age is Marc Freedman's calling. He founded a nonprofit organization that not only builds social engagement, but directs it toward building a better society, too. Check out www.CivicVentures.org, and then read *Prime Time: How Baby Boomers Will Revolutionize Retirement and Transform America* (PublicAffairs, 2002). His sequel explores the growing societal trend of second careers—not just for a paycheck, but for fulfillment, too: *Encore: Finding Work that Matters in the Second Half of Life* (PublicAffairs, 2008).

On a much more personal level, take a peek into the work of John Gottman. He invites couples to stay in his university "Love Lab," and then videotapes them. (It's not what you think!) By studying the social interactions that many of us don't notice, he's identified the characteristics of stronger and weaker relationships. He can predict in advance whether couples are more likely to stay together or split up! See *Ten Lessons to Transform Your Marriage: America's Love Lab Experts Share Their*

Strategies for Strengthening Your Relationship (Three Rivers Press, 2007), coauthored with his wife, Julie Schwartz Gottman. He takes a wider view in *The Relationship Cure: A 5 Step Guide to Strengthening Your Marriage, Family, and Friendships* (Three Rivers Press, 2002).

Acknowledgments

In terms of inspiration, my coauthor Dick Bolles is the deep underlying force behind the creation of this book. Dick's unique approach to the original *What Color Is Your Parachute?* provided both the motivation and the guidance for this companion volume. Likewise, Dick's playful persistence (or persistent playfulness?) is the model for the ongoing updates. To put it simply, this book would not exist without him! Thank you, Dick and Marcie, for your encouragement and your kindness.

In terms of execution, Sara Golski, Betsy Stromberg, George Young, Aaron Wehner, and the staff at Ten Speed Press are the drivers behind this edition. Without them, it would have been merely an interesting possibility.

In terms of ideas, many people from many fields have influenced the development of the Well-Being Model, which provides the essential structure for this book. My advisor at the University of Wisconsin, Alan Knox, lit the match by introducing me to the concept (and practice) of "boundary spanning." Betty Hayes added fuel to the fire, by granting me the freedom to design a doctoral course of study that makes sense only in retrospect.

I've learned from many revolutionary thinkers and teachers, whether through single seminal conversations or longer courses of study. Across the geo-financial, bio-medical, and psycho-social domains, my appreciation goes to Carol Anderson of Money Quotient, Don Ardell, Robert

Atchley, David Cooperrider of Case Western, Mihaly Csikszentmihalyi, Marc Freedman of Civic Ventures, Matt Greenwald, George Kinder, Gregg Levoy, Harry "Rick" Moody of AARP, Chris Peterson of Michigan, David Rakel of Wisconsin, Martin Seligman of Penn, Steve Vernon, Lois Vitt of ISFS, and Richard Wagner. Special thanks to Shalom Schwartz of Hebrew University.

In terms of support, many people have serendipitously appeared with just the right help at just the right moment. My gratitude goes to Lee Eisenberg, Jan Fulwiler, Sally Hass and Andy Landis from Weyerhaeuser, Neal Mayerson and Deb Pinger of the VIA Institute, Betty Meredith of InFRE, Tim Nuckles of Olive Consulting, Al Sommers from AARP, Marv Tuttle of the FPA, and Mary Willett.

Joseph Campbell cautioned us that the journey to adventure invites both fulfillment and fiasco. But he might have added that while on the journey, it's often difficult to tell the two apart! In both fulfillment and fiasco, my deepest acknowledgement and love always goes to my family. Thank you, Cheryl, Erik, Sean, Evan, Don, Russ, and Amanda Nelson; and Sharon, Gordie, Heidi, Camron, Hannah, and Hunter Johnson. We're all on the journey together.

—John E. Nelson

Index

G

H

N

O

P

R

S

T

About the Authors

John E. Nelson is a speaker and seminar facilitator on life stage planning, well-being, and core values.

He is the creator of the Well-Being Model, which integrates emerging concepts from psychology, economics, medicine, and other fields. It was selected as the structure for the retirement education program for the federal workforce, the employees of AARP, and other organizations. For more information and resources, visit www.retirementwellbeing.com.

John is currently pursuing a PhD at the University of Wisconsin, where he is also an instructor for undergraduate courses and continuing education workshops. He lives in Madison, Wisconsin, with his wife, Cheryl, and their sons, Erik, Sean, and Evan.

Visit www.johnenelson.com.

Richard N. Bolles is the author of the best-selling job-hunting book in the world, *What Color Is Your Parachute?* He has been a leader and the #1 celebrity in the career development field for more than thirty years.

Richard was trained in chemical engineering at MIT; in physics at Harvard University, where he graduated cum laude; and in New Testament studies at the General Theological (Episcopal) Seminary in New York City, where he earned a master's degree. He is the recipient of two honorary doctorates, is a member of MENSA, and is listed in *Who's Who in America* and *Who's Who in the World*. He lives in the San Francisco Bay Area with his wife, Marci.

Visit www.JobHuntersBible.com.